RÉSUMÉS FOR EXECUTIVES AND PROFESSIONALS

by
Robert F. Wilson
Director, Career Clinics, Inc.
New Canaan, Connecticut and
San Francisco, California

and

Adele Lewis
Former President and Founder,
Career Blazers Agency, Inc.

BARRON'S EDUCATIONAL SERIES, INC.
New York • London • Toronto • Sydney

All inquiries should be addressed to:
Barron's Educational Series, Inc.
250 Wireless Boulevard
Hauppauge, New York 11788

Library of Congress Catalog Card No. 83-15789

International Standard Book No. 0-8120-0872-3

Library of Congress Cataloging in Publication Data

Lewis, Adele Beatrice, 1927-
  Résumés for executives and professionals.

  1. Résumés (Employment)   I. Wilson, Robert F.
II. Title.
HF5383.L49   1983   650.1'4   83-15789
ISBN 0-8120-0872-3

PRINTED IN THE UNITED STATES OF AMERICA

9012   100   15 14 13 12

Contents

Introduction

If you are reading these words in a bookstore or library, trying to decide whether this book is worth your time and money, let us help you telescope the decision-making process.

We assume that, having turned to this page, you are either an executive or a professional with an interest in improving or changing your career. We assume you know that a powerful, effective résumé is one essential tool toward accomplishing your goal.

We assume also that you want to continue working in your current career area; or you are changing career fields but know precisely in what new area you want to apply past career interests, skills, and accomplishments. (If you are less than sure of your next career move, you will find valuable tips in Chapter 5. You may want to read that chapter first and conduct further research on your own before using the rest of the book.)

From these assumptions we frame our entire universe of prospective readers, and we welcome you among them. Good luck in your new or improved career.

Some time ago a retail executive came to Career Clinics for help. For a man in his early thirties, his record of accomplishments bordered on phenomenal. He had risen dramatically in two prestigious corporations, and had left the second for an expected division presidency of a large midwestern chain of more than two hundred stores.

Six months into his new job it was apparent that the promised presidency was not forthcoming—at least in the immediate future. He was angry, frustrated, and wanted to leave. We talked of several opportunities, including one he had rejected just before accepting the midwestern position.

The résumé that emerged from our conversations boosted his confidence significantly. It was the first time he had seen an organized, succinct record of his professional history. Because he had been personally recommended for his two previous positions, there had been no need for a résumé.

The payoff? No, he didn't get a new, more lofty position the first time he used the résumé in an interview. What he did do, though, was convince his current employer that, based on what he had accomplished and what he could accomplish, he was being wasted in his current staff position. He was given the elusive division presidency within the month. That's **résumé power**!

And though it may be rare indeed that you will use a new résumé to improve your present position, it is the single most important self-advertisement for any executive or professional on the move. A résumé is your advance communication to generate interviews. It is your mini-business or professional dossier, to be distributed among prospective colleagues for review, comment, and recommendation. It is your statement of self, which says as much to a potential boss as anything can about your tastes and values—short of a personal meeting—as it does about your responsibilities and accomplishments.

If you are not known to a prospective employer, a good résumé—or occasionally, just a good letter of introduction—is essential to getting the interview. And without the opportunity of meeting a possible boss face to face, your chances of getting hired are nonexistent.

Some career management consultants recommend withholding the résumé as a trump card in generating interviews. If asked, they advise, stall. The longer you can avoid showing your résumé, apparently, the better.

The supposition seems to be that once an employer has seen your résumé, all your weaknesses will have been exposed, which puts you just moments away from a rejection. We have to believe that anyone as reluctant as this to use a résumé must not know how effective a good one can be.

This is not to say that résumés should *always* be used. One legitimate reason for not using a résumé, or delaying its use as long as possible, would apply to anyone who wants to make a career change so drastic that previous experience bears no relationship whatsoever to the intended new direction.

One client in his early forties had a background he was quite sure would be of interest to a number of corporations, but after a dozen telephoned inquiries and several weeks of research, he was fairly certain *they didn't know it yet*. He had recently returned from six years in Morocco, where he taught French, German, English, Russian, and Spanish to children of high-ranking government officials. Before this, he had spent ten years as a U.S. Naval officer. He was widely read and had traveled all over the world. Most prospective employers, though, would throw out a résumé from a man in his forties with no corporate experience. We decided on a different strategy—more appropriately described in Chapter 6.

For just about every other situation, however, we emphatically recommend the preparation, use, and frequent updating of the best written and designed résumé possible. If you are going after more than one kind of job you may need more than one résumé. But you do indeed need a résumé. In today's business and professional world the résumé is almost universally to be viewed as indispensable as the calling card. Don't apply for a job without it.

In Search of the Perfect Résumé

Résumés are used, for the most part, in only three kinds of situations: 1. to generate an interview for an open position; 2. to determine whether an opening exists—either immediately or in the near future; or 3. as part of a presentation to *create* a position.

But no matter which of these situations applies to you, the only effective résumé is one that leads to interviews. The résumés you will see in this book—including the one you learn to write—are designed to generate interviews.

Several years ago Career Clinics took a survey to find out how line and staff executives evaluated résumés. We interviewed the interviewers themselves; more than fifty corporate officers, line managers, and human resource executives in a wide variety of Fortune 500 and smaller companies. Here's what we asked them:

☐ How many résumés do you receive a day?
☐ How much time do you take to read each one?
☐ What determines how much time you spend on each one?
☐ How long do you believe a résumé should be?
☐ What information do you think a résumé should convey?
☐ What résumé format do you prefer (chronological, functional, other)?
☐ How would you describe a "good" résumé?
☐ How would you describe a "bad" résumé?
☐ What do you think are the most frequent mistakes people make when writing résumés?
☐ What information do you think a cover letter should contain?

The point about which there was virtually unanimous agreement was this: *A résumé must communicate—totally and instantly.*

Let's say you're responding to an advertisement, or have knowledge from other sources about a position known also to other candidates. By definition you are in competition with anywhere from several dozen to many hundreds of other men and women who want the job. Under these circumstances, our experts say, ten to twenty seconds is about all the time you have to persuade a prospective employer to read every word—or at least to absorb most of what you have to offer. It must be clear immediately, they say, that you know precisely where you are going with your career, and that you have just the right background at your current level to qualify for the position.

Or let's say you're making a "cold call" on a company—either because you've heard there was an opening, or because your capabilities and experience uniquely qualify you for an opening you've heard is likely to break. Here too a strong résumé, backed up by an equally strong cover letter, is the first step you need to get in the door.

Chronological vs. Functional

Before getting to specific résumé components that help to achieve total communication, let's spend a few paragraphs comparing the two most common résumé formats: the chronological and the functional.

The basic difference between the two is that the chronological résumé stresses accomplishments and responsibilities tied closely to specific positions and employers, and the functional résumé stresses a profile of your experience based on professional strengths or skills groupings, irrespective of any particular jobs held while attaining them.

With few exceptions, the chronological résumé format was preferred by the corporate executives we interviewed as doing the best job of indicating an individual's direction, skills, accomplishments, and promotion record.

The only situations in which the chronological format should be modified or discarded in favor of the functional, say our experts, are these:

- ☐ You have a spotty work record—four jobs in six years for example.
- ☐ You are re-entering the corporate or professional world after several years of freelancing, consulting, homemaking, or unemployment.
- ☐ You are making a dramatic change of careers—from personnel management to computer sales, as an extreme and unlikely example.

One Career Clinics client, a wife of a career diplomat, had done only volunteer work twelve years before returning to the United States. She wanted to use her pre-marital travel experience (with a tour company, an airline, and a trade association) in some way to get back into a salaried position in travel sales or sales promotion. As it turned out, after she had completed our questionnaire (parts of which are quoted in Chapter 3) we had enough data—including her three years as president of the International Women's Club of Copenhagen and as Business English lecturer at a Brussels secretarial school—for a résumé that led to an interview and subsequent promotion job for a major international hotel chain. As you can see from her résumé (all résumé identities in this book have been changed) on pages 172-173, she was able legitimately to list the magazine she founded and published for the women's club, including the thousands of dollars of advertising she sold to keep it going and the managerial experience she gained by supervising a staff of twelve.

A freelancer's accomplishments can be chronicled the same way; likewise the consultant and the self-employed entrepreneur. An impressive client list, detailing specific accomplishments and an ability to bring projects in on time and to budget, can offset the stigma of a largely noncorporate work history. (See pages 18-19 for examples.) Similarly, a business sold for a profit is a rare phenomenon. If you can count it among your accomplishments, highlight it prominently.

If you've held too many jobs in too few years, however, you face a more challenging problem; similarly so if you have not worked for some time—either for pay or in volunteer positions. In these instances you will be better off with either a functional résumé or no résumé at all.

The functional résumé stresses career-wide accomplishments, responsibilities, and skills, and it avoids a complete chronology of employment—with a list of employers and inclusive employment dates often the last entry.

Even though your reasons for going to the functional résumé are sound, you face a risk in using it. According to most of the corporate executives we surveyed, it raises more questions than it answers, and makes many prospective employers suspicious. Functional résumés should be used only in situations where the "whole truth"—that is, an all-inclusive chronological format—will kill any chance of an interview.

What Makes Good and Bad Résumés

To do its job—get you the interview—a résumé must clearly and forcefully make the best possible case for your ability to meet the needs of the targeted prospective employers. Obviously there are other factors to consider. One résumé cannot be an all-situation solution. Occasionally a specially written résumé is called for. An individual going after two different but related types of positions may want to distribute two or three variations of the same résumé. The list of individuals receiving the résumé of course is key, as is the letter that accompanies the résumé. These two stages we'll cover in Chapters 5 and 6, respectively.

None of this, however, takes away from the power of a well written, well designed résumé. Put in the form of negative example (and taken directly from responses to the Career Clinics corporate survey), let's imagine an employer "Hit List" of résumé characteristics, any one of which will ensure that a candidate is a candidate no more. For ease of discussion, we'll divide the characteristics into the categories of Appearance, Clarity, and Content. They break down like so:

Appearance
☐ Tacky typing or reproduction job
☐ Poor paper quality
☐ Vibrant, bizarre, or otherwise offbeat paper color
☐ Typographical errors
☐ Gratuitous, attention-getting visual effects (wild or mixed type styles, brochure format, photographs)
☐ Paper size other than 8½ by 11 inches
☐ Length of more than two pages (with exceptions, of course; see Chapter 3)
☐ Inappropriate format for level (middle manager with typeset body copy; corporate vice-president without same)

Clarity
☐ Description of jobs or accomplishments longer than four lines, causing difficult reading
☐ Position objective or experience summary not clearly stated
☐ Grammatical or syntactical errors or inconsistencies

- [ ] Personal data (name, address, phone numbers) not immediately identifiable
- [ ] Job history not stated in reverse chronological order

Content

- [ ] Excessive space devoted to items not directly related to career (hobbies, detailed personal data, detailed descriptions of jobs related to former careers)
- [ ] Employment gaps not sufficiently played down or explained
- [ ] Sequence of major headings inappropriate to level (for example, education listed first for person with solid, career-related experience)
- [ ] Career-related volunteer experience not effectively treated or developed
- [ ] Accomplishments insufficiently treated, or not quantitatively stated, where appropriate

In Chapter 3 we'll go into more detail about these characteristics and the inevitable exceptions to the rule, take a look at predominant résumé types and styles, and determine when to use them.

Résumé Nuts and Bolts

All successful authors write with a specific audience in mind. A successful résumé writer should be no less selective. Your target may be an individual hiring for the only position in the world for which you would consider leaving your present job. Or, it could be every vice-president of marketing in the bottled water industry with sales over $10 million in Southern California, Texas, and Florida. No matter. Know him, her, or them as well as you can, and write a résumé addressing specific needs.

An ability to write directly to needs rests on the mastery of three essential levels of information: 1. knowledge of industry; 2. knowledge of company; 3. knowledge of position or function.

The simplest, most easily managed goal is to move up the ladder in a relatively straight line—assuming more or broader responsibilities in your function and staying within your industry. If this is so, your job is to demonstrate—either directly or indirectly—your awareness of industry trends, problems, and promise. The "knowledge-of-company" level should be dealt with only in terms of your present company. Your awareness of the idiosyncrasies of other specific companies can be handled in the cover letter accompanying the résumé.

As to "knowledge-of-position," chances are the job you want is much like the one your boss has. In this case you need to be clear your *prospective* boss can see which of your *current* boss's responsibilities you either have handled or can handle. This, we repeat, is the simplest, most easily managed challenge. Those of you changing functions, industries, or both will find it tougher, but the strategy remains the same.

Writing your best résumé requires the assemblage of all pertinent professional, personal, and educational data. At Career Clinics we use a detailed questionnaire, completed by each client and augmented by a one-on-one "drawing out" session based on responses to specific questionnaire questions. We'll reproduce salient portions of the Career Clinics questionnaire here, as they apply to specific sections of the résumé.

Objective

After identifying yourself by name, address, and phone number at the top of page one, the first item of information should be your immediate career objective. This and the entry that follows—the Summary—provide the direction, tone, and major emphasis of the entire résumé. Every succeeding word will be read in light of these few words at the beginning of the document.

We ask clients to identify both short- and long-term objectives on our questionnaire to determine whether the individual has thought about a career path. In some instances (especially for younger executives), it may be wise to mention your immediate objective *in terms of* your long-range objective. ("Telemarketing Sales, leading to sales management position," for example.)

In many instances, though, it may be that just a specific title will serve. If this is precisely what you want and fully suits your needs, you are lucky and this is all you *should* use. For example:

> Operations Vice-President
> Senior Corporate Counsel
> Foundation Executive Director

They have a certain crisp purity to them, don't they? Let's hope it's this easy for you—but it may not be. If you have most recently held a vice-presidency, for example, some well-paying positions of power may be perfectly acceptable to you and not carry a company or corporate officership. Corporate structure may not so warrant, or it may be that industry-wide the job may not necessarily call for a vice-presidency, division presidency, or whatever. If this is so, broaden your base. For example:

> Senior Management—Sales/Merchandising
> Health Care Financial/Administrative Management
> Orchestral Conductor or Choral Director

If your field is relatively new or quickly evolving, you may need to cast your net wider still:

> Telecommunications Programming Management
> Director of Development, Major University
> Information Systems Management

The maxim to remember, though, no matter what your objective, is to state it broadly enough to embrace all acceptable closely related positions, but not so broadly that you diffuse your focus and appear to be willing to accept anything out there. A prospective employer may infer lack of direction—or worse, that you're in a panic situation and will take anything you can get. Better to write two or three résumés, varying the objectives as necessary.

Summary

The purpose of the objective is to succinctly describe the position you want, by level, function, and/or industry. The Summary (or "Background," or "Professional Highlights") section is a companion entry indicating those achievements and skills justifying your ability to handle the position sought.

Anywhere from two to five brief, powerful sentences will be enough, highlighting those aspects of your background of most appeal. The beauty of a Summary is that it offers the advantages of a functional résumé with none of its disadvantages. You have the opportunity to combine and build on similar aspects of your work experience that may go back ten or twenty years.

The real possibility exists that an achievement you are particularly proud of may date back far enough—if you are using straight reverse chronology—to appear on the second page of the résumé and thus never be seen by a large number of prospects.

One Career Clinics client had a strong financial background spanning three industries over eighteen years. Among his achievements was that of originating the airline credit card which was eventually imitated by every major airline. The problem was that his airline experience came immediately after his 1965 M.B.A., and would have been buried near the end of the résumé if treated chronologically. We decided to use a one-sentence general summary, followed by a Highlights section that would cause selected accomplishments to "pop out" visually. It read like this:

SUMMARY: Fourteen years experience in financial and business planning, marketing, and controlling functions for a manufacturer, an airline, and a brokerage firm.

HIGHLIGHTS:
- Conceived and implemented TWA "Getaway" credit card system, now the most popular of all airline credit cards
- Assisted in negotiating the transfer of TWA control away from the Hughes organization
- As media liaison, used marketing and advertising to make general public aware of negotiability of industrial diamonds
- Developed capacity for improving relations between factory and office workers to increase production and cut costs
- As general manager, tightened financial controls and directed short- and long-term business planning

The best way to get a handle on writing a good Summary is to go back over your career and list all of the skills, responsibilities, and achievements that you feel will qualify you for your next position. Pare down your list to the top six or seven points, and then combine those that are similar in scope or function so that you wind up with a brief narrative that has a little bit of flow to it.

Choose your words carefully. If your Summary sustains the reader's interest, more likely than not the rest of the résumé will, too. Don't be flowery. Your chances of getting the interview will not be improved by any records set in the use of adjectives or polysyllables. Make every word count. Rewrite your first drafts, striking out unnecessary words and phrases and tightening sentences until they say exactly what you mean. Then have one or more friends who know you well professionally read what you've written, and suggest accomplishments you either have forgotten or perhaps have dismissed as unimportant.

If you are changing careers—even slightly—don't mention the function or industry *being* changed. One client with a strong sales and marketing background wanted to minimize the fact that his excellent record had been compiled for the past seven years in the catering industry, a field he wanted to leave. So although we went into considerable detail relating his experience in terms of specific employers later in the résumé, it was more effective to write the Summary stressing more generic skills and accomplishments, as follows:

SUMMARY: Extensive experience in sales and service of major industrial and commercial accounts. Outstanding record in acquiring direct accounts and initiating client contact at top management levels. Comprehensive background conceptualizing and implementing advertising campaigns.

An industry-changing executive, then, can encourage a prospective employer to consider his "pure" strengths first—at the top of the résumé—before revealing that those strengths were attained in what might be viewed as an alien industry.

Such a Summary, in fact, can be used with two or more specific Objectives to provide résumés with as many differing orientations as opportunities warrant. Two used by the marketing executive whose Summary appears above are:

> Executive Management, Hotel Industry
> Television Time Sales/Marketing Management

So in essence he has three résumés, to be used for situations that have already come up, with the option of preparing others pointed toward slightly differing situations as needed.

Experience

The heart of the résumé is the organization and presentation of your job history. If you have selected the chronological format as the one best for you, your goal is to make as much as you can out of every position you have had. Describe your major responsibilities, to be sure, but concentrate most heavily on accomplishments you can legitimately own or share. As a memory refresher, the Career Clinics questionnaire utilizes a "Problem/Action/Results" inquiry for every position held and with every employer for whom a client has worked.

The key (to quote from the questionnaire) is to "think of as many problems as you can that you both faced and were able to solve to some satisfaction. Briefly describe the problem; next, the action you took to solve or alleviate it; then, the results or consequences of that action. Specifically mention, for example, situations or conditions that improved, dollars saved or earned for the firm, ideas adopted by the firm, dollars in increased sales for the firm, etc."

This will give you a nucleus of data from which to frame a powerful, achievements-oriented Experience section. Concentrate on utilizing achievements consistent with your career direction, and spend as little space as possible on aspects of previous positions that have no bearing on the kind of job you're after now. Similarly, devote more attention to current or recent career-related positions than on those held earlier in your professional life. Don't appear to be dwelling in the past. If you attained similar goals early in your career as well as more recently, load them in your current experience and keep the past relatively spare.

The obvious exception to this advice is if you are in the process of a career change back to one held when you were younger. In this instance the wiser course is to list first those positions, responsibilities, and accomplishments from the career you want now under a heading such as RELEVANT EXPERIENCE, and try to use the entire first page to chronicle this part of your professional background. You will then be following your stated Objective and Summary with experience that backs up your intentions. The only possible negative to this strategy is that the inclusive dates in the margin relative to employment may go back a decade or more. Defuse this by a parenthetical note or asterisked footnote after the dates, such as: "See page 2 for current experience."

One Career Clinics client had spent five years managing restaurants after a successful retail career, and wanted to go back to the field he realized was his first love. We accomplished this by filling the entire first page with retail experience without ever referring to his more recent restaurant experience on page 2—except for a footnote. Page one of the résumé is shown on page 12.

Sequence is important not just for career changes, however, but for anyone interested in the most effective possible résumé. Think of your résumé as a script, for both you and the interviewer. This is particularly true of the Experience section. Each entry is a cue to be picked up by the interviewer as he or she wishes, and singled out for elaboration if it piques interest and as it relates to the position available.

The accomplishments should be broken up in bite-size entities for the interviewer to spot and absorb quickly. The interviewee, on the other hand, should view each entry as the basis for a leading question, about which he or she has rehearsed responses of anywhere from one to fifteen minutes, determined by interviewer interest.

This being so, it is extremely important not only to include those points of maximum appeal, but to sequence them by degree of importance—almost the way you learned to write a topic outline in your first composition course. Where appropriate, buttress or quantify an accomplishment to further whet the reader's interest. Follow a main point with appropriate sub-points. Let's take an example from another retail executive.

- Developed marketing programs to reposition corporation as necessary
  —Created 120-store test to analyze customer buying patterns for purpose of maximizing inventory investment (later implemented in all 320 stores)
  —Initiated and implemented merchandise line plan to fully develop previously nonformalized corporate policy

and later in the résumé:

OBJECTIVE: RETAIL SENIOR MANAGEMENT

SUMMARY: Eight years strong retail managerial experience -

                 including two years ownership of own gift shop -

                 embracing sales promotion, inventory control and

                 purchasing responsibilities. Multilingual.

RETAIL
EXPERIENCE: J. W. MAYS DEPARTMENT STORE, New York, NY
                 <u>Senior Buyer</u>

1972 to 1975*   * Supervised ordering, pricing, display and marketing
                   of all giftware, crystal, glassware, silverware,
                   china figurines and imported merchandise

                 * Devised incentive plan responsible for sales increase
                   of 15% on volume of $3.5 million annually

                 * Supervised 10 assistant buyers and sales personnel

                 * Identified and assigned new vendors to anticipate
                   market trends

                 LINAS GIFT SHOP, Oakhurst, NJ
                 <u>Owner</u>

1970 to 1972   * Overall bottom-line responsibility; established and
                   maintained overhead; supervised bookkeeping

                 * Hired, trained, and managed three salespeople

                 * Attended regional and national gift shows to determine
                   trends and generate merchandising and marketing ideas

                 MOHANS, LTD., Cedar Grove, NJ
                 <u>Sales Manager</u>

1967 to 1970   * Ordered, displayed, priced and advertised all ladies'
                   and men's clothing

                 * Supervised 18 salespeople

                 * Increased sales by 30% in first year; responsible for
                   25% of volume of $2.5 million

                 * Achieved 13½% profit sharing, highest in company

* For current experience, see page 2

- Assumed total responsibility for start-up and opening of individual store
    —Led and managed all areas (merchandising, operations, personnel and inter-community relations) to achieve sales volume and profit objectives
    —Trained, developed, and managed Assistant Managing Director, 6 Operational Department Managers, 13 Merchandising Managers
    —Established environment of full employee input preparatory to store opening, keeping motivation and morale at optimum levels

The chief point to remember in writing and laying out this section is: Make all key aspects of every entry as visible as possible to permit the reader to take in your strengths at a glance, and to select for more careful reading those that relate closely to the target position. The layout, in fact, is as important as the writing. Don't underestimate it. Sound data presented in a sloppy or unclear manner are as ineffective as a badly written résumé. As you go through the sample résumés in this book, look as closely at the design as you do the writing.

Education

Start with your most advanced degree, and include the name and location of the institution, your major, year of graduation (if you're under 45), and all career-oriented scholarships and academic awards. Mention of any fraternity or sorority affiliations may hook you into the social-academic version of an Old Boy network; on the other hand, it may irritate a former Independent who considers all college social organizations snob factories. You might want to wait and work this into the interview if you think you're being interviewed by a Brother or Sister.

List any career-related extracurricular activities. Include all career-related courses or programs completed, whether company-sponsored or paid for by you. If you are a non-college graduate, list institutions attended anyway, with inclusive dates but without additional comment; this may be perceived as defensive.

Licenses and Certifications

Include only those that are career-related, without elaboration.

Additional Personal Data

Career-related hobbies—yes.

Marital status, height, weight, number and ages of children, state of health (it's always "excellent" anyway; at least on the résumés we've seen), availability of references (when they want them they'll ask)—no.

Sample Résumés

4

The résumés reproduced in this chapter have been categorized among the following standard corporate functions and services:

Communications
Finance
Human Resources and Development
Information Systems
Legal
Marketing
Operations
Research and Development

This creates a few awkward catchalls, among them the inclusion of all educational and health care positions under "Human Resources and Development," and some engineering and science-oriented positions under "Research and Development." Similarly, we have included under "Communications"—perhaps arbitrarily—most art and design, public relations, film, television, museum, music, editorial, and writing positions.

Check the back cover to see if the particular job you are after is included in the appropriate function or service area—or perhaps one or more close to it—and you will likely be able to draw what you need from more than one example. Better yet, if you have the time, skim all of the samples in this chapter. It may well be that suggestions for several of your résumé entries will appear in career fields completely different from your own.

Communications

PAUL TOWNSAND   118 West 87th Street, New York, NY 10024   212-873-7721

OBJECTIVE   <u>PRODUCTION EDITOR</u>

SUMMARY   Editor with production expertise and the ability to schedule and
            manage the activity of art, editorial and production staffs. Knowledge-
            able in all phases of production editing including consultation with
            authors and work assignments for in-house and free-lance staff members.
            Able to remain unruffled and maintain a steady, concentrated work flow
            despite tight scheduling and other pressures. Background in medical,
            scientific and foreign language books and periodicals.

EDITING EXPERIENCE

1975 - 1981 FREE-LANCE EDITOR, New York, NY

     * In-house editorial production supervisor for Macmillan's Medical
        Books Division, Free Press, Schirmer and other publishers

        - Managed projects from design survey on concentrated
          manuscript through all phases of proof, to final checks of
          blueprints and press sheets
        - Assigned work to free-lancers and in-house copy editors
        - Corresponded and consulted with authors
        - Collaborated with manufacturing supervisors

     * Copy editor of 12 to 15 titles per year for such clients as Jason
        Aronson, Inc.; Time, Inc.; and Arthur D. Little, Inc.

        - Copy edited manuscripts, jacket copy and promotional
          material
        - Handled proofreading, slugging and checks on repros,
          blueprints and press sheets

     * Guided and supervised editorial staff of 12 on four-volume
        <u>Encyclopedia</u> <u>of</u> <u>Bioethics</u> (a popular title at a $250 price tag)

        - Drew up five-page style guide, which was widely copied
          and circulated throughout parent company
        - Checked over all copy editing of 3,000-page manuscript

     * Reviewed and corrected manuscripts copy edited by others whose
        work did not meet professional standards

1969 - 1975 PRAEGER PUBLISHERS, New York, NY
            <u>Copy Editor</u>

     * Production and copy editing for 15 to 18 projects annually

        - Copy edited manuscripts, jacket copy and promotional material
        - Handled proofreading, slugging and checks on repros,
          blueprints and press sheets
        - Assigned work to free-lancers and in-house copy editors
        - Corresponded and consulted with authors

     * Responsible for two of Praeger's most popular titles: <u>The Life</u>
        <u>and Death of Adolf Hitler</u> by Robert Payne and <u>The Wall Street Gang</u>
        by Richard Ney

PAUL TOWNSAND/2

1959 - 1969   CURRENT DIGEST of the SOVIET PRESS, New York, NY
<u>Managing Editor, Current Digest/Co-Editor, Current Abstracts</u>

* As Managing Editor, <u>Current</u> <u>Digest</u> <u>of</u> <u>the</u> <u>Soviet</u> <u>Press</u>
    - Supervised staff of 12 translators, copy editors and indexers
    - Selected and abridged material in Russian for translation
    - Wrote headlines and captions

* As Co-Editor, <u>Current</u> <u>Abstracts</u> <u>of</u> <u>the</u> <u>Soviet</u> <u>Press</u>
    - Instrumental in the inauguration of new monthly magazine
    - Surveyed about 24 Soviet periodicals for articles of compelling interest to academic, government and media subscribers
    - Capsulized selected material and copy edited other articles
    - Selected graphic art for reproduction
    - Wrote headlines and captions

EDUCATION   COLUMBIA UNIVERSITY GRADUATE SCHOOL of JOURNALISM
1959 - MS, Journalism

PRINCETON UNIVERSITY
1955 - BA, Art and Archeology (graduated <u>cum</u> <u>laude</u>)

US ARMY LANGUAGE SCHOOL, Monterey, CA

US ARMY INTELLIGENCE SCHOOL, Fort Holobird, MD

LANGUAGES   Russian - Reading, writing, conversation, translation
French - Reading, conversation

WILLIAM A. POST

20 Waterside Plaza, New York, NY 10010   212/889-1427 (home)   212/867-0530 (office)

OBJECTIVE: EDITORIAL/MARKETING MANAGEMENT, EDUCATIONAL
                    PUBLISHING

SUMMARY: Comprehensive experience editing and publishing
                    educational textbooks at elementary and secondary levels.
                    Recruit, contract and motivate authors; direct, motivate
                    and correlate work of editors and writers on multi-
                    grade projects running concurrently. Initiate conceptual
                    programs and designs. Demonstrated ability to solve
                    problems, meet challenging goals and expedite production.

EXPERIENCE:

1972-Present   ACADEMIC MAGAZINE, INC.
                    New York, NY
                    Editorial Director, Reading and Language Arts Departments
                                  Text Division (1977-Present)

                    * Recruit and supervise senior authors for development
                       of text programs in basal reading, spelling, grammar
                       and composition.

                    * Directed four editors and 25 freelance writers in
                       development and publication of industry-leading
                       remedial reading system.

                       --Comprises 150 published novels and seven instructional
                         kits for grades 4-10 (additional 25 novels in work)

                       --First program to offer high-interest reading material
                         to elementary school students reading at first grade
                         level

                    * Conducted teacher focus groups and worked with outside
                       consulting firm to prepare market research study
                       reports for presentation to senior management.

                    * Explore and research programs produced by other publishers
                       in the field.

                    * Represent company at state and regional curriculum and
                       subject area meetings; conduct state and regional
                       workshops in reading and language arts.

                    * Effectively discharge responsibility for implementing
                       projects accounting for 50% of division revenue.

Associate Editorial Director, Reading Department
School Division (1976-1977)

* Supervised material for and publication of "Kicks," elementary level reading magazine

* Initiated and developed "Speed," a secondary level magazine

* Developed and published remedial math program for grades 4-6 (Academic has no math department)

Supervising Editor (1974-76)

* Directed staff of three division editors in Kicks Libraries, Kicks Reading Skills Program and Academic Listening Skills program, from manuscript acquisition through publication

Editor, Kicks Libraries (1972-74)

* Acquired manuscripts, assessed readability level and edited material for publication

| 1971-72 | NEWTON COLLEGE OF THE SACRED HEART Newton, MA |

* Assistant Professor of Education

| 1968-69 | CLINTON JOB CORPS Clinton, IA |

* Teacher, basic education

| 1967-68 | J.B. YOUNG JUNIOR HIGH SCHOOL Davenport, IA |

* Teacher, 8th Grade English

EDUCATION:

| 1971 | Harvard Graduate School of Education, M.A.T., English Education |

| 1969 | University of Nebraska, Lincoln, NE B.S., English Education |

AFFILIATIONS:

American Association of Publishers, Social Issues Committee

Chairman of Education Committee and member of Publications Committee, St. Peter's Church

HENRY EDMONDS
400 East 85th Street   New York, NY 10022
(212) 688-2251

OBJECTIVE: <u>EDITORIAL MANAGEMENT</u>

SUMMARY: Fifteen years' experience in production of texts, magazines and multimedia instructional programs for leading publisher. Excellent understanding of components controlling manufacturing costs and generation of editorial revenues. Responsible for significant number of text publishing success stories.

EDITORIAL EXPERIENCE:

1965 to   McGRAW-HILL, INC., New York, NY
Present   <u>Project Editor, Text Division</u> (1971-Present)

* Plan and budget multimedia instructional programs accounting for more than 10 percent of divisional revenue

* Achieve product goals through supervision of staff varying from 14 to 25 on any given project, including free-lance writers and consultants

* Participate in sales campaigns aimed at securing text adoptions in key states

* Conduct workshops for secondary teachers; led two statewide seminars and conducted five regional National Council of Social Studies workshops

* Member, typesetting computer committee charged with streamlining and scheduling of text typesetting and production

* Work closely with rights and permissions department both in drafting of authors' contracts and in obtaining permissions from other publishing houses

* Now developing on-level, basal text entry for high school U.S. history market, possibly the most competitive social studies market in pre-college text publishing; program tested positively in 1980 field surveys

* Refashioned <u>American Adventures</u>, best-selling multimedia history program, into basal format (both soft and hard cover) without sacrificing popular appeal

   - Extensive rewriting, re-editing and additions resulted in adoption by 15 states and most dramatic sales increase on a text program in company's history

   - Convinced upper management that regional variations were unnecessary, thus decreasing manufacturing costs by approximately 50 percent

* Produced simplified world history multimedia program, which is a steady seller with loyal following among teachers

   - Selected and guided ten writers, ten consultants, a designer, illustrator, and several indexers and caption writers, all working against tight deadlines

* Co-authored <u>Tropical and Southern Africa</u> (currently in seventh printing), one of seven original volumes in World Cultures Program

Concurrent Free-Lance Projects

- Contributing editor for 250-page book on basic legal principles for lay public in association with American Bar Association and scheduled for publication by Elsevier/Dutton

- Author, Junior Scholastic articles on California history and government (1979) and Presidential qualifications (1976)

- Wrote and produced four-page adult discussion guide for NBC-TV News to accompany three-hour telecast on American foreign policy, 1976

- Editor for one unit of Webster McGraw-Hill world history, Echoes of Time

- Wrote numerous Scholastic teleguides on such subjects as Alistair Cooke's America, David Copperfield, and New York City ca. 1880-1990

- Co-authored nine "map-paks" for W.H. Sadlier, Inc., 1973-1974; more than 370,000 copies of these skills-oriented study materials are still in print

Senior Associate Editor, School Division - Magazines (1965-1971)

* Hired as Assistant Editor in 1965; in quick succession of promotions, became Associate Editor, Managing Editor, then Senior Associate Editor within five years

* As Senior Associate Editor of American Observer, researched and wrote one or two articles weekly

* As Managing Editor of Junior Scholastic, brought about circulation turn-around of one of company's two highest-circulation magazines

    - Worked to give magazine a clear, lively style and brighter appearance; edited lead articles

    - Supervised staff of twelve including writers, artists and production personnel

1963-1965   MEDICAL ECONOMICS, INC., Oradell, NJ
Associate Editor

1962-1963   TIME, INC., New York, NY
Head Copy Boy, TIME Magazine

EDUCATION: STANFORD UNIVERSITY, Palo Alto, CA
M.A., United States History (University Scholarship)
B.A., History

COLUMBIA UNIVERSITY, New York, NY
Course work in Accounting

LANGUAGES: Some Spanish and very limited Japanese

AFFILIATIONS:

Sigma Delta Chi Professional Journalism Association

Willing to relocate

ROBERTA LOWREY

21 Fairfax Gardens, Hackettstown, NJ 07840   Home: (201) 852-6413
                                                Office: (201) 852-4225 Ext. 51

OBJECTIVE   NEWSPAPER EDITOR

To apply my newspaper experience in a position offering variety of
assignments and challenge with opportunity for growth

SUMMARY   Astute interviewer and reporter capable of handling varied assignments. Experienced in editing and page makeup. Creative assessor
of story ideas and material and able to visualize concepts for news
value publicity. Knowledge of basic photography. Willing to accept and carry out travel assignments.

EXPERIENCE

2/79 -   THE FORUM - Bi-Weekly Newspaper
Present   State Publishing Company
          Hackettstown, NJ

Copy Editor

* Edit copy for four reporters, write headlines, size pictures and
  help with page makeup

* Cover municipal beat

Special Sections Writer

* Charged with responsibility for three sections of the paper:
  Real Estate, Leisure, Fashions

  - Covered and wrote stories, rewrote releases and took photos
  - Made up sections

2/76 -   ARGUS OBSERVER - Daily Newspaper
8/78   Matheur Publishing Company
          Ontario, OR

Reporter

* Covered county beat and improved coverage (and subsequent circulation) by introducing additional beats

  - Economic Development
  - Health Planning
  - Municipal
  - Extended Zoning and Planning

* Wrote feature stories and took own photos

* Filled in for wire editor and did other desk work as needed

* Filled in for editor last 6 weeks

Society Editor

* Put together daily Family Page from the bottom up

  - Covered and wrote stories, edited releases, took photos
  - Handled correspondents' news
  - Made up page and wrote headlines

EXPERIENCE
(Cont'd.)

5/75 -   STATE OF OREGON, Disability Prevention Division
2/76   Portland, OR

           * Typed psychology reports for therapy program

EDUCATION Willamette University, Salem, OR
           1975, BA, English

              - Received Helen S. Pearce Award as outstanding senior woman
                English major
              - Worked as reporter and composition manager for newspaper
              - Worked as aide in public information office
              - President, Alpha Phi Sorority
              - Secretary, Mortar Board

           Portland State University, Portland, OR

              - Course in Reporting I

MEMBER   Ontario Press Club - served as secretary

TRAVEL   Backpacked through England, Ireland, Scotland, Germany, Italy,
           Spain, and Austria (8/74 - 12/74)

                    TEARSHEETS SUBMITTED UPON REQUEST

MARTIN DUPRÉ
20 Oakwood Court
Rockville Centre, NY 11570

Home (516) 764-1520
Work (516) 536-7500

OBJECTIVE: NEWSLETTER EDITOR

SUMMARY: Writer and editor with ability to simplify the complex, and solve publication and scheduling problems. Record of successful new publication
introductions. Expertise in taxes, fringe benefits, pensions, personal
finance, estate planning, insurance, trusts.

EXPERIENCE: BARNSWORTH PUBLISHING, Rockville Centre, NY
Director of Publishing

1979 to
Present

* Write and edit three highly successful monthly newsletters of steadily
  increasing circulation through better coverage of material.

* Positioned company in banking field by creating a pamphlet program,
  thus expanding market beyond insurance field.

* Placed company in lucrative pension and profit-sharing market via
  creation of sophisticated syndicated pension trust letter.

* Revitalized previously lagging pamphlet program by editing on-shelf
  material.

Free-lance Writer (Concurrent with position at Barnsworth)

American Institute of Certified Public Accountants; Warren, Gorham &
Lamont; Main, Hurdman & Cranstoun; Estate Planner's Quarterly; Dental
Management; Physician's Management.

MATTHEW BENDER & COMPANY, New York, NY
Chief Editor - Insurance & Pensions

1972
to
1979

* Created and wrote four-page syndicated monthly insurance newsletter
  accompanied by 50-page technical analysis, which became leading newsletter in field.

* Created and wrote pension trust syndicated monthly newsletter for
  banks--despite lack of in-house expertise--by thoroughly researching
  field and interviewing experts. Circulation grew to 50,000 (40 banks)
  within one year.

* Wrote classic, highly successful booklet for insurance industry after
  Tax Reform Act of 1976 by utilizing in-house material and special
  knowledge of insurance.

* Aided in writing bank (non-pension) trust letters.

DUNKIRK ASSOCIATES, Latham, NY
Vice President, Editor-in-Chief (1970-1972)

1967
to
1972

* Editor-in-Chief directing staff of 15 editors; responsible for all aspects of 12 insurance publications, including writing, editing, production scheduling and promotion.

* Raised quality and consistency of copy while maintaining tight production schedule.

* Increased productivity and accuracy of staff by assigning key writers to subject areas rather than publications.

COPLEY INTERNATIONAL, New York, NY
Editor

1965
to
1967

* Wrote weekly newsletter and brochures on topics of international business investment throughout world.

BUSINESS INTERNATIONAL, New York, NY
European Editor

1964
to
1965

* Wrote portion of weekly newsletter and brochures dealing with investments in Europe.

1960
to
1964

LEHMAN BROTHERS, New York, NY
Economist (1962-1964)
Trainee Economist (1960-1962)

NEW YORK STATE DEPARTMENT OF LABOR, New York, NY
Labor Speechwriter

1956
to
1958

* Wrote policy speeches for Gov. Averill Harriman and Industrial Commissioner Isador Lubin.

INTERESTS: Biking, walking, jazz, reading

Writing samples available on request

SUSAN JANE CLEMONS   415 West 96th Street #3H   Home: 212-666-5216
                                  New York, NY 10027   Work: 212-694-0200

OBJECTIVE   <u>TECHNICAL WRITING</u>: Position closely allied with research department of
                 pharmaceutical manufacturer

SUMMARY   Technical writer with sophisticated medical and chemical laboratory
                 experience. Talent for comprehensible and stimulating presentation of
                 highly complex technical data. Doctorate in Chemistry and post-doctoral
                 research at Columbia University College of Physicians & Surgeons. Co-
                 authored four articles in the field of bio-organic chemistry published by
                 <u>Journal of the American Chemistry Society</u> and <u>Photochemical Photobiology</u>.

PUBLICATIONS   S.J. Clemons, V. Haughton, J.S. King, K. Blevins, "A Non-
                 bleachable Rhodopsin Analogue Formed from 11,12-Dihydroretinal,"
                 J. Am. Chem. Soc., <u>89</u>, 6210 (1979).

                 K. Blevins, V. Haughton, S.J. Clemons, M. Cole, M. Lukens,
                 B. Randall, "Double Point Charge Model for Visual Pigments; Evidence
                 for Dihydrorhodopsins," Photochem. Photobiol., <u>39</u>, 875 (1980).

                 B. Randall, U. Goettl, K. Blevins, V. Haughton, S.J. Clemons,
                 M. Cole, M. Lukens, "An External Point Charge Model for Wavelength
                 Regulation in Visual Pigments," J. Am. Chem. Soc., <u>201</u>, 6684 (1981).

                 R. Linder, S. West, K. Blevins, S.J. Clemons, V. Haughton,
                 "Incorporation of 11,12-Dihydroretinal into the Retinae of Vitamin
                 A Deprived Rats," Photochem. Photobiol., <u>43</u>, 91 (1983).

RESEARCH AND TECHNICAL COMMUNICATIONS EXPERIENCE

1978 to   COLUMBIA UNIVERSITY COLLEGE OF PHYSICIANS & SURGEONS, New York, NY
Present   <u>Postdoctoral Fellow, Arteriosclerosic Research Training Program</u>

                 * Summarize experimental work in one-hour semi-annual presentations
                    for medical doctors, biologists and other researchers

                    - Developed format which dramatically increased comprehension
                       and interest in experiments by audience with little knowl-
                       edge or enthusiasm for synthetic chemistry

                    - Wrote and distributed summaries which emphasized objectives,
                       expected and observed results, and explanations of possible
                       discrepancies in and interpretations of experiments

                    - Supplemented written work with flow charts and tables

                 * Design and conduct independent experimental research on Vitamin A
                    metabolism; evaluate results

                    - Successfully isolate critical factors affecting experimental
                       results through careful recording and analysis of procedures
                       followed in sensitive process not easily duplicated

SUSAN JANE CLEMONS/2

       * Equipped unused biological/clinical laboratory with instruments to perform synthetic reactions and other chemical procedures

         - Negotiated for instruments specially designed and produced by Chemistry Department; acted as liaison between Director and Chemistry Department and set up account for payment

1974 - 1976   COLUMBIA UNIVERSITY, DEPARTMENT of CHEMISTRY, New York, NY
               Teaching Assistant

       * Closely supervised 15 students in general chemistry lab, evaluating students' mastery of general laboratory techniques and giving help where needed

       * Prepared sample time schedule and suggestions for saving time to encourage timely, neat and organized completion of student work

1975 - 1979   Writing & Research Experience gained in conjunction with work for doctorate, Columbia University, New York, NY

       * Presented paper at 1978 meeting of American Chemical Society in Chicago under title of "A Nonbleachable Rhodopsin Analogue Formed from 11,12-Dihydroretinal"

       * Prepared and referred manuscripts for publication in technical journals

       * Presented two departmental seminars

       * Prepared 190-page doctoral thesis on "Bio-Organic Studies in Visual Pigments; Formation of 11, 12-Dihydrorhodopsin from 11,12-Dihydroretinal"

         - Thesis included background of project, literature review, description of original research and results, and detailed experimental section

EDUCATION   COLUMBIA UNIVERSITY, New York, NY

         1978 - Present   Postdoctoral Research Fellow, College of Physicians And Surgeons

         1979   Ph.D., Chemistry

         1976   M.S., Chemistry

         DOUGLASS COLLEGE of RUTGERS UNIVERSITY, New Brunswick, NJ
         1974   B.A., Chemistry
                       Graduated with High Honors
                       Elizabeth Laudenslager Clark Scholarship
                       President, Rutgers Chapter, Iota Sigma Pi Chemistry Society

         WATERS ASSOCIATES, New York, NY
         1979   Course in use of high pressure liquid chromatograph

LANGUAGES   Working knowledge of French and German

MICHAEL HERRICK   •   214 47th Street   •   Lindenhurst, NY 11757

Res: (516) 226-1829   Bus: (212) 374-3254

OBJECTIVE: To transfer my expertise and experience as a FORENSIC COMMUNICATIONS SPECIALIST to the private sector

SUMMARY: Highly skilled in administration and operation of audio laboratory with special emphasis on techniques of voice identification and tape enhancement. Intimate knowledge of uses and adaptation of technical equipment to investigations. Practiced and effective lecturer. Creative designer of strategic training programs. Thorough researcher. Capable organizer and implementer of innovative systems and procedures.

CAREER HIGHLIGHTS:

1953 to Present   NEW YORK POLICE DEPARTMENT, New York, NY

Commanding Officer - Tape and Records Unit   (1971-Present)

Administration

* Proposed, researched, established and currently supervise Forensic Audio Laboratory of the Communications Division

  - Provide NYPD with speaker identification and tape enhancement capability

  - Provide prosecutors with admissible evidence

  - Procedures have resulted in cost saving of more than $250,000 over past three years; more effective utilization of investigator man-hours in major criminal investigations and terrorist activities

  - Supervise 15 tape and audio technicians and voiceprint examiners

* Responsible for 911 Tape Logging System (largest in world - 200 channels)

  - Organized, refined and maintain system which supplies more than 5000 tape recordings per year in cooperation with investigators and officers of the court

* Proposed, established and supervise correlated records unit enabling efficient and timely pinpoint recovery of specific crime information (from 911 master reels and computer printouts reduced to microfiche)

* Maintain efficiency and integrity of specialized electronics equipment valued at more than $300,000; initiated, implemented and maintain security procedures

Training/Lectures/Presentations

* Coach attorneys in effective introduction of sound recordings to assure their admissibility as evidence; instruct employees in use and application to investigative and prosecutorial process

  - Conducted on-going 911 seminar program for district attorneys resulting in more effective use of 911 tapes and records in New York criminal court proceedings

* Lecturer - forensic communications course: biennial Homicide Investigations Course attended by FBI and State Police personnel from all over country; biennial Criminal Investigators' Course structured for local law enforcement agencies

Training/Lectures/Presentations (cont'd)

* Guest lecturer at 1980 NY State District Attorneys' Assn. workshop
* Co-authored status report on development of audio laboratory for presentation at 1980 convention of American Academy of Forensic Sciences in New Orleans

Investigation and Consultation

* Act as departmental consultant on forensic and 911 communications with all departments and with officers of the court
* Act as consultant in liaison with state and federal agencies
* Continue research in legal and scientific considerations through consultation with private sector and academic researchers to maintain state-of-the-art technological proficiency
* Conducting investigation into technique of using sound spectrograph to determine if subject is actually under hypnosis
* Conducting investigation on the effects of aging in speaker identification

Career Progression - NYPD

1953 - Joined department - assigned to routine patrol duties
1960 - Assigned to Emergency Service Division - rescue and sniper work
1963 - Assigned to Detective Division - served in Bureau of Identification as fingerprint technician
1968 - Promoted to sergeant-supervisor of tactical patrol force unit of 30 officers charged with riot control and special weapons tactics
1969 - Transferred to Communications Division with supervision and training of 911 operators and dispatchers

EDUCATION: Specialized Training and Certification

1979 - Advanced Voice Identification Course, Michigan State Police
1976-79 - Annual International Association of Voice Identification Seminar (different location each year)
1978 - Magnetic Tape Analysis Course, FBI Laboratory, Washington, DC
1978 - Security Management Course, New York Police Academy
1977-78 - Specialized Spectrum Analysis, Queens College
1976-78 - Annual Carnahan Crime Countermeasures Conference University of Kentucky
1977 - Spectrum Analysis Techniques, FBI Course, New York City
1976 - Voice Identification Techniques, Voice Identification, Inc. Laboratory, Somerville, NJ
1973 - Management Techniques and Principles, New York Police Academy
1972 - American Management Association Course, New York Police Academy
1961 - Basic and Advanced Fingerprint Identification, NYPD
Criminal Justice Courses, John Jay College

MILITARY: 1956-57 and 1960-61 - U.S. Army, Sergeant First Class
NCO Academy, Munich, Germany - 6-week Leadership Course
Communications Section Leader

MEMBER: International Association of Voice Identification
Acoustical Society of America

QUALIFIED: Certified Voice Print Examiner

JACK L. GRIMES

670 MANNAKEE STREET   ROCKVILLE, MD 20850
Home: (301) 340-4801   Office: (202) 389-1602

OBJECTIVE

**MANAGER, DEPARTMENT of PUBLIC AFFAIRS
or GOVERNMENT RELATIONS**
Scientific or other technologically oriented corporation

SUMMARY

Extensive experience working directly with heads of Fortune 500 corporations, federal agencies and the Congress. Skilled in assessing importance of specific issues and designing successful issues-oriented actions.

PROFESSIONAL HISTORY

1974-Present

NATIONAL ASSOCIATION of SCIENCES/NATIONAL RESEARCH COUNCIL, Washington, DC
Executive Director, Board on Minorities in Engineering & Sciences

- Direct planning, organization and administration to implement science manpower policy utilizing $4,000,000 annually
  - Coordinate efforts of 65 corporations, 15 federal agencies and 112 universities participating in program
  - Establish national priorities and initiatives, guide development and allocation of resources, and monitor achievement of goals

- Influence federal policy and action through communications, negotiation and the creative utilization of human resources
  - Work with Cabinet and agency heads, and members of Congress, in formulating and implementing appropriate laws and regulations
  - Provide significant linkages between academic research facilities, The National Science Foundation and federal departments

- Increased corporate contributions to university minority engineering projects to $11 million, effecting a 400% expansion in corporate participation within six years
  - Facilitated participation of AT&T, DuPont, Exxon and General Electric as corporate pace-setters

- Established national initiatives which increased minority undergraduate engineering enrollment to 7% from 4.5% of the total undergraduate engineering population within six years

- Organized national symposium with 800 prominent leaders from government, industry, academic institutions and civic organizations; coordinated semi-annual meetings for 35 corporate leaders to address national manpower problems
  - Produced national reports used as guides by corporations and funding agencies in establishing funding priorities

- Prepare budgets and plan and staff all functions

Part-Time Consultant
- Assisted in key management at AT&T, Ford Motor Company, Olin Corporation, General Electric Company, RCA Corporation, Rockwell International and Xerox Corporation

—Advised corporate leadership on recruitment of employees to expand technical base, distribution of funds in minority-related areas, regional manpower development activity and corporate-academic linkages

—Organized corporate-financed regional and professional engineering societies

1969-1974

NEW YORK INSTITUTE of TECHNOLOGY, Albany, NY
Director, Engineering Opportunity Program

• Conceived and developed first successful university recruitment and educational program in engineering for women and minority students; created model written up by Departments of Labor and Education for use as national referent

• Placed minority enrollment at NYIT within country's top ten institutions by implementing 75% increase in successful minority matriculation

• Expanded services while maintaining quality through development of first external fundraising activity for university minority programs
—Obtained $15,000 from Alfred P. Sloan Foundation and other corporations
—Established financial aid office and received federal grants for needy students; obtained grant from New York Department of Higher Education

1965-1969

EXPERIMENTAL EDUCATION PROJECT, Paterson, NJ
Director (Part-time)

1960-1969

EASTSIDE HIGH SCHOOL, Paterson, NJ & C.A. JOHNSON HIGH SCHOOL, Columbia, SC
Chairman — Mathematics Department, Science Instructor, Guidance Counselor

EDUCATION

SYRACUSE UNIVERSITY, Syracuse, NY
1968: MS, Chemistry — National Science Foundation Fellowship
ALLEN UNIVERSITY, Columbia, SC
1960: BS, Chemistry

Management Training

General Electric Management Development Institute: Management of Time, Manpower & Money, 1974
University of California at San Diego: Institute for Management Training (sponsored by Department of Defense), 1973

PUBLICATIONS

"Parity for Minorities in Engineering: Myth or Reality," **Engineering Issues,** April, 1980.
"The Image and Relevance of Engineering in the Black and Puerto Rican Community," **New Jersey Science Teachers Journal,** 1971.
"Engineering Opportunity Program: A Special Program for Disadvantaged Students," April, 1973 issue of **Engineering Education.**

PROFESSIONAL AFFILIATIONS

Arthur S. Flemming Awards Committee
American Society for Engineering Education
American Association for the Advancement of Science
National Society of Black Chemists and Engineers

ELIZABETH R. LINTON · 302 North Chestnut Avenue, Livingston, NJ 07039 · (201) 992-9726

OBJECTIVE: PUBLIC RELATIONS/CORPORATE COMMUNICATIONS

To apply my expertise in publicity/public relations in the editorial, music and arts field to a position with a corporation involved in community affairs.

SUMMARY: More than 15 years' experience in writing, publicity, public relations and media placement. Ten years with publishing houses. Creative designer of promotional concepts. Excellent coordinator of diverse groups working toward single goal. Discerning interviewer and organizer of material and campaigns.

CAREER HIGHLIGHTS:

1979 to   CLOVER PUBLICATIONS, INC., New York, NY
Present   Director of Publicity

* Conceive and follow through on promotional campaigns for major books

* Place publicity in national publications; set author interviews on radio and TV; negotiate store tie-ins

   - First full-length Clover review in New York Times; national recognition of Clover

   - Special in-store displays at FAO Schwartz and Lord & Taylor

   - Constantly develop reviewer lists

* Work closely with editorial and sales

1977-78   AMERICAN FEDERATION OF TELEVISION AND RADIO ARTISTS, New York, NY
              Committees Coordinator

* Established committees of varied segments of membership; successfully attained positive communication

   - Maintained liaison between local members and executive staff and between AFTRA and "outside" influences

* Worked with highly confidential information

1975-76   DISTRICT COUNCIL 37, EDUCATION DEPARTMENT, New York, NY
              Writer/Administrative Assistant

* Publicized courses offered by Council to its members; coordinated with educational institutions relative to scheduling and registration

* Wrote and published course handbook (became standard literature for department)

1972-75   SIMON & SCHUSTER, New York, NY
              Associated Director of Publicity

* Wrote and designed all publicity and sales promotional material; selected and placed visuals

   - Increased press coverage and sales through copy frequently acclaimed by reviewers and authors

* Booked authors on network and local television and radio shows

Continued

34

SIMON & SCHUSTER (Continued)

* Promoted from Assistant Director in 1974

1974-77   SCHRIMER BOOKS, New York, NY
Freelance Editor

* Handled all editorial production functions for this division of
MacMillan Company, from manuscript through blues

1969-71   MERCURY PHILLIPS RECORDS, New York, NY
Director of Publicity, Classical Division

* Brought relatively unknown label to attention of national music media

- First complete recording of Berlioz' Les Troyens named "Recording
of the Year" for 1971

* Set up interviews with newspapers and magazines, appearances on
radio and TV for recording artists; promoted open recording sessions
and parties

* Maintained still existing liaison with press agents, reviewers, radio
stations and press agents

1967-69   WASHINGTON NATIONAL SYMPHONY, Washington, DC
Editor, Program Book

* Wrote 95% of program notes for concert repertoire and laid out weekly
program book published for concert audiences

* Maintained liaison between printer and concert office

1966-67   THE CHRISTIAN HERALD, New York, NY
Assistant Editor

* Read manuscripts for publishing potential; read books and manuscripts
for Book Club potential

* Edited articles: copyreading, proofreading, rewriting, cutting

1964-66   AVON BOOKS, New York, NY
Editorial Assistant

* Read hardcovers and manuscripts for potential paperback publication

* Wrote cover copy

* Put together two anthologies: opera, vampire literature

EDUCATION: Columbia University, New York, NY
1964 - MA, Music/English

Hofstra University, Hempstead, NY
1962 - BA

SCHOOL
ACTIVITIES: Represented Music Department at Long Island Contemporary Arts Festival
Worked on college newspaper and literary magazine
Participated in symphony orchestra and chorus

LANGUAGES: Read, speak and translate German

MEMBER: Publishers Publicity Association

KIT LOUX

33 West 95th Street, New York, NY 10024   212/580-6620

OBJECTIVE: <u>RECORDING INDUSTRY - PUBLIC RELATIONS/PROMOTION</u>
To offer my recent experience and my training in the music business in an entry level job leading to a position at the level of assistant in promotion, with growth potential in the promotion area.

SUMMARY: Knowledgeable in area of artist promotion. Trained in music and stagecraft, including writing of lyrics for special occasions. Relate well with people. Competent director of employees and contract talent. Eager to learn music business "from the ground up." Free to travel.

RELEVANT EXPERIENCE:

1978-1979   MUSICBOX, INC.
London, England

Managing Director, U.K. Branch

* Introduced firm to United Kingdom and managed entire operation: consisting of personal delivery of singing telegrams for special occasions.

* Auditioned, hired, and directed singer-artists.

* Arranged for and secured radio and television appearances/interviews as publicity and procured and placed all advertising.

* Sold service to prestigious clients many of whom were in the recording business in London.

* These included: Polydor Records, Pink Floyd Music, The Who, Island Records, CBS Records, EMI Screen Gems Music, BBC Radio & Television, Chrysalis Records.

* Wrote successfully received lyrics for songs used in telegrams.

* Handled all office procedures and finances and secured and trained replacement director.

1977-1978   MUSICBOX, INC.
New York, N.Y.

Courier/Lyrics Writer

* Initiated and promulgated innovative singing telegram service for company and delivered first in-person message in costume.

* Appeared on TV and in press interviews in recognition of service's news value.

* Sold orders over phone and wrote lyrics for customers.

1977 Part Time	AMERICAN MANAGEMENT ASSOCIATION New York, N.Y.

Market Research

* Secured information for sales department.

1972 Summer	VOCATIONAL FOUNDATION, INC. New York, N.Y.

Job Developer

* Phone communication with top management of business firms to secure jobs for unemployed youth. (Successfully placed about 100 youths during summer.)

1969-1972 While in School	CHILDRENS HOSPITAL Washington, D.C.

Volunter - 4-10 year olds

* Worked well with debilitated children, getting them to eat and keeping them entertained and happy.

U.S.CONGRESS
Washington, D.C.

Office Assistant

* Attended Senate and House meetings with Congressman Jack Lee (Arkansas). Worked office machines under supervision of his secretary.

FAIRFAX COUNTY PUBLIC SCHOOLS
Fairfax, Va.

Teacher's Aide

* Supervised children and gave them extra scholastic aid.

EDUCATION:

Chatham College, Pittsburgh, Pa.
   Drama major; Music and French minor
Royal Academy of Dramatic Art, London, England
Graduated 1975

CAREER RELATED COURSES AND ACTIVITIES:

Theater Productions - performing and stage managing
Choir Touring - performing and managing
Photography - Pittsburgh Film Institute
Acting/Scene Study - Lee Strasberg Theatre, New York
Acting/Scene Study - HB Studio, New York
French - Read, Write, Speak
Also, have traveled extensively

MEMBER OF: Actors Equity

CHARLES A. SLABAUGH
930 Third Avenue, New York, New York 10022
(212) 758-9929

OBJECTIVE: **MEDIA PLACEMENT SPECIALIST/ACCOUNT SUPERVISOR**

SUMMARY: Six years public relations experience in both private and public sectors. Excellent broadcast and print media placement record. Good writer and researcher with strong orientation to deadline and detail. Familiar with state-of-the-art technology in film, video and multimedia. Particularly skilled in organizing and managing special events. Maintain consistent reputation for integrity with producers and editors.

EXPERIENCE:

1979 to Present

CHARLES SLABAUGH ASSOCIATES, INC., New York, NY
President

- **National Marine Manufacturers Association** — Initiate radio, television and print promotion for eight industry-owned and operated boat shows nationwide

  —Supervised National Boat Show broadcast media coverage four consecutive years, culminating in 16 placements in 1983 (local, network and syndicated, including CBS Morning News, INN, PM Magazine, Entertainment Tonight, Satellite News Channel, Cable News Network; ABC, NBC and Mutual radio networks; etc.)

  —Generate economic/business stories and publicity for boat shows in Norwalk (CT), Chicago, Philadelphia, Baltimore, Minneapolis/St. Paul, including the Today Show and Good Morning America

  —Created ticket giveaway programs to increase market penetration of regional boat shows; developed Boating Radio Network, providing audio material on boating industry

- **Worrell 1000**—Handle pre-race publicity and press operation of 1,000-mile sailboat race from Ft. Lauderdale to Virginia Beach with extensive print and broadcast coverage in Florida, North Carolina, South Carolina, Georgia and Virginia; supervise television crews and print media traveling with race, including CBS Sports, *Sports Illustrated,* 60 Minutes, AP, UPI, *Miami Herald* and various boating publications

- **The Rath Organization** — Total responsibility for two monthly newsletters (writing, editing, design and production, photography supervision, article solicitation); created seminar program for Pitney Bowes

- **Direct national publicity tours** — for variety of clients:
  —Gerry Spiess (*Yankee Girl,* smallest boat to cross Atlantic and Pacific)
  —Curtis and Kathleen Saville (hold transatlantic rowing record)
  —David Ganz, *World of Coins and Coin Collecting* (Scribners)
  —Jim Hendricks, owner of *African Queen*
  —Joe Franklin, "Memory Lane Nostalgia Convention"

EXPERIENCE:
(Cont'd)

1977 to   **SLABAUGH'S RARE COINS, New York, NY**
1979   **Manager,** Sales Promotion

- Bought, sold and cataloged rare coins to wholesale and retail clientele

- Trained in auction sale promotion, including advertising, releases, catalog preparation and coin photography

1975 to   **GERALD A. ROGOVIN PUBLIC RELATIONS, INC., Boston, MA**
1977   **Writer/Researcher**

                 AGNEW ASSOCIATES, INC., Boston, MA
                 Account Coordinator

                 REP. PETER HARRINGTON (MA)
                 Legislative Aide

                 GOV. MICHAEL DUKAKIS (MA)
                 Student Intern

EDUCATION: **UNIVERSITY OF PENNSYLVANIA, Philadelphia, PA**

- Wharton School of Business, Executive Education Program, 1982

                 SYRACUSE UNIVERSITY, Syracuse, NY

- Master's Candidate in PR Administration

                 BOSTON UNIVERSITY, Boston, MA

- B.S., Public Relations (Cum Laude), 1977

                 NEW YORK UNIVERSITY, New York, NY

- Film Production Workshop
  (200-hour intensive program)

                 NEW YORK INSTITUTE OF TECHNOLOGY, New York, NY

- Television Production Workshop
  (200-hour intensive program)

AFFILIATIONS: Public Relations Society of America
                   Publicity Club of New York (Recipient of Distinguished Service Award)
                   International Association of Business Communicators

ANDREW GARVERICK • 900 West End Avenue, 8E • New York, NY 10025 • (212) 865-6690

OBJECTIVE   PRODUCER/MEDIA PROGRAMMING

SUMMARY   Experienced media producer with high degree of artistic and technical
               expertise. Trained in total approach to use of media. Fully informed
               on state-of-the-art in media production, including the latest video
               editing techniques. Excellent interpersonal skills. Experienced writer,
               producer and supervisor of creative and technical personnel.

EXPERIENCE

1978 to   MERCER MC DONALD (Public Relations), New York, NY
Present   Manager, Audio-Visual Department (1979-1981)

               * Organized and developed Audio-Visual Department of nation's
                  third-largest PR firm

               * Direct day-to-day operations of department, including preparation
                  of budgets, purchase of new equipment and supervision of both
                  creative and administrative personnel

               * Produce, direct and script media programs, including videotapes
                  and multi-projector slide shows

                  - Clients include Sun Company, Inc.; Honeywell; Children's
                     Television Workshop; U.S. Department of Energy (Solar
                     Energy Project); Merle Norman Cosmetics; Emery Air Freight

                  - Awarded John Starr Writing Award - 1980

               * Work intensively with clients to develop programs to fulfill
                  publicity objectives within scheduling and budgeting requirements

                  - Present array of concept proposals from which
                     clients can choose most suitable program

                  - Develop production budgets and schedules, in-
                     cluding services of photographers, graphic
                     artists, video editors and other media vendors

                  - Rated consistently high by clients for expertise,
                     on-schedule performance and follow-up

               * Instrumental in generating substantial new business by working
                  closely with both internal account staff and clients

               * Select, supervise and coordinate efforts of vendors in film and
                  video; work with top-quality editors, utilizing state-of-the-art
                  facilities

               Technician (1978-1979)

               * Wrote proposal outlining methods for improving Audio-Visual
                  Department's profitability and capabilities based on analysis
                  of client needs; resulted in promotion to Manager

1980 to Present	FREE-LANCE MEDIA PRODUCER, New York, NY

* Client list includes CBS Publications Group, <u>Interface Age</u> Magazine, Park Avenue Mall Association and Chacma, Inc.

* Produced radio commercial campaigns for nationally distributed computer magazine

  - Scripted, edited and coordinated all aspects of production

* Directed and wrote sales and motivational slide presentations

  - Scripted, edited and coordinated talent, recording, photography, production of special effect slides, sound mixing and cueing

* Produced promotional videotape for management consulting firm

  - Co-wrote script and coordinated all aspects of production

1975-1976	PACE UNIVERSITY, Pleasantville, NY <u>Media Coordinator</u>

* Coordinated production-oriented program to develop nursing media curriculum; developed and wrote scripts; designed program and supervised television production

1974-1975	UNIVERSITY OF WISCONSIN MEDIA CENTER, Madison, WI <u>Assistant Coordinator, Multi-Media Laboratory</u>

* Produced media programs, including color videotapes and multi-image slide programs; acted as cameraman in color studio and co-produced several productions

* Supervised use of sound studio and four-room presentation facility

* Proposed ideas for new work and methods for improving programming

EDUCATION	Columbia University, New York, NY 1978 - MS, Public Media
	University of Wisconsin, Madison, WI 1974 - Graduate courses in film production
	University of Wisconsin, Madison, WI 1972 - BA, Philosophy/Psychology

PROFESSIONAL AFFILIATIONS:

National Academy Television Arts and Sciences

JOE GUARINO • 150 Great Pine Lane • Pleasantville, NY 10570

OFFICE: (212) 765-2967   HOME: (914) 769-3296

OBJECTIVE	**PROGRAMMING/MANAGEMENT — TELECOMMUNICATIONS INDUSTRY**
SUMMARY	Ten years' experience developing and managing international artists for live performances and television programming. Skilled administrator and supervisor of creative and technical personnel. Excellent track record creating and expanding domestic and international markets. Thorough knowledge of media advertising and publicity. MBA in International Marketing.

MANAGEMENT EXPERIENCE

1973 to Present

JOE GUARINO ENTERPRISES, LTD. (entertainment management), NY, NY **President**

- Management and Marketing Development—promotion, publicity, touring and production—for over 20 contemporary recording artists

- Budget, plan and organize record productions and concert tours; negotiate recording and publishing contracts, personal appearances, advertising endorsements and TV appearances

- Supervise staff of eight, including five account executives; initiated successful system for providing full service to clients while reducing overhead

- Executive producer for precedent-setting engagement of major comedian on Broadway

- Created separate TV division for additional client exposure

  — Produced, packaged or created concept for more than two dozen international and domestic television programs or series, sponsored by BBC, CBC, French Television, German Television, Japanese Television, Australian Television and Los Angeles Cable Television

  — Booked various artists for more than 30 television appearances, including Merv Griffin Show, Dinah Shore Show, Dick Cavett Show, Mike Douglas Show, Don Kirschner's Rock Concert (NBC), Midnight Special (ABC) and Dick Clark's New Years Rock & Eve (ABC)

1971 to Present

GREAT SOUNDS, LTD., NY, NY
President   (1972-Present)
Director, Business Affairs (1971-1972)
- Chief Administrator of 20-person staff responsible for organization and planning of concert tours, personal appearances, record production, publicity and marketing campaign

- Determine annual budgets and both short- and long-range cost projections to sustain profit levels

GREAT SOUNDS, LTD. (Continued)

- Instrumental in expansion of gross revenues to peak of $4 million

  —Developed video productions and advertising endorsements, creating $250,000 in new income; obtained world video rights for distribution to national independent TV stations

  —Generated $450,000 in guaranteed annual income after analyzing audience demographics of major rock group

  —Executive Producer for rock group's appearance at New York Metropolitan Opera

  —Developed international markets, coordinating personal appearances with record exports and publicity campaigns, increasing revenues by $500,000 annually

  —Arranged three-week tour behind Iron Curtain sponsored by Department of State

1978 to Present

ATV MUSIC (publishing), NY, NY
Management Consultant

- Supervise and guide ten songwriters and arrangers through creative and production problems

- Develop and implement marketing strategies

  —Arranged for writers to co-write songs with artists who have recording contracts

  —Increased ad agency awareness of coterie of song writers available for creation of original jingles

  —Brought about 50% increase in advanced income by negotiating international publishing agreements

EDUCATION

NEW YORK UNIVERSITY GRADUATE SCHOOL OF BUSINESS, NY, NY
1971 — MBA, International Marketing

ADELPHI UNIVERSITY, Garden City, NY
1969 — BBA, Business & Finance

Dean's List, 1968-1969
President, School of Business Student Council
Vice President, Marketing & Advertising Club

ALICE BRANDEL   225 East 86th Street, #8-B   Home 212-755-0434
                     New York, NY 10022   Work 518-474-1029

OBJECTIVE   <u>TV WRITING/PRODUCING/DIRECTING</u> - Commercial, cable, public or
             industrial television

SUMMARY   Award-winning writer/producer/director of televised programs, public
           service announcements and closed-circuit programs employing nationally
           known talent. Skilled at developing production budgets and hiring and
           directing creative staffs. Adept at designing program packages and
           software to fulfill specific client requirements.

TELEVISION EXPERIENCE

1969 to   CENTER FOR LEARNING TECHNOLOGIES, NEW YORK STATE EDUCATION DEPARTMENT
Present   Albany, NY

* Write, produce and direct television and closed-circuit training
  programs for adults and children combining studio and electronic
  field production

  - Administer budgets of $3,000 to $100,000
  - Hire and direct production and creative staffs

* Created, produced and directed award-winning, three-part media
  package to promote good nutrition

  - Package included 15 radio and 15 TV announcements, 30-minute
    public TV program and 20-minute closed-circuit TV program
  - Received medal of excellence, International Film and TV
    Festival of New York

* Designed, produced and implemented interactive 40-hour children's
  TV series

  - Broadened and modernized curriculum through use of entertainment
  - Positive response by students evidenced in significant learning
    results

* Developed and produced ongoing statewide teleconferences

  - Programs are "live" and broadcast by all New York State
    public television stations
  - Toll-free call-in provides direct answers to viewers'
    questions

* Consulted with diverse school districts, providing in-service
  training and recommending software and hardware specifications
  to achieve instructional objectives

* Created the "video memo" format as a way to disseminate information
  to staff at 756 locations

ALICE BRANDEL/2

1961-1968   ROCHESTER CITY SCHOOL DISTRICT, Rochester, NY
               TV Instructor (1967-68)
               Business Education Instructor (1961-67)

               * Conceived, wrote and served as on-camera host for 42-lesson,
                  self-instructional TV series in business education used by
                  100 districts statewide

                  - Wrote three manuals to accompany the series
                  - Series was telecast by public and cable TV stations and is
                    used by the State Education Department employee training
                    center
                  - Established reputation of Rochester Televised Instruction
                    Center and resulted in further awards of contracts for
                    videotape production
                  - Series resulted in effective replacement of classroom
                    instruction with 79% pass rate and reduction of instructional
                    costs by almost 50%

               * Assistant Producer for five videotapes featuring the Rochester
                  Philharmonic

EDUCATION   Syracuse University, Syracuse, NY
               1964 - MS, Business Education

               Russell Sage College, Troy, NY
               1961 - BS, Business Education
                      Graduated cum laude with high honors in Business

               University of Hawaii, Honolulu, Hawaii
               1967 - Six credits in Television Production

               Indiana University, Bloomington, Indiana
               1966 - Nine credits in Television Production
                      Awarded H. Wilson Scholarship

               New School for Social Research
               1976 - Developing Programming for Children's Television

AWARDS   Ohio State Broadcasting Award for "Visual Learning" with Gene Shalit,
                  Walter Cronkite, and Betty Furness
               International Film and Television Festival of New York Medal for
                  "The Breakfast Connection" with Lendon Smith, MD, and Marilyn
                  Michaels

Partial list of productions available upon request

WILLIAM MONROE
417 E. 58th Street, Apt. 18D, New York, N.Y. 10022   (212) 935-1725

OBJECTIVE   <u>COMMERCIAL INTERIOR DESIGN</u>

SUMMARY   Interior designer with ten years of commercial and residential design
              experience. Thorough knowledge of trade sources. Understanding of
              city codes and building department routine and bureaucracy. Compre-
              hensive knowledge of commercial planning systems and office land-
              scaping.

DESIGN EXPERIENCE

1977 to   DANIEL STERLING, INC., New York, NY
Present   <u>Head Designer</u> (1978-Present)
              <u>Assistant Designer</u> (1977-78)

       *   Design commercial and residential spaces and direct all facets
           leading to completion of projects. Supervise assistants,
           assuring on-schedule production of quality work. Negotiate with
           architects, vendors and tradesmen, scheduling and coordinating
           their activities.

       *   <u>Achievements</u>

           The Discotheque Parfait, New York City
           Executive business offices, Exemplar International Insurance Co.
             Fort Lee, NJ
           Rare Form contemporary restaurant, New York City
           Solarium for president of Perrier Water Co.
             (featured in TOWN & COUNTRY magazine)
           Private residences for leading social figures in New York City
           Solarium for Richard Todd of the New York Jets, New York City

1979 to   FREE-LANCE PROJECTS
Present
       *   Packaging concept for Alan Fortunoff (owner of Fortunoff's),
           New York City

       *   Textile design collection for Schumacher Decorators Walk,
           Riverdale Fabrics, New York City

       *   Kent Bragaline, New York City

       *   Album cover logo and publicity T-shirts for Darryl Hall and John
           Oates, Arista Records, New York City

       *   Skating Club set and costume design - Utica Figure Skating Club,
           Clinton Figure Skating Club, Hamilton Figure Skating Club, Ice
           Club of Syracuse

1976-1977   TABER INTERIORS, New York, NY
             Assistant Designer

    *   Developed designs, conceptualizations and renderings of floor
        plans, elevations and layouts under tutelage of Head Designer.
        Coordinated design elements and became acquainted with trends
        in design field.

1975-1976   BLOOMINGDALES, New York, NY
             Designer

    *   Created residential interiors, utilizing existing retail
        product lines

1973-1975   SELF-EMPLOYED DESIGNER
             (Concurrent with pursuit of MFA)

    *   Designed and conceptualized various boutiques, shopping plazas
        and restaurants

1970-1972   CARRIER CORPORATION, Syracuse, NY
             Assistant Designer, Corporate Planning

    *   Drawing, drafting, rendering

EDUCATION   COLUMBIA UNIVERSITY, New York, NY
             1981 - MFA   (GPA - 3.8/4.0)

             SYRACUSE UNIVERSITY, Syracuse, NY
             1970 - BFA, Interior Design (GPA - 4.0/4.0)
             Dean's List, eight semesters

CERTIFICATION

             Permanent Certified Design Instructor, New York State Board of Regents

SALLY MARCUS
340 EAST 57th STREET
New York, N.Y. 10022
(212) 730-2196

OBJECTIVE

To employ my professional training in
architectural design in the area of
planning and designing private residences
and public spaces.

SUMMARY

Creative spatial planner with ability for combining function and aesthetics in a variety of
environments. Broad background in architectural history and theory, human factors and urban
studies. Studied under prestigious experts in
fields of city planning, contract, residential
and lighting design, and landscape architecture.

EDUCATION

Parsons School of Design, New York, NY
1980 - BFA Program, Environmental Design

Columbia University, New York, NY
1975-76 - Urban Studies

DESIGN EXPERIENCE
1975-80

o Spatial planning for bazaar: The Burke
  Institute fund-raising

o Interior design consultant to Mrs. Rebecca
  Noonan, New York

o Design consultant and spatial planner for
  Deanne, Bellow and Roth, Inc.

o Apprentice to Rita Blass, AIA, South Salem,
  NY

DESIGN ASSIGNMENTS
1977-80

PINE ISLE RESORT HOTEL, Gainesville, Georgia
    Design of Winter/Summer resort

MIDTOWN POCKET PARK, Newark, NJ
    Design of two-level public plaza in center
    of business district

SEAMEN'S RESTAURANT, New York, NY
    Renovation of three-story residence, Upper
    East Side

SOLAR ENERGY-EFFICIENT HOUSE
    Typical two-family brownstone home adapted
    for energy efficiency

OTHER EXPERIENCE
1974-79

Stony Brook Day Camp, Dover, NJ
    Camp counselor (four summers)

YW/MHA, West Orange, NJ
    Hotline Phone Counselor

St. Louis, MO Public Schools
    Tutor

Extensive travel throughout Europe and
    United States

Yvonne C. Miller

207 Hudson Street, Apt. 5N, New York, N.Y. (212) 226-5525

GRAPHIC ARTIST AND ILLUSTRATOR

OBJECTIVE: To apply my artistic talent as an illustrator in a position with growth potential to design responsibility

SUMMARY: Experienced in broad spectrum of commercial art including technical and advertising graphics. Have capacity for fast learning.

EXPERIENCE:

1978-80   Technical Illustrator - VOLT INFORMATION SCIENCES, INC., Syosset, NY

* Coordinated in-house and farmed-out steps in production process, including assigning artists, camera and proofing

* Illustrated viewgraphs, flowcharts and forms; adapted photos as graphic illustrations; cartooning, flipcharts, lettering and posters

* Did layout, page makeup and paste-up for manuals and graphs; paste-ups for trade magazine and telephone company publication ads

* Charged with responsibility for complete production of company display from rough layout to finished art

1977 to   SELECTED FREELANCE ASSIGNMENTS
Present
Graphs - CBS Radio Sales Research Department, New York, NY
Brochure and consumer ad illustration - Jasper Industries, Oyster Bay, NY
Ink illustrations, Xerox and color photo adaptation - New Community
     Theatre, Huntington, NY
Murals - Gent's World, Madison, WI
Posters and murals - Concourse Hotel, Madison, WI
Display ads and billboards - Sel Metals Corporation, Holbrook, NY
Textbook illustrations - McGraw-Hill Book Company, Inc., New York, NY

EDUCATION: University of Wisconsin, Madison, WI
1973-75 - Fine Art

Technical College, Old Westbury, NY
1973 - Course in Photography

State University of New York, Farmingdale, NY
1971-72 - Art Advertising

MARGARET YORK

78-20 Austin Street   Kew Gardens, New York   11415   (212) 847-6721

OBJECTIVE: Long-term commitment to reputable consumer magazine as an associate, assistant, copy or contributing editor.

SUMMARY: Skilled in all aspects of handling manuscripts: rewriting, copy editing and proofreading. Experienced in judging manuscripts and dealing with authors. Expert speller and grammarian.

RELEVANT EXPERIENCE:

Nov. 1978-
Present

<u>Associate Editor</u>, MACFADDEN WOMEN'S GROUP

* Evaluate, rewrite and edit new manuscripts

* Proofread galleys, check page proofs and final pages

* Maintain close liaison with Home Service, art and production departments

June 1978-
Nov. 1978

<u>Production Editor</u>, JOHN WILEY AND SONS

* Edited and proofread copy for four technical magazines

* Checked final pages and incorporated authors' corrections onto proofs

* Logged manuscripts, used Greek symbols and type specifications

April 1974-
June 1977

<u>Production Editor</u>, AMERICAN SOCIETY OF MECHANICAL ENGINEERS

* Solely responsible for journal

--Copy editing, proofreading, transferral of authors' corrections onto final pages

--Page layout, sizing of figures and photographs, pagination, check of final pages

Jan. 1973-
June 1973

<u>Traffic Editor</u>, SIMPLICITY PATTERN COMPANY

* Controlled flow of pages to and from printer

* Informed art and design departments about changes in page sequence

April 1972-
Oct. 1972

<u>Assistant Copy Editor</u>, AMERICAN INSTITUTE OF AERONAUTICS AND ASTRONAUTICS

(Duties similar to those at John Wiley)

EDUCATION: Molloy College, B.A. in English, 1969

LANGUAGES: French and Latin

FRANK LOYKOVICH

3275 West 33rd Street
Brooklyn, NY 11224

Home: (212) 946-6695
Office: (221) 889-2875
Ext. 246

OBJECTIVE: <u>ART DIRECTOR/CORPORATE COMMUNICATIONS</u>

Seeking corporate position where my expertise in editorial design will be employed in communications media for both external and internal circulation.

SUMMARY: More than 12 years experience in graphic design for production of magazines, brochures, annual reports, conference displays, newsletters, book jackets, house organs, and other collateral units. Capable production strategist in selecting freelance talent, interfacing with vendors, editorial and public affairs departments, and overseeing production budgets. Knowledgeable of broadcast media advertising and public relations requirements. Discerning in adapting research to specific markets.

CAREER HIGHLIGHTS:

1977 to
Present

EARL E. GRAVES LTD. & SUBSIDIARIES
New York, NY

<u>Associate Art Director</u>

* Assist Art Director in producing visuals for total packaging of 260,000 circulation magazine

* Select freelance talent, negotiate fees, oversee average $15,000 monthly budget, supervise five-member staff

* Expedite workload traffic flow to meet camera ready processing deadline

* Conceive and design print ads and collateral for company-owned radio stations

* Conceive and design brochures and other collateral material for station public affairs director for exhibitions and presentations

* Conceive and design material for publisher's public policy presentations

* Research demographics and create chart material in marketing to the community

1974 to
1977

FREELANCE GRAPHIC DESIGNER
New York, NY

* Sold own talents successfully to clients for design of corporate stationery, promotional brochures, book jackets, inside book design, conference displays, newsletters, house organs, trade ads and general advertising

* Maintained customer relations with advertising agencies, publishers and corporate art directors

1973 to 1974	**LIVING TOGETHER PUBLICATIONS, INC.** New York, NY

Media Representative

* Advertising account executive for 200,000 circulation magazine supplement in top 20 markets newspapers

* Established new major accounts for personal care and cosmetic products (including Clairol) as new entries into ethnic market

1972 to 1973	**VIZMO PRODUCTION, INC.** New York, NY

Staff Designer

* Created and designed graphic presentation for NBC-TV including national and local newscasts and The Today Show

* Created and designed weather maps, slide titles and promotional material for media sales department

1971 to 1972	**PERFECTION PHOTO, INC.** New York, NY

Associate Designer

* Designed typography for packaging, print ads, direct mail, brochures and magazines

1968 to 1970	**MCGRAW-HILL, INC.** New York, NY

Staff Designer, Corporate Art Department

* Correlated book jacket and sales collateral with editorial, advertising and marketing departments

* Designed annual reports and slide presentations

OTHER ACTIVITIES:

- Worked with editor in refocusing editorial content of NAACP's "The Crisis"; redesigned and restructured features and departments of the publication

- Consulting art director and lecturer, New York University - editorial design; production of magazine as term project

EDUCATION: New York City Community College, Brooklyn, NY
              Advertising and Design Theory

              School of Visual Arts, New York, NY

MEMBER: Graphic Artists Guild
              Society of Publications Designers
              New York Type Directors Club

AWARDS: New York Art Directors Club, 1979 Merit Award

HOWARD D. PAPPAS
10 Hall Avenue
Freehold, NJ 07728
(201) 780-1576

OBJECTIVE: CHORAL DIRECTOR - COLLEGE OR UNIVERSITY

SUMMARY: Ten years experience as choral director in schools at elementary, secondary and college levels, including three years as church minister of music. Creative teacher with ability to motivate students in appreciation of and participation in all phases of music. Skillful conductor in training and performances. Active and artistic performer.

RELEVANT EXPERIENCE:

1975 to Present   MARLBORO TOWNSHIP PUBLIC SCHOOLS, Marlboro, NJ

Teacher of Music

*   Train and direct school chorus and prepare students for assembly and public performances

    -   Also teach classes for trainable impaired children

    -   Assist classroom teachers in program preparation

*   Initiated change in curriculum to include related arts approach to teaching music as prescribed by the Orff-Schulwerk Method

    -   Coordinate the study of singing, dance, speech, playing musical instruments and ear and sensitivity training

*   Compose and arrange songs for children (both words and music)

*   Introduced conceptual approach to general music program, giving students a more defined insight into music

*   Served as curriculum consultant to school district in Orff techniques; served on Related Arts Committee to develop multi-discipline, multi-media experiences

Concurrent 1978-79   FAIRLEIGH DICKINSON UNIVERSITY, NJ

*   Directed university chorus (25 students for credit courses) on part-time basis; conducted two public concerts

1974-75   MOORESTOWN FRIENDS SCHOOL, Moorestown, NJ

Teacher of Music

*   Directed high school and junior high school chorus; taught music as elective to high school students and general music in grade school

*   Created a course in 8th grade general music based on Rock history, through both styles and performers

1975-76   PLACERVILLE PRESBYTERIAN CHURCH, Placerville, NJ

Minister of Music

*   Trained and directed adult choir; developed outstanding repertoire of sacred music; trained and directed junior choir

*   Conducted choir for Sunday services; presented two cantatas at Christmas; presented Bach motet at Spring Concert

HOWARD D. PAPPAS/2

1971-73   JUILLIARD SCHOOL, New York, NY
               <u>Teaching Fellow</u>

               * Assisted choral director in all aspects of managing department (served
                 in his stead during several four-to-six week absences)

               * Charged with responsibility for concert arrangements, library, attendance,
                 grades and interoffice communications

               * Conducted and rehearsed Juilliard Chorus while director was on tour for
                 professional engagements

               * Prepared Juilliard Chorus for historic production of opera "Macbeth" by
                 Ernest Block

               * Instructed classes in choral conducting

               * Only candidate accepted for enrollment in 1969

                 - Recipient of Frank Damrosch Prize

1970-73   THE NEW JERSEY CHORALE, Rutherford, NY (While attending school)
               <u>Conductor</u>

               * Developed chorale into a prestigious company with a repertoire that
                 attracted sponsors for more lucrative contracts

               * Conducted chorale's first concert featuring a full length classical work
                 with orchestra

               * Substantially improved chorale's financial condition through removal of
                 deficit by increased bookings

OTHER WORK: * Professional freelance soloist and choral singer

               * Recordings of educational records for:

                 - Victor Kayfetz Productions, 1971

                 - American Book Company, 1973

               * Solo recital for Monmouth Symphony League, March 1978

                 - Eight sound filmstrips for HEW-funded elementary music program

               * Private instruction in voice, piano and theory

EDUCATION: The Juilliard School, New York, NY
               1973 - MM, Choral Conducting

               Trenton State College, Trenton, NJ
               1968 - BA, Music Education (Vocal)

               1978 - Conducting Fellowship, Aspen Music Festival; Singer Aspen Choir

               Concert Westminster Choir College, Princeton - Orff-Schulwerk Courses

MEMBER: College Music Society
               Music Educators National Conference
               New Jersey Music Educators Association
               National Education Association
               New Jersey Education Association
               American Orff-Schulwerk Association
               Central New Jersey Orff-Schulwerk Association

CERTIFICATE: New Jersey Permanent Teaching Certificate

ELEANOR GOLDMAN

250 West 89th Street   New York,   NY 10025   (212) 580-6692

OBJECTIVE: MANAGEMENT - OFFICE/PERSONNEL

SUMMARY: More than ten years experience in supervision of office procedures and
            personnel recruitment and management. Creative designer of work flow
            systems to eliminate duplication of effort and increase proficiency and
            productivity of staff. Administer confidential projects with dispatch
            and discretion. Astute negotiator with vendors of supplies, equipment
            and services.

BUSINESS HIGHLIGHTS:

1973 to   INTEGRATED RESOURCES, INC.
Present   New York, NY

            Office Manager and Personnel Manager

            Office Manager

            * Supervise staff of 152 secretarial and clerical personnel

               - Serve as liaison for middle management with executive suite

               - Train clerical personnel in procedures and office equipment

               - Administer vacation policies and schedule vacations

            * Purchase office supplies, equipment, furniture and services

               - Supervise maintenance crew for two floors and suites on
                  four other floors of 41-story building

               - Maintain liaison with New York Telephone Company relevant to
                  equipment and service for this office and 14 subsidiaries of
                  company

               - Supervise all communications invoices

            * Initiated Mag card system of word processing

            * Have complete responsibility for special projects

               - In process of moving offices: supervising decor, purchasing
                  furnishings, consulting on phone installation, allocating office
                  assignments, arrangement of files and equipment, selection and
                  supervision of movers and expediting printing of new stationery

               - Administer maintenance of corporate apartment for visiting VIP's

            Personnel Manager

            * Recruit, interview and hire clerical personnel (in last six months,
               interviewed 300, hired 50 and trained 15)

            * Negotiate contracts with personnel agencies

            * Maintain confidential records; supervise benefits; process insurance
               claims

            * Prepare payroll (EDP), bi-weekly input sheets, quarterly reports for
               WHT and unemployment insurance and W-2's

            * Designed and implemented smoothly operating personnel system

            * Wrote personnel manual and developed records systems

1968 to 1973	RESTAURANT ASSOCIATES INDUSTRIES, INC. New York, NY

Central Files Supervisor

* Set up central files system and supervised clerical personnel
* Maintained confidential employment and labor contracts

Summer 1968	BOARD OF EDUCATION, CITY OF NEW YORK Brooklyn, NY

Teacher's Aide

* Supervised school students on day camp trips; assisted in classroom work

1967 to 1968	UNITED STATES TESTING COMPANY Hoboken, NJ

Consumer Tester

* Administered consumer testing program for food items
* Persuaded casual shoppers to participate by responding to test and filling out questionnaire

1965 to 1966	WILBUR ROGERS DEPARTMENT STORE Port Authority Bus Terminal, New York, NY

Cashier/Sales Clerk

* Assisted customers with purchases
* Handled cash and ran register check at close of business

SKILLS: Train employees in typing, dictaphone, telecopier, Mag 2, memory typewriter

EDUCATION:

Allen University
Katherine Gibbs School of Business
W & J Sloan School of Interior Decorating
American Management Association: Getting Ahead in Personnel

INTERESTS:

Fashion, interior decorating, dancing, sports and travel

RICHARD SPOSITO . 200 East 33 Street Apt 6A . New York, NY 10016 . (212) 532-4455

OBJECTIVE: To offer my expertise in the field of music to a publishing house
as editor or technical consultant

SUMMARY: More than 15 years experience in all phases of music: Composer,
Arranger, Conductor, Performer, Instructor and Business Manager.
Compositions have been performed in Carnegie Hall. More than ten
students have become stars, hundreds have become professional
musicians and singers. Play piano and flute; knowledgeable about
all instruments.

PROFESSIONAL HIGHLIGHTS:

1972 to   NEW YORK SCHOOL OF MUSIC, New York, NY
Present
Chairman of Music Theory Department/Instructor

* Instruct both graduate and undergraduate students in music theory

  - Organized courses of study

  - Originated new courses in Advanced Ear Training

* Oversee auditions for prospective applicants

* Recommend instructors and substitutes for hire

* Train new instructors

* Hundreds of former students have gone on to play or sing professionally

* Currently in joint authorship of a music theory workbook for
beginning high school students in the Preparatory Division of
Manhattan School of Music (September, 1984 projected publication
date)

Concurrent Leader of Jazz Combo
1976 to
Present   * Write and arrange compositions, direct appearances and perform on
the piano and flute

* Book appearances in New York Metropolitan Area for weddings, bar
mitzvahs, cocktail parties and holiday events

* Manage all financial affairs and arrangements for group, including
billing and collection

Concurrent BROOKLYN COLLEGE, Brooklyn, NY
1973-80
Adjunct Lecturer

* Taught assigned music theory and music appreciation courses to
music and non-music majors

1965-79   SEAMAN'S METHODIST CHURCH, Brooklyn, NY

Music Director

1970-72   NEW YORK CITY COMMUNITY COLLEGE, Brooklyn, NY

<u>Adjunct Lecturer</u>

* Taught assigned music appreciation courses to non-music majors

1962-69   NEW YORK CITY BOARD OF EDUCATION, Brooklyn, NY

<u>Teacher of Orchestral Music</u>   (1966-69)

* Trained students on all orchestral instruments

* Instituted home use of instruments to increase interest in orchestra

* Developed orchestra from ten poorly trained players into well disciplined musical group of 60 instrumentalists

<u>General Music Teacher</u>   (1962-66)

* Taught music appreciation to general classes

* Trained and rehearsed school Glee Club

EDUCATION: Manhattan School of Music, New York, NY
              1972 - MM, Music Theory/Piano
                    Thesis: "Ear Training Program for College Freshmen"

              New York University, New York, NY
              1967 - MA, Master of Music Education

              Howard University, Washington, DC
              1959 - BA, Music Education (cum laude)

HONORS: - Inducted into Pi Kappa Lamda, Howard University
              - Elected president of student council
              - Received Lucy E. Moten Fellowship for European study and travel - 1958
              - Achieved highest score on Regular Teacher Examination (orchestral music), Board of Education of New York - 1966

ORIGINAL COMPOSITIONS:

              Serenity for Solo Flute
              Theme and Variations for Piano and Bassoon
              Piano Sonata in One Movement
              Woodwind Quintet No. 1
              Woodwind Quintet No. 2 (performed at Carnegie Hall)
              Theme and Variations for Woodwind Quintet

MEMBER: American Music Center
              Music Theory Teachers of New York State

CERTIFIED: Music Teacher for New York State

RAYMOND W. CLANCY . 6518 Grant Place . West New York, NJ 07093 . (201) 867-7777

OBJECTIVE: <u>MUSEUM DEVELOPMENT/PROGRAM ADMINISTRATOR</u>

A position employing my experience in educational program development and knowledge of anthropology, classical antiquity and presentation and promotion.

SUMMARY: MA, Anthropology. Experienced in program development in anthropology, American History, language and humanities and enrichment programs for gifted and talented students. Adept at negotiation, persuasion and promotion. Knowledge of fund raising, budget development, organization and production.

HIGHLIGHTS:
- Magazine Production - coordinated all aspects including design, layout, editing and printing

- Film and Theatrical Production - from conception to production including scripting, casting, lighting and direction

- Fund Raising and Special Promotions - conceived and directed money raising events through use of film, sales, and theatre

TECHNICAL SKILLS:

* Audio visual equipment (super 8 film and 1/2" video cameras, projectors, voice recorders, copy stands, Repronar, slides and filmstrips)

* Darkroom facility: 35 mm color and black and white (develop and print)

* Holography

PROGRAM DEVELOPMENT EXPERIENCE:

1969 to Present   DUPONT BOARD OF EDUCATION, Dupont, NJ

<u>Instructor</u>

* Anthropology, Latin, American History, Humanities

* Developed and implemented six new curricula in Anthropology, Latin and Political Science

* Conceived, developed, and initiated first school wide anthropology course

* Achieved full enrollments in elective courses through intense promotional campaigns; maintained enrollment by combining humor and drama with solid exposure to subject matter

* Assisted with development of humanities program

DUPONT SCHOOL DISTRICT

* Participated in setting district and school-wide goals to ensure enhanced education and special programs for gifted and talented children

- Developed specialized curricula in science, art and communications

- Conducted intensive research into existing programs for gifted and talented students

(continued)

DUPONT SCHOOL DISTRICT (continued)
* Advisor to school literary and art magazine:
  - Directed unique fund raising ventures
  - Prepared budget and selected vendors within budgetary outlines
  - Supervised staff of 20
  - Coordinated production, including design, layout, editing and printing
* Active in school organization:
  - Elected chairman of eight-member Faculty Council
  - Member of committee on development of educational goals for entire district
  - Member of Committee for Faculty Evaluation
  - Advise and oversee budget distributions of student language, science, theatre, athletic, newspaper and chef's clubs
  - Secured favorable increases and benefits in negotiations with district Board of Education
  - Convinced Board of Education to publish official policy book to clarify personnel policies
* Produced three 15-minute films and directed two full-scale theatrical productions for fund raising and promotion

RESEARCH AND WRITING EXPERIENCE:

1968   STATEN ISLAND INSTITUTE, New York, NY

            Foundation Researcher

1967   WNYC RADIO, New York, NY

            Free-Lance Writer/Researcher

            * Researched and wrote programs on consumer frauds and exposés on home service industries and food pricing

EDUCATION:

            Montclair State College, Montclair, NJ
            1976 - MA in Anthropology

            St. Peters College, Jersey City, NJ
            1969 - BA in American History
                  Multiple minors in English, Latin, Philosophy and Education

LICENSES:

            Licensed to teach American History, English, Latin and Anthropology by the State of New Jersey

LANGUAGE: Latin - Reading and Translation

INTERESTS: Photography, classical music, jazz

KATHERINE SINORADZKI
River Bend Road, New Canaan, Ct. 06840
(203) 966-0318

OBJECTIVE: CRUISE DIRECTOR

SUMMARY: Six years intermittent experience as cruise director and
             passenger on voyages of from 18 to 90 days in Caribbean,
             Mediterranean, South Seas, Trans-Pacific and the Greek
             Islands. Strong background planning, budgeting and super-
             vising daily on-board activities. Assist passengers in
             familiarization of ship's facilities and activities, as well
             as ports of call. Particular facility for "people matching"
             to see that greatest number of passengers meet those of
             similar interests and tastes, thus ensuring enthusiastic
             repeat passengers and referrals. Widely traveled in Europe,
             Near and Far East, Caribbean, South America, Australia,
             New Zealand and South Sea Islands. Nine-year resident of
             Japan. Fluent in Spanish; read and interpret Japanese.

RELEVANT   FINNISH AMERICAN LINE, New York, NY
EXPERIENCE: Cruise Director, SS Kungsholm

(while em-   Planned, budgeted and supervised eight to ten recreational
ployed at   and social activities daily for approximately 500 passengers
New York   of widely varying interests and energy levels.
Stock Ex-
Change--see   - Scheduled and oversaw ship-wide tournaments (cribbage,
page 2)   deck tennis shuffleboard, scrabble, etc.).

                  - Dropped or added activities in mid-cruise as necessary
                    to accommodate unique passenger interests.

                  - Provided activity information and other "ship's news"
                    to passengers through cabin-delivered daily programs,
                    posters and public address announcements.

              Developed ability to introduce passengers of like interests
              to one another, thus encouraging friendships that led to
              large number of repeat passengers and referrals.

                  - Organized "Captain's sit-down cocktail parties," so
                    arranged to permit optimum passenger introductions.

                  - Conducted "special interest" parties bringing together
                    "Repeaters," "Singles," "Masons," etc., to permit meeting
                    of people of like interests.

              Acted as "liaison officer" between passengers and ship's
              staff, conveying questions, complaints, comments and sugges-
              tions; worked closely with purser, dining room staff, etc.

              Also worked closely with entertainment staff, special activi-
              ties staff and land tour staff in disseminating information
              to passengers about their various functions.

NEW YORK STOCK EXCHANGE, New York, NY
Gallery Director, Public Relations Department

1952
to
1958

Served frequently as Exchange spokeswoman in contacts with media; worked with print and broadcast media representatives to keep Exchange functions and brokerage office procedures in public eye.

- Worked with newsmen and feature writers on articles on Exchange.

- Wrote and delivered daily radio broadcast on WNYC on various aspects of Exchange and financial operations; gave daily price quotations on selected list of stocks.

- Made guest TV and radio appearances on behalf of Exchange (e.g., the "Today" show).

Designed, organized and supervised Stock Exchange exhibit in U.S. Pavillion at Exposition International in Brussels.

Supervised 13 tour guides in overseeing operations of Visitors' Gallery, including conducting tours for up to 2,000 visitors daily.

- Escorted special individual and group visitors on in-depth tours of Exchange and financial area; entertained individuals and groups during visits to New York (as escort to shops, theatres, restaurants, etc.).

- Arranged luncheons for guests of the Exchange, working with chefs on menus and occasionally working as hostess.

CURRENT
EXPERIENCE:

SELF-EMPLOYED, New Canaan, CT
Landscape Designer

Design, execute and supervise construction of gardens and garden structures (principally Japanese), such as rock gardens, pool houses, tea houses, bridges, waterfalls, decks, dams and swimming pools for clients nationwide.

EDUCATION:

PARSON'S SCHOOL OF DESIGN, New York, NY
NEW YORK INSTITUTE OF FINANCE, New York, NY
MISS PORTER'S SCHOOL, Farmington, CT

LICENSES AND
CERTIFICATIONS:

Registered Representative and Security Analyst,
    New York Stock Exchange
Private Pilot's License
Radio Operator's License

LANGUAGES:

Fluent in Spanish; speak and interpret Japanese.

Finance

COLLEEN MC DONALD
4021 Snyder Avenue
Brooklyn, New York 11203

Home: (212) 856-7321   Office: (212) 489-6300

SUMMARY   Fifteen-year banking career with eight years in branch operations
management capping seven years in varied ground-floor services.
Adept at control of cash losses and forgeries and able to structure
work assignments for maximum efficiency and customer service.
Fully knowledgeable of NOW accounts, money market accounts and
safe deposit procedures. Experienced in use of NCR 270 and IBM CRT.

BANKING AND FINANCE EXPERIENCE

1968 to   UNITED MUTUAL SAVINGS BANK, Brooklyn, NY
Present   Branch Manager and Officer (1979-Present)

* Structure and supervise functions of 20 branch employees to ensure
  maximum efficiency and security

  - Charged with direction of daily work assignments of nine tellers,
    new accounts and safe deposit personnel, clerical, maintenance
    and security staffs

  - Restructure work flow depending on daily requirements

  - Conduct salary reviews

* Decreased annual overtime costs by nearly $10,000 and increased
  efficiency by revamping Tellers' Department

  - Trained tellers in all facets of unit; wrote training outline
    for execution by Head Teller

* Eliminated cash losses and forgeries over past five years through
  vigorous implementation of security measures

  - Conduct bi-monthly meetings to assure good security practices
    among tellers

  - Maintain minimum total cash and working drawer levels

  - Execute frequent internal audits of cash, travelers' checks and
    bonds

* Able to take on expanded responsibilities and troubleshoot during
  emergencies

  - Assume Assistant Vice President's functions during periodic
    absences of up to three weeks' duration

  - Substitute for managers in other branches on emergency basis

  - Troubleshoot computer malfunctions and improper data entries

* Performed above responsibilities since 1973, beginning as Banking
  Operations Assistant; promoted to Assistant Manager in 1976 and
  Manager in 1979

Head Teller (1970-1973)

* Supervised 11-member Teller Department, completely restructuring Department to increase efficiency and customer service

    - Organized work flow and staggered hours based on analysis of customer traffic patterns

    - Centralized equipment and supply locations for increased utility

New Accounts Clerk (1968-1970)

* Opened regular savings and society accounts; sold travelers' checks and bonds; stopped payments on checks and money orders

* Administered estate and guardian accounts, securing and completing necessary tax waivers, letters of administration and court orders

* Issued personal savings and demand loans; proved daily balances for all loans

Teller (1968)

* Performed full range of teller services: Conducted deposit and withdrawal transactions; issued money orders and tellers' checks; cashed checks and travelers' checks; accepted loan payments

* Maintained bank security through close scrutiny of all transactions

1959 - 1962   MERRILL, LYNCH, PIERCE, FENNER & SMITH, New York, NY
                Cashier

* Accepted payment for stock margin accounts; acted as liaison with salespeople; operated teletype and PBX switchboard; responded to telephone and mail inquiries from customers

1957 - 1959   MANUFACTURERS HANOVER TRUST COMPANY, New York, NY
                Operator, Check Sorting Machine

EDUCATION   Professional Seminars (study sponsored by United Mutual Savings Bank)

                Financial Institute of Studies, Fairfield, CT
                1980 - Intensive one-week seminars on Branch Management, Women in Management

                AIB, New York, NY
                Six-week course in Life Insurance

                1957 - Graduate, Bishop McDonnell High School, Brooklyn, NY

CERTIFICATIONS

                Certified by State of New York as Notary Public and Life Insurance Agent

AFFILIATIONS   Savings Bank Women

ANDREW K. MELON . 1600 Hitchcock Road . Wantagh, NY 11793 . (516) 781-7321

OBJECTIVE: **VICE PRESIDENT - COMMERCIAL/INDUSTRIAL LENDING**

(Commercial bank, commercial finance company or leasing company)

SUMMARY: 14 years industrial lending management experience, including 10 as vice president with three major commercial banking institutions. Thoroughly experienced in all aspects of credit, administration, development, collection and legal. Particular expertise in equipment financing and leasing. Managed $74 million portfolio, which increased 250% over five-year period.

EXPERIENCE:

1975 to Present

LONG ISLAND TRUST COMPANY, Garden City, NY
Vice President - Commercial/Industrial Credit

* Develop, originate and administer direct and indirect loans; successfully increased portfolio from $30 million (1975) to $74 million (1980)

* Develop major customers and new business in coordination with branches

* Serve as member of credit committee acting on commercial and industrial loan requests and line of credit renewals

* Administer all activities of department; prepare and monitor budget; oversee collections; direct solicitation of new business

* Direct personnel administration; supervise staff of five

* Conceived and implemented simplified procedures and improved communications with resulting increased work flow and departmental capability

1975

JANLIN LEASING CORPORATION, Melville, NY
Vice President - Credit/Marketing

* Initiated credit investigations and established documentation procedures for processing lease and finance paper

- Arranged for discounting paper

1971-1975

SECURITY NATIONAL BANK, Melville, NY
Vice President - Monthly Payment Business Loan and Equipment Finance Departments

* Originated, coordinated and processed direct branch loans, and indirect loans through equipment dealers and leasing companies (lending authority, $250,000)

* Increased loan portfolio from $14 to $33 million; achieved balanced mix of industries

* Prepared and periodically analyzed budget

* Reviewed recommendations on loans which exceeded staff authority limits

* Coordinated legal, accounting and personnel functions within department; supervised staff of nine

(continued)

SECURITY NATIONAL BANK (continued)

* Directly negotiated loans with other bank officers, bank customers, attorneys and accountants

* Evaluated computer reports; implemented new forms, reporting procedures and follow-up systems; created departmental operating manual

1967-1971   FRANKLIN NATIONAL BANK, New York, NY
Assistant Vice President - Metropolitan Division of Industrial Credit

* Managed loan portfolio of $25 million, increasing loan volume by 25%

* Solicited new industrial loan customers; introduced new loan customers to other bank services including payroll accounts, trust services, letters of credit, accounts receivable financing and real estate financing

* Supervised staff of six

1959-1967   FEDERATION BANK AND TRUST COMPANY, New York, NY
Assistant To Vice President - Industrial Credit Department

* Beginning as credit investigator and documentation clerk, was promoted to assistant cashier with medium five-figure line of credit; then to assistant vice-president with low six-figure line of credit

* Responsibilities included budget preparation, development of branch loans, overall management and personnel direction

EDUCATION: New York Institute of Credit, New York, NY
1963 - Business and Banking courses

Moberly Junior College, Moberly, MO
1956-1958 - Business Administration

New York Institute of Technology, New York, NY
Business courses (continuing professional education)

JOHN TUMINO, 25 NORTHRIDGE ROAD, OLD GREENWICH, CONNECTICUT 06870
Home: (203) 637-6653   Office: (212) 980-8573

OBJECTIVE: **SENIOR MANAGEMENT — BANKING**

SUMMARY: Highly motivated and creative international banker with distinguished service and profitability record in New York, London, Paris and Amsterdam.

CAREER HIGHLIGHTS:

1975 to Present   CITICORP INTERNATIONAL
New York, NY

Vice-President for Europe, Mideast and Africa
New York, NY (December 1978 to Present)

- Direct all Edge Act marketing and account service for EMEA-New York

- Control demand balances in excess of $75,000,000 and 90% of 40,000-plus monthly transaction volume

- As senior credit officer for both parent bank and Edge Act subsidiary, govern EMEA-New York exposure

- Contributed substantially to design of deposit-based earnings credit system for Islamic clients, offsetting cost of future credit services

- Principal force in redesign of accounting and profitability models

Vice-President and Representative (December 1977 — December 1978)
Assistant Vice-President (January 1976 — December 1977)
Amsterdam, The Netherlands

- Managed corporate and correspondent relationships throughout 23-nation area, coordinating efforts with U.S. associates

- Directed compilation and analysis of data relative to the economics of developing nations; wrote acceptable business plans accordingly

- Met with senior ministers and heads of state throughout Africa, and developed strategies for establishment of credit limits with French West Africa

- Designed and implemented special correspondent agreements with compatible European banks, effectively creating a branch network overseas for Citicorp

- Consistently surpassed annual goals set for deposit gatherings, loan volume, profitability and staffing

Assistant Vice-President, Corporate Finance
London, England (February 1975 — January 1976)

- Responsible, as part of team effort, for origination and implementation of new merchant and corporate capabilities for Citicorp in Europe

June 1974
to
Jan. 1975

BANK OF AMERICA INTERNATIONAL, LTD.
London, England

Manager

- Set up and managed umbrella administration for credit, loan services and syndication areas

Jan. 1972
to
June 1974

BANK OF AMERICA INTERNATIONAL S.A. (LUXEMBOURG)
Paris, France

Assistant Vice-President and Loan Officer
Banque Ameribas

- Member of original team that formed aggressive new merchant bank. Assembled portfolio in excess of $250,000,000 over three-year period, on nominal capital

Sept. 1969
to
Jan. 1972

IRVING TRUST COMPANY
New York, NY

Assistant Manager

- Coordinated, with treasurers and finance vice-presidents, bridge loans and stock option financing programs for major corporate relationships

Oct. 1968
to
Sept. 1969

TRADE BANK AND TRUST COMPANY
New York, NY

Assistant Credit Manager

Feb. 1967
to
Sept. 1968

BANKERS TRUST COMPANY
New York, NY

Retail Platform Associate; Branch Operations Supervisor; Collection Clerk; Teller

EDUCATION: Columbia University, BA Economics, 1971
University of Geneva (Switzerland), 1962 — Certificate French Language and Civilization

Joint Studies Program, Stanford University/Crocker National Bank: Advanced Techniques of Credit and Financial Analysis

New York Institute of Credit: Accounting Survey Lecture Series; Credit and the Uniform Commercial Code Lecture Series

National Credit Office: Applied Course in Credit and Financial Analysis

LANGUAGES: Bilingual French-English; read Dutch and Spanish

CITATION: **Who's Who in the World**

MEMBERSHIPS: New York Institute of Credit (former)
New York Credit and Financial Management Institute (former)
American Chamber of Commerce (NL) (present)

FRED BUXTON • *212 West 79th Street* • *New York, N.Y. 10024* • *(212) 873-5123*

CONTROLLER/FINANCIAL MANAGER

OBJECTIVE: To fully utilize my experience in management, planning and financial control.

SUMMARY: Fourteen years in financial and business planning, marketing and controller functions for a manufacturer, an airline and a brokerage firm.

HIGHLIGHTS:
* Conceived and implemented TWA "Getaway" credit card system, now the most popular airline credit card

* Assisted in negotiating the transfer of control of TWA away from the Hughes organization

* As media liaison, used marketing and advertising to make general public aware of the negotiability of industrial diamonds

* Developed capacity for improving relations between factory and office workers to increase production and cut costs

* As a general manager, tightened financial controls and directed short- and long-term business planning

EXPERIENCE:
1975 to 1979 — Controller reporting to the President
SCOMILL MANUFACTURING COMPANY, Brooklyn, NY

--Responsible for entire financial structure in a manufacturing environment

--Managed $22.3 million budget for both manufacturing and administration

--Implemented ADP data processing system for payroll and for A/P-A/R: system reduced time interval between shipment and receipt of payment

1971 to 1975 — General Manager, reporting to President & Executive Vice President
GEMCO EQUITIES, INC., New York, NY

--Developed and managed $4.6 million budget

--Guided long-range planning as well as day-to-day operations, reporting to the Executive Vice-President and President

EXPERIENCE: --Directed new product development and product
(con't.)   introduction strategies

                --Established liaison between the industry and the
                  public through effective marketing and advertising

                1965 to   Director of Corporate Planning
                1971   reporting to Operations VP
                                TRANS WORLD AIRLINES, New York, NY

                --Analyzed business trends and profits on short- and
                  long-term basis

                --Designed and implemented profit plans and control
                  systems

                --Developed and implemented TWA "Getaway" credit card

EDUCATION: Columbia University, New York, NY
                MBA in Business Finance (1966)

                Georgetown University, Washington, DC
                BBA Magna cum laude in Business Finance (1964)

                --President of student body

                LaSalle Extension University
                Dale Carnegie Course

MILITARY   1957 to   U.S. Navy
SERVICE: 1961   Rank: Lieutenant (JG)

SPECIAL   Licensed pilot (Multi-engine instrument rated)
SKILLS:

SUSAN FISHER   1400 Ocean Avenue   •   Brooklyn, New York 11230   •   (212) 258-6575

Financial officer and operating executive with expertise in institutional administration and financial development. Functional experience in human resources management and computer accountancy.

PROFESSIONAL
EXPERIENCE:

1977-1979   Director of Business & Financial Operation, BENNINGTON COLLEGE
                                                    Bennington, VT

As chief financial officer of the college reporting directly to the President, I administered all non-academic financial services including personnel, budget, data processing, plant administration, auditing, purchasing, investments, real estate and insurance administration.

--Effected savings of $250,000 annually in plant maintenance by adopting sub-contracting system

--Instituted energy conservation program that reduced use of oil by 50% (300,000 barrels annually--a current cost avoidance of approximately $200,000 per annum)

--Elected Treasurer of Board of Trustees (first time in school history a non-trustee named to this position)

--Re-negotiated food service contract resulting in $12,000 annual savings, a 25% cost reduction

--Revised health and pension package to provide improved coverage at reduced cost

--Member or Chairman of 14 operational, planning or advisory committees

--Served as ERISA coordinator and Affirmative Action Officer

1966-1976   QUEENS COLLEGE, Flushing, NY

Business Manager (1971-1976)

In this position I acted as Bursar and was responsible for all accounting functions, purchasing, budget, payroll, personnel, benefits administration, auxiliary enterprises and warehouse operations.

--Chief operations manager during period of operational budget growth from $16 million to $60 million in 5 years

--Personally supervised office staff of 180 people including 4 Assistant Business Managers and 10 other professionals

--Planned and implemented Queens College's first computerized budget; negotiated unionization of food service staff

--Negotiated HUD contract for $15 million as part of three-man team

--Member or Chairman of 21 operational, planning or advisory committees

--Established principles for joint faculty-student action, and supervised revision of college legislative structure as administrative member of the Ad Hoc Faculty-Student Committee of campus governance; prepared final draft of college restructuring plan

QUEENS COLLEGE (Con't.)	<u>Assistant Business Manager (1967-1971)</u> <u>Assistant to Business Manager (1966-1967)</u> (Budget Officer)

--Completely revised budget system, purchasing procedures and accounting methods to comply with newly passed CUNY Construction Fund Law. Overhaul required close collaboration with all university departments

1965-1966	WOODMERE ACADEMY, Woodmere, NY <u>Assistant to Headmaster (Business Manager)</u>

--Administered all fiscal affairs

--Responsible for budget, payroll, purchasing, food service, plant maintenance, student transport, general accounts

--Administrative member of Parents' Board, requiring empathy with non-academic viewpoint

1958-1964	ADELPHI ACADEMY, Brooklyn, NY <u>Assistant to Headmaster</u>

--Appointed acting Chairman of English Department (1958) Within a year was made Director of Development and Fund Raising

--Conceived and directed program for tracing lost alumni: boosted funds raised by 1000%; revived contact with more than 1,000 potential donors

--Supervised financial affairs and physical plant

OTHER EXPERIENCE:

1964-1965	BROWN UNIVERSITY CLUB

--Elected to Board of Governors as full-time volunteer

--Organized 3 fund raising performances--raised more than $25,000

--Chairman of Brown University Bicentennial Program in New York

EDUCATION:	Columbia University: Graduate Study in School Administration
	University of Michigan Graduate School of Business: Institute in Program Budgeting
	Brown University: AB, English and American Literature

PROFESSIONAL MEMBERSHIPS:

National Association of College and University Business Officers

Eastern Association of College and University Business Officers

Practicing Law Institute

American Association of Higher Education

PETER SEATON
60 East Tenth Street
New York, NY 10003
(212) 673-7321

OBJECTIVE: FINANCIAL ANALYST

SUMMARY: Three years with active and diverse private trust. Emphasis on investment and management of assets. Evaluate investment potential of venture capital situations and going concerns, monitor holdings, troubleshooting assignments. Exposure to financial analysis in many industries and business situations.

EXPERIENCE:

1978 to Present

A.T.C. COMPANY, New York, NY
Asset and Investment Analyst

VENTURE CAPITAL PROJECTS

Evaluate opportunities for equity participation in new ventures; comprehensive project analysis; analyze long-run growth and profit potential; recommend action.

Example: Recommended financing cosmetics company with innovative product concept

Result: Company now making an operating profit on annual sales of over $1,000,000; employs 600 sales personnel in 13 states.
(Subsequently appointed to board of directors with full participation in financial planning and policy decisions)

Example: Advised creation of a company to utilize patented Biophonics technology in greenhouse food production.

Result: Twenty-five production units now in operation; cost-efficient technology gives company international franchise potential.

REAL ESTATE ASSIGNMENTS

Cash flow and R.O.I. analysis, purchase and sale evaluations, pro forma and operating statement preparation, and determination of real estate development potential, and troubleshooting.

Example: On-site in Anchorage, AL, developed turn-around plan for 19 building apartment complex with 55% vacancy rate.

Result: Improved financial procedures, negotiated financing, repositioned property for the market. Vacancy rate reduced to 40% after only three months; purchase offer under consideration is $1.5 million higher than offer received prior to turn-around plan. (Definitive market survey now used by Anchorage banks)

Example: Evaluated offer for one of the trust's shopping centers in Pennsylvania

Result: Analysis utilized in negotiating 29% increase in offer; resulted in sale of the property.

INVESTMENT MANAGEMENT	Charged with monitoring the performance and security of current holdings and analyzing other investment opportunities.

Example: Evaluated acceptability of common stock offered in lieu of note repayment by manufacturer of Pay-TV hardware

Result: Identified financial weaknesses caused by confused management and marketing efforts; recommended holding the note to secure priority claim on promising technology in case of default or bankruptcy

Example: Analyzed opportunity to invest in regional operations of national fast food chain.

Result: Showed profit-margin projections of investor group to be greatly overstated. Prevented potential $700,000 loss.

OTHER ASSIGNMENTS

Acquisition analysis of company engaged in air and ground transport for the entertainment industry

Monitor and manage securities portfolio

Negotiate distribution of assets in order to dissolve a corporation

Evaluation of proposal to develop Florida Cable-TV station

PRIOR EXPERIENCE

Court Liaison for New York County, Court Referral Project, New York, NY
Supervised staff of 14 (1973-1976)

Supervisor, Legal Department, Samaritan Halfway Society, Inc., New York, NY
Supervised staff of eight (1970-1973)

High School Graduate Trainee Program, Citibank, New York, NY
Trusts and Securities Operations (1968-1970)

EDUCATION:

New York University, New York, NY (1/76 - 2/80)

Jan. 1980 — BA, Economics/Philosophy
Recipient, Arts and Sciences Scholarship
Earned 100% living expenses; worked 30 hours per week

Jan. 1981 — Candidate for January admission to MBA Program at NYU

FINANCIAL PLANNING MANAGER

DONALD CHU . 100 Hidden Lake Drive Apt. 18L . North Brunswick, NJ 08902
Home: (201) 297-4340   Business: (215) 293-5261

OBJECTIVE: MANAGER OF FINANCIAL/ECONOMIC PLANNING

SUMMARY: Directed and trained an economic and financial planning group which
               functions as internal consultants to senior management. Demonstrated
               expertise in:

               - financial analysis and management reporting
               - systems design and development
               - short range budgeting, expense control and forecasting
               - productivity analysis; long range asset and resource utilization
               - operations consolidation and divestiture
               - oral and written communications to senior management

               Group activities have resulted in significant regional productivity
               improvements and direct expense savings of over $500,000 in the
               past six months alone.

EXPERIENCE HIGHLIGHTS:

1977 to Present   MOBIL OIL CORPORATION
Supervisor, Systems and Financial Analysis   Valley Forge, PA (1979-Present)

Manage, train and develop group of eight MBA analysts responsible for systems
development and financial planning to optimize return on investment, review long
range resource requirements and coordinate management sciences activities

* Successfully implemented politically sensitive departmental reorganization
   which consolidated all economic planning within controller's portfolio

* Initiated proposal to optimize manufacturing facility, which, when implemented,
   will pay back in 1 1/2 years and realize savings of $400,000 annually

* Achieved 200% productivity gain within planning unit by computerization of
   delivery fleet statistical reporting

* Proposed centralization of internal and external computer activities with
   anticipated saving of $40,000 annually

Senior Financial Analyst   Scarsdale, NY (1979)

* Developed computer model to analyze profitability of existing business
   - Application resulted in a service station divestment program and district
     consolidation
   - annual savings of $300,000 in overhead and salaries

* Designed and implemented a control system to ensure efficient utilization of
  outside timesharing vendors and internal operations; savings of $5,000 annually

* Restructured supervisory span of control within credit department to improve
  internal communications. As a result:
  - firm priorities were established
  - past due balances were sharply reduced

* Established credit appraisal system for evaluating financial risk which was
  implemented by regional controller

78

MOBIL OIL CORPORATION (continued)
<u>Staff Analyst</u>
(1978)

* Increased unit productivity by over 100% through computerization of routine
  management reports

* Monitored regional service station operations budget and introduced computerized
  reporting system which pinpointed variances and trends
  - provided sales management with improved tools for sensitivity analysis

* Significantly improved sales forecasting techniques

<u>Controller Trainee</u>
(1977)

* Prepared budget forecast of $11,000,000 depreciation expense, 18 months in
  advance; actual 1978 expense was under projection, with variance of .2%

* Developed control and monitoring procedures for new engineering maintenance
  centers which:
  - reduced administrative workload and paperflow
  - established financial controls

9/74 to 5/77   KENDALL, BOWERS & COMPANY, INC.
<u>Consultant</u>   Stamford, CT (Part-time)

Performed statistical analysis for management consulting firm specializing in
employee relations counseling

9/72 to 8/74   MOBIL PIPELINE CORPORATION
<u>Pipeliner</u>   Rochester, NY

Supervised 5-10 contracted hourly employees and was responsible for planning,
organizing, directing and controlling a five-month pipeline maintenance project.
Surpassed management objectives.

EDUCATION: New York University, New York, NY
                  1978 - MBA, Corporate Finance - Quantitative Analysis
                  Thesis: <u>An Analysis of the Impact of Vertical Divestiture on the
                           Financial Environment of a Fully Integrated Petroleum
                           Organization</u>

                  New York University, New York, NY
                  1976 - BS, Operations Management/Behavioral Science

                  University of Miami, Miami, FL
                  1970-72 - Statistics/Psychology

HONORS: Founders Day Award - New York University
                  Deans Honor Roll - New York University

PROFESSIONAL   Beta Gamma Sigma Honorary Business Society
ASSOCIATIONS: Alpha Kappa Psi Professional Business Fraternity

John Hawkins, C.P.A. • 250 Main Street, Apartment 3-G • Millburn, New Jersey 07041
Home (201) 379-4761   Office (212) 790-5206

OBJECTIVE

A senior financial management position with a publicly owned company or a large privately owned company which will utilize my experience in financial accounting and reporting, auditing, and administration.

EXPERIENCE SUMMARY

Twelve years' experience with Deloitte Haskins & Sells, an international public accounting firm. For the past two years assigned to Executive Office in New York where responsibilities include writing for publication and departmental administration. The previous ten years assigned to the Audit Department of the Memphis office with client responsibilities, teaching assignments and office administration.

EXPERIENCE

Executive Office of Deloitte Haskins & Sells　　　　　　**1978-1979**
1114 Avenue of the Americas
New York, New York 10036
212-790-0716

- Wrote the firm's booklet *Audit Committes: A Director's Guide* describing the activities of the audit committee and presenting the firm's view toward its evolution.

- Assisted international and domestic offices in such activities as writing proposals, making contacts, and furnishing information on other firms.

- Edited practice development publications about the firm, its services, and topics of current interest to the profession and clients.

- Participated in the development of the Deloitte Haskins & Sells advertising campaign, including research in connection with the benchmark study.

- Prepared practice development programs for presentation at all national and regional firm meetings.

- Assisted in the supervision of the department, including assignments of personnel, budget preparation, and coordination of departmental activities with other departments.

Deloitte Haskins & Sells
165 Madison Avenue
Memphis, Tennessee 38103

1967—1977

- Supervised audit engagements of publicly and privately owned companies. Client industries included manufacturing, insurance companies and agencies, real estate development, leasing, agricultural, retail and professional athletic organizations.

- Prepared constructive service letters and internal control comments for presentation to officers and directors.

- Supervised engagements for registration statements on Form S-1 and for annual reports on Form 10-K.

- Performed a special investigation for a brokerage client into the use of bond proceeds by a public utility district.

- Taught at six of the firm's national and regional seminars. Topics included technical accounting, auditing, and management training.

- Designed uniform accounting system and ticket sales system for each franchise of a professional athletic league. Wrote audit programs and supervised engagement to audit gate receipts for each game played.

- Handled various administrative responsibilities for the office including manager in charge of recruiting, assignment director, and staff counsellor.

EDUCATION

Bachelor of Science Degree with major in Accounting, Mississippi State University, 1967.

Member of Beta Alpha Psi and Beta Gamma Sigma honor societies.

ORGANIZATIONS

American Institute of Certified Public Accountants and Memphis Chapter of Tennessee Society of CPA's.

Junior Achievement of Memphis; former Member of Jaycees, Kiwanis, and Planning Executives Institute; Vice President and Treasurer of a private school.

MARY OLSON
2660 Sedgwick Avenue
Bronx, NY 10468

Home: (212) 298-7725

OBJECTIVE: Responsible position with an organization specializing in taxation
and/or accounting

SUMMARY: More than 20 years experience in tax accounting, preparation and
consultation with full knowledge of federal, state and local
compliance statutes. Proven ability to interact with company
presidents and controllers in effecting compliance with regulations.
Expert investigator and interviewer. Capable motivator of personnel
with definitive training experience. Additional experience as insurance field representative and assistant sales manager.

PROFESSIONAL HIGHLIGHTS:

1970 to   NEW YORK STATE TAX DEPARTMENT, White Plains, NY
Present   Tax Agent

One of 18 agents to service five-county area of Westchester, Rock-
land, Putnam, Sullivan and Orange Counties

* Investigate and interview taxpayers, taxpayers' representatives
and corporate executives regarding problems in compliance with
tax laws

  - Secure and verify financial statements; analyze statements
  for accuracy; investigate claims of indebtedness

  - Interview relevant parties (bank officers, attorneys, county
  clerks, landlords, etc.) to determine validity of statements

  - Handle caseload of more than 1,000 annually (majority are
  business clients)

* Upon completion of investigation, write reports with recommendations (accepted 95% of time)

  - Payment Arrangement: lay out all terms for payment

  - Seizure Procedures: notify taxpayer; complete warrant; participate in confiscation actions; reverse seizure order when
  payment plan with sufficient control has been instituted

* Complete returns for taxpayers without accounting help

  - Assures compliance and helps them avoid prosecution

* Assist in training new agents in enforcement proceedings

(Continuing involvement in tax return preparation and record keeping
for family and friends on gratis basis)

1961-1970   TAX CONSULTANT (Self-employed), Bronx, NY

Kept business records and prepared tax returns for clients throughout New York metropolitan area and various other states

*   Consulted with clients on all types of taxes; completed returns

    -   Forms included federal, state and local returns for taxes on payroll, sales, withholding, real estate and personal property

*   Developed clientele of more than 50 clients concurrent with Prudential employment

1949-1970   PRUDENTIAL INSURANCE COMPANY, Bronx, NY
             <u>Assistant Manager</u> (1959-1961)

*   Motivated staff to stimulate sales

    -   Gave descriptive and motivational speeches to 50 agents in office dealing with aspects of successful sales techniques

*   Recruited and trained new agents

*   Served as mediator of complaints against agents

*   Directly supervised six representatives

<u>Field Sales Representative</u> (1949-1959; 1961-1970)

Sold policies for Life and Health Insurance and pension plans

*   One of youngest agents ever hired by company

*   Wrote more than $100,000/week four times; received numerous awards for superior salesmanship

    -   Invited to annual business meeting and convention (restricted to top 20% of representatives) every year, 1949-1970

*   Became No. 1 salesman in New York in one year; remained in top category all 20 years of employment

EDUCATION: Westchester Community College, Valhalla, NY
             1974-1975: Two years of Accounting

PROFESSIONAL CERTIFICATIONS:

             New York State Life Insurance License
             New York State Insurance Broker's License

MILITARY: U.S. Marine Corps

PERSONAL: Date of birth - July 18, 1927. Willing to travel

MORGAN JONES, 250 Central Park West, New York, N.Y. 10010   PL 3-4370

OBJECTIVE   INVESTMENT/MONEY MARKET PORTFOLIO MANAGEMENT

SUMMARY   Money market economist with background in Commercial/Investment banking; areas
              of expertise include: Financial futures markets; Cash markets; Foreign ex-
              change; Interrelationships among domestic and foreign markets; Development of
              quantitative techniques as aids to trading

EXPERIENCE

1980 to   PETERS-JONES, INC., New York, NY
Present   Vice President, Director of Research

              PRODUCT DEVELOPMENT:

              * Yield value of 1/32nd for GNMA's of different coupons and paydown rates
                 Product useful for cash/futures positioning

              * Futures parity table for various deliverable T-Bonds for futures contracts

              * Hedge ratio table for cash/cash arbitrage taking into account yield and
                 maturity effects

              * Developed new formula for hedge ratio for T-Bond spread vs. T-Bill futures
                 trades

              * Developed innovative weekly chart package for firm's trade/sales personnel
                 permitting "ahead of the pack" Fed's policy monitoring

              * Developed Implied Repo Rate table for deliverable T-Bonds taking into
                 account accrued interest

              * Analyst and strategist on use of multiple hedging simultaneously of Euro-
                 dollar time deposit, T-Bill, CD, T-Bond futures

              RELATED PROFESSIONAL ACTIVITIES:

              * Lecturer to financial professionals under the auspices of the American
                 Management Association and the Financial Executives Institute

              * Designed and implemented course on money markets for firm's trainees

              * Conducted weekly information sessions for firm's trade/sales personnel
                 on Fed's monetary policy and economic developments and their impact on
                 financial markets

              * Authored articles on short-term money market investments, use of financial
                 futures, and SDR's for The Money Manager, Pension And Investment Age, Cash
                 Flow Magazine and Lombard-Wall's in house-financial markets newsletter

1966 to   MORGAN GUARANTY TRUST COMPANY, New York, NY
1980   Vice President, International Money Management Group (1978-1980)

              * Conducted international cash management studies

              * Introduced innovative procedures -

                 - quantitative technique useful to MNC's
                   exposure management function
                 - a new approach to evaluation of a firm's cash
                   management phase (resulting in indicated potential
                   savings to client up to $125,000 annually)

              * Performed risk analyses of hedging decisions which utilized forward
                 foreign exchange markets

MORGAN GUARANTY TRUST COMPANY (Continued)

Vice President/Money Market Economist
Treasurer's Division, Portfolio Investment Research Group (1973-1978)

* Performed trade-off analysis of borrowing/lending decisions for bank's international treasury management

* Developed interest rate tracking models and forecasting techniques applicable to foreign exchange, domestic Euro/currency, and foreign money markets as aids to traders

* Organized seminar on fundamentals of portfolio management including spread and risk analysis and interest rate forecasting resulting in increased effectiveness of sales staff

Senior Operations Research Officer-
Consultant to Treasurer's Division
Operations Research Department (1966-1973)

* Supervised and motivated staff of analysts charged with research into aspects of portfolio management

* Developed simulation models-
  - for U.S. government bond market, used by portfolio manager for optimum bidding
  - for federal funds market as aid to managing bank's daily money position

* Advised pension trust department on portfolio performance evaluation techniques

1963 to 1966	GRUMMAN AIRCRAFT ENGINEERING CORP., Bethpage, NY Research Mathematician
1961 to 1963	UNITED AIRCRAFT RESEARCH LABORATORIES, East Hartford, CT Senior Mathematician
1958 to 1961	STEVENS INSTITUTE OF TECHNOLOGY, Hoboken, NJ Research Engineer/Lecturer
EDUCATION	1967 - MBA, Economics, New York University 1958 - MS, Applied Mathematics, Stevens Institute 1956 - BS, Mechanical Engineering, Stevens Institute Additional studies include: 1958-1961 - PhD studies in Applied Mathematics, NYU; 1961 - Credit and Financial Analysis Course, Dun & Bradstreet
LANGUAGES	Fluent in Russian and German Familiar with French and Yugoslavian
MEMBER OF	New York Association of Business Economists

LUCY OSTRAHAND
250 Oak Drive
Philadelphia, PA 19012
(215) 547-1234

OBJECTIVE: SECURITIES MANAGEMENT

To employ my expertise in stock research and trading portfolio investment and estate management in the trust department of a major bank.

SUMMARY:
- Ten years experience in marketing and sale of industrial and bank stocks as member

- Exhaustive researcher of growth potential of particular stocks in complete customer relations service

- In-depth knowledge and marketing expertise of industrial and bank issues

- Ninety-five percent successful selling stocks considered unmarketable

BUSINESS HIGHLIGHTS:

1970 to Present

MANN SECURITIES Philadelphia, PA
<u>Bank Stock Trader</u>   (1973 to Present)

* Initiated and instituted bank stock trading company in 1973, in addition to industrial stock trading

* Developed list of prospective customers; responsible for start-up and management of department

* Locate markets for inactive regional bank issues

* Trade stocks of 3,500 banks throughout country

* Maintain liaison with Commerce Clearing House in keeping bank quotes current and customer service timely

* Advise bank trust departments on buy/sell feasibility of illiquid issues

LUCY OSTRAHAND/2

                     *   Research and evaluate stocks for growth
                            potential

                     *   Responsible for increase in departmental profit
                            from $15,000 in 1973 to more than $150,000
                            in 1979 with negligible additional expense to
                            company and minimum increase in capital

                      <u>Industrial Stock Trader</u>   (1970 to 1973)

                     *   Traded inactive industrials for clients

                     *   Researched companies for appreciation in growth,
                            seeking out undervalued issues and marketing
                            to investment buyers with in-depth studies of
                            company operation and production

                     *   Located and traded expired tender offers

                     OTIS MARSHALL, INC. New York, NY
1965 to   <u>Over-the-Counter Trading Department</u>
1970

EDUCATION: Wagner College, Staten Island, NY
                     1965 - BA, Marketing/Accounting

                     Pace College, New York, NY
                     Advanced study in Industrial Psychology and Marketing

MEMBER: National Association of Security Dealers

                     will relocate; will travel

STEPHEN BOGS · 91-48 79 Road, Apt. 6G · Woodhaven, NY 11421 · (212) 441-6620

OBJECTIVE: INVESTIGATOR - CLAIMS/COLLECTIONS
               To apply in-depth experience with highly sophisticated collection
               and investigation procedures on behalf of corporate financial
               institution

SUMMARY: More than seven years with Internal Revenue Service as an officer in
               charge of investigation and resolution of business and personal tax
               problems. In-depth understanding of businesses, including collection,
               investigation, interviewing and bookkeeping procedures. Knowledge of
               computer programming. Capable administrator and supervisor of personnel.
               Skills transferrable to corporate application.

HIGHLIGHTS OF EXPERIENCE:

1972 to   INTERNAL REVENUE SERVICE
Present   New York, NY

               Revenue Officer

               Charged with independent responsibility for investigation and deter-
               mination of tax claims against large accounts ($50,000 or more) with
               full authority to resolve problems

               * Perform complex credit analyses in connection with tax liens,
                  collateral agreements and uncollectable accounts

               * Conduct intensive investigations of large corporations and prominent
                  high-income individuals to uncover hidden assets, analyze financial
                  condition and determine valuation of properties

               * Maintain comprehensive and practical knowledge of current collection
                  techniques including -

                  - Laws on rights of creditors
                  - Forced assessment and collection
                  - Lien priorities and bankruptcies
                  - Summons procedures
                  - Interpretation of public records

                  - Application of such laws and procedures in extremely complex and
                     often delicate situations

               * Originated new techniques and creative approaches in application of
                  general tax and collection guidelines

               * Developed keen ability to influence, motivate, interview and educate
                  persons who are generally fearful and uncooperative, through use of
                  sophisticated interpersonal skills

               * Assist taxpayers in understanding of regulations; negotiate payment
                  schedules to fulfill obligations

               * Serve as technical expert in matters before the tax court

               * Serve as classroom instructor in training of IRS personnel; evaluate
                  courses and recommend changes

               * Received steady promotions to highest level in job category

3/71-7/71
and
8/68-3/69

DEPARTMENT OF SOCIAL SERVICES
New York, NY

<u>Caseworker</u>

* Investigated and assisted people on welfare

    - Determined need for assistance and made recommendations

* Worked independently in the field

MILITARY: United States Army, West Germany
             4/69-1/71 - Personnel and Administrative Specialist (Spec/5)

EDUCATION: St. John's University, Jamaica, NY
             1968 - BA, Social Sciences

             1971 - Graduate School (courses in Accounting, Statistics,
                                    Business Management)

             Control Data Institute, New York, NY
             1971-72 - courses in Computer Programming (FORTRAN, COBOL)

PAUL CHANG

625 West 110th Street
Apt. 10E
New York, NY 10025

Tel. Numbers:
(212) 866-2513
(212) 483-9875

OBJECTIVE: PORTFOLIO MANAGER/FINANCIAL MANAGEMENT

SUMMARY:
- Three years experience as an aggressive, sales-oriented brokerage house account executive
- Creative securities manager in developing options trading strategies in profitable customer service activity
- Thorough and definitive researcher into viability of market as a whole and of individual stocks
- Bilingual: English-Chinese

BUSINESS HIGHLIGHTS:

1978 to
Present

MOORE & SCHLEY, CAMERON & CO., New York, NY

Account Executive

* Initiate research and development of options trading strategy for list of 50 clients; advise on covered writing
* Develop special portfolio strategies for individual customers
* Inaugurated advertising campaign in Chinese media; doubled market in Chinese community from 100 to 200 clients ($60,000 in earnings)
* Successfully developed strong leads from general advertising with 20% conversion to sales
* Redesigned brokers' desks for maximum utility at minimum cost

1977 to
1978

MERRILL, LYNCH, PIERCE, FENNER & SMITH, New York, NY

Account Executive

* Promoted to account executive after short training period and charged with developing options trading strategy for account executive group
  - Completed training program in least time of any trainee

EDUCATION: Columbia University, Graduate School of Business
1977 - MBA, Finance/Accounting

Columbia University, Graduate School of Arts and Sciences
1975 - graduate study, Mathematical Sociology
President, Columbia Pine Society

National Taiwan University
1969 - BA, Sociology/Economics

OTHER EXPERIENCE (in Taiwan):

1970-72   CHINA AIRLINE - Supervisor, Traffic Department

1967-69   ACADEMIA SINICA - Quantitative analysis of population survey of Taiwan

1965-67   CHINA DAILY NEWS - Frequent analysis of foreign press articles

Human Resources & Development

JUDITH AARONSON   84 Apple Road, Jamaica, N.Y. 11432   (212) 523-3082

OBJECTIVE: PENSION SPECIALIST

To fully utilize my experience in the field of pension benefits in a challenging position as a pension consultant or administrator.

EXPERIENCE: HARRY ALLAN CONSULTANTS, INC., New York, NY
Research Assistant

Current   Conduct pension and actuarial research as it relates to company's actuaries, consultants and clients

- Review, digest and abstract articles from newspapers and magazines pertaining to pension law

- Read and review articles from wide variety of industry and government publications dealing with health, life insurance and actuarial studies

- Conduct telephone and written surveys based on client needs

METROPOLITAN LIFE INSURANCE COMPANY, New York, NY
Issue Technician (January 1980 to July 1980)

June
1979
to
June
1980

Issued Deposit Administration and Immediate Participating Guarantee contracts for roster of corporate clients

Drafted specimen plans, summary plan descriptions, plan amendments to comply with client request for IRS final regulations

Prepared IRS forms 5300, 5301, 5302

Heavy ERISA research and analysis, utilizing experts in the field, and government regulations

Valuation Technician (June 1979 to January 1980)

Prepared actuarial valuation reports, summary annual reports, employee benefit statements, employee census reports

Worked with Entry Age Normal and Frozen Initial Liability methods

JUDITH AARONSON/2

        Prepared IRS Schedules A, B and 5500-C

        Used EDP input/output for valuation analysis

        NEW ENGLAND LIFE INSURANCE COMPANY, New York, NY
        Pension Benefit Analyst

1976
to
1979
        Analyzed pension benefit plans and contracts

        Calculated benefits for quotations and retirements

        Worked with deferred annuities and deposit adminis-
          tration cases

        Trained new employees in calculation formulas and
          benefits purchase

EDUCATION: LONG ISLAND UNIVERSITY, MA, Political Science, 1977
              JOHN JAY COLLEGE, BA, American Government/Constitutional
              Law, 1976

SEYMOUR GOLDMAN • 1500 York Avenue, Apt. 5B • New York, NY 10021

(212) 249-6625   (212) 249-1523

OBJECTIVE: **ORCHESTRAL CONDUCTOR/CHORAL DIRECTOR**
To devote my broad experience and expertise to conducting an established orchestra, or to developing and conducting a concert orchestra and/or chorale that may only be at the conceptual stage

SUMMARY: More than 15 years as musical director and conductor for prestigious organizations including symphony orchestras, opera companies and university and church chorales. Frequently toured Europe and South America for concert engagements. Possess full repertoire of classical and semi-classical scores.

EXPERIENCE

CONDUCTOR:
Current

WHITTENBURG CHOIR COLLEGE, Princeton, NJ
Music Director
• Conduct University Symphony Orchestra
• Member, piano faculty

NATIONAL COUNCIL OF THE ARTS, New York, NY
• Commissioned to organize Latin-American Symphonic Choir

1972-76
THE MONTAUK ORCHESTRA, Long Island, NY
• Music Director and Conductor

FIRST METHODIST CHURCH, Setauket, NY
• Choral Director with 10-15 concerts per year

1973-75
HOPE OPERA COMPANY, Long Island, NY
• Orchestral and Choir Director
• Directed and conducted operatic performances including *I Pagliacci, Tosca, Magic Flute* and *Cavalleria Rusticana*

1970-72
STATE UNIVERSITY OF NEW YORK AT STONY BROOK, NY
• Served as Assistant Conductor for four semesters

1962-65
BUENOS AIRES CONSERVATORY, Buenos Aires, Argentina
• Conductor for orchestra and chorale; piano instructor

TOURING CONDUCTOR:
1972 to
Present
• Guest conductor in South America and Europe (Italy, France, Poland)
  — Conducted 15 concerts in South America (July/August, 1979) with engagements in Chile, Argentina, Uruguay, Paraguay and Bolivia

INSTRUCTOR:
1966 to
Present
PRIVATE INSTRUCTOR, New York, NY
• Instruct in piano and conducting; coach voice
  — Currently coaching 15 professionals; have coached 60-65 professionals
  — Have instructed more than 120 non-professionals

1967-70	NEW YORK INSTITUTE FOR THE EDUCATION OF THE BLIND, New York, NY • Member of the piano faculty
1965-66	PRIVATE INSTRUCTOR, St. Louis, MO • Taught piano and solfege
1961-65	PRIVATE INSTRUCTOR, Buenos Aires, Argentina • Taught piano, solfege, ear training and harmony
JUDGE:	NEW YORK STATE SYMPHONIC MUSIC ASSOCIATION • Annual Spring Festival for entries in piano, chorus and orchestra NEW YORK STATE MUSICAL EVALUATION CENTER • (First National Competition, 1980-1981)

EDUCATION

DEGREE PROGRAMS:	STATE UNIVERSITY OF NEW YORK AT STONY BROOK, NY (Full Scholarship) 1972 — MM, Orchestral Conducting/Choral Conducting CONSERVATORY NACIONAL OF MUSIC GENERAL URQUIZA, Buenos Aires, Argentina (Full Scholarship) 1965 — PhD, Conducting 1964 — MM, Music, Orchestral and Choral Conducting 1961 — BM, Piano/Analysis

ADDITIONAL TRAINING:

STATE UNIVERSITY OF NEW YORK, Oneonta, NY
1979 — Seminar in Choral Conducting and Analysis

MARIANO SIJANEK, Buenos Aires, Argentina
1977 — Opera seminar (6 weeks)

PRIVATE INSTRUCTION, St. Louis, MO
1965-70 — Orchestral and Choral under professional directors

PROFESSIONAL AFFILIATIONS:

American Symphony Orchestra League
Musical Educators National Conference
Musicians Club
Piano Teachers of New York

LANGUAGES:	Fluent in Spanish, Italian and French; working knowledge of Portuguese and German
CITED:	*Reader's Digest,* Oct., 1979 (Also published in all 15 foreign language editions) *People* Magazine, June 5, 1980 *To Live Again,* Ana Maria de Bottazzi, Dodd, Mead, 1978. Various magazine and newspaper articles, U.S. and abroad

DORA MARTINEZ
80-12 180th Avenue
Howard Beach, NY 11414
212-845-6695

OBJECTIVE: DIRECTOR OF HUMAN RESOURCES

Personnel Manager with nine years' experience in human resources
administration. Demonstrated ability to work effectively and
congenially with employees at diverse levels. Comprehensive
knowledge of recruitment, screening and interviewing; policy
implementation; benefits administration; and staff supervision.
Adept at labor negotiations. Innovator with ability to increase
employee morale and improve communications. Experience includes
management, staffing and establishment of personnel procedures
for two new facilities of a major corporation.

PERSONNEL EXPERIENCE:

1972 to   PERMITRON ULTRASONICS, DIVISION OF PERMITRON CORPORATION
Present   Long Island City, NY
                  Major manufacturer of bio-medical, dental and surgical equip-
                  ment and industrial applications of ultrasonic technology
                  (union shop with 160 employees)

             Personnel Manager
             * Responsible for recruitment, screening and interviewing of
                exempt, non-exempt and hourly personnel for diversified
                employment areas

                - Maintain staffing of technical, electronics, research,
                   medical, production instrument assembly, plant management
                   and general clerical functions

             * Also responsible for staffing of New Jersey acquisition and
                new Connecticut facility while handling full personnel manage-
                ment functions in Long Island City office

             * Extensively involved in labor relations, including participation
                in contract negotiations, administration and interpretation
                of union contract and close interface with union

             * Interpret and oversee implementation of all personnel policies;
                control administration of comprehensive employee benefit
                programs

             * Introduced measures to improve communications and establish
                employment incentives

                - Created and issued first policy manual

                - Established ten-year service award club to promote better
                   relationship between labor and management

                - Initiated company newspaper

             * Establish and maintain EEO guidelines, ensure compliance with
                federal and state regulations

                                                      Continued

PERMITRON ULTRASONICS (Continued)

* Conduct wage and salary analyses to assure competitive compensation position in industry

* Regularly achieve 30% under budget allocation for placement advertising and employment agency commissions

* Supervise three-person department; delegate work flow to 15-person clerical staff

1971-1972   THE SINGER COMPANY, New York, NY
            Assistant, Compensation & Benefits Department
            * Assisted Director of Compensation & Benefits with office administration; processing of benefit action forms and payroll action forms on terminations, transfers, salary increases and new employees; and all related correspondence

            * Oriented employees relocating overseas regarding cultural, social and psychological adjustments

1965   EQUITABLE LIFE ASSURANCE COMPANY, New York, NY
            Administrative Assistant
            * Assisted Director of Group Insurance Department

            * Tour guide responsible for orientation tours for new employees and visitors

EDUCATION: Queens College, Queens, NY
            Business Major

            1972 - Present - Numerous seminars on personnel and management sponsored by AMA and other institutions

PROFESSIONAL AFFILIATIONS:

            International Association of Personnel
            Women Queens Personnel Management Association

MAY NELSON
10 Maple Avenue
Bedford Hills, NY 10507
Home: (914) 241-3420   Office: (212) 719-9233

OBJECTIVE   CORPORATE PERSONNEL - Position in recruitment coordination with
              excellent potential for growth into personnel management

SUMMARY   BA in Psychology/Business and continuing record of successful
              personnel experience. Adept at interpersonal and interdepart-
              mental communications. Fully knowledgeable of laws governing
              recruitment procedures. Exceptional recruitment and counseling
              abilities. Strong organizational skills.

PERSONNEL EXPERIENCE

1980 to   CAREER BLAZERS PERSONNEL SERVICES, New York, NY
Present   Branch Manager, Career Blazers Learning Center (Feb. 1981 to Present)

        * Recruit permanent and temporary word processing specialists,
          administrative assistants, secretaries, and other clerical
          personnel for client corporations

            - Screen and interview applicants to match
              client specifications

            - Have achieved exceptionally high level of client
              satisfaction through astute recruitment and
              perceptive counseling of personnel

        * Enhance marketability and curriculum of Learning Center by
          counseling graduates regarding business etiquette and
          procedures

            - Increase confidence levels of graduates through
              placement in low-risk temporary employment slots
              in client companies

            - Coach graduates in telephone etiquette, proper
              dress and grooming, and behavioral expectations

        * Call on clients and assist in coordinating evening seminars
          to establish awareness of Learning Center, create climate of
          acceptance, and increase utilization of available facilities

            - Reactivated approximately 25 resigned accounts
              as direct result of calls

        Assignment Manager, Career Blazers Temporary Services (10/80 to 2/81)

        * Recruited temporary applicants for client firms in areas of
          finance, marketing, advertising and manufacturing

        * Coordinated long-term project for R.J. Reynolds Tobacco Company
          requiring 50-60 models weekly for large-scale public relations
          project

1979 - 1980   UNIONMUTUAL INSURANCE COMPANY, Elmsford, NY
              Disability Benefit Specialist

              *   Interviewed approximately 40 prospective employees through
                  company's College Recruitment Program and hired 15 for
                  entry-level positions in sales and disability benefits

              *   Conducted full field investigations to determine validity
                  of questionable claims

                  - Worked closely with physicians, lawyers
                    and other professionals to determine
                    eligibility of claims

              *   Upgraded communications between sales and benefits departments,
                  bringing about substantial improvements in client services

                  - Set up monthly meetings between sales and
                    benefits departments at 12 district offices
                    and clearly defined long-term goals and
                    short-term objectives

                  - Gave lecture and participated in sales seminar
                    for 200 employees

              *   Simplified insurance policy terminology for benefit of policy
                  holders and claimants

              *   Invited to apply for supervisory position normally requiring
                  a minimum of three years after only one year with company

EDUCATION

              State University of New York at Oneonta
              1978 - BA, Psychology/Business and Economics

              Willing to relocate

TRAINING COORDINATOR

LISA HOHMANN · 73 Bleecker Street, #4-B · New York, NY 10012 · (212) 260-8950

OBJECTIVE: TRAINING COORDINATOR

SUMMARY: Ten years experience as trainer, manager and occupational therapist designing rehabilitation and training programs for individuals and corporations. Knowledge of affirmative action legislation as it applies to both private and public sectors

BACKGROUND: NEW YORK UNIVERSITY, Current

Coordinator, National Interpreter Training Consortium

$300,000 grant program for training development throughout the U.S.

* Responsible for collection, evaluation and dissemination of information

  - Provide resource information

    · On national level conceived on-site internship program for Executive Director of National Registry of Interpreters for Deaf

    · On local level conducted training workshops throughout Northeast area

    · Preparation of quarterly and annual reports to H.E.W.

* Designed policy guidelines for disabled students and interpreter services involving all the schools adjunct services of New York University

* Supervise staff of 20

* Production of training videotapes (produced by Ted Estabrook) available commercially throughout the U.S. to state and civic service organizations and private business sector

    · Wrote script for 35 minute tape

    · Cast tape using over 20 people

GOODWILL INDUSTRIES, New York, NY, 1977-78

Program Development/Deafness Specialist

* Served as liaison between Office of Vocational Rehabilitation and Goodwill Industries

    · Responsible for counseling 60 clients regarding employment, training, medical and other support services

    · Supervised internship program for graduate students

* Developed program for disabled clients and employees

    · Secured cooperation from business sector in providing individualized job orientation

    · Secured interpreters for clients and arranged for special tutors at no cost to Goodwill through effective use of available human resources

    · Developed human resource orientation program for corporations

LISA HOHMANN/2

FEDERATION EMPLOYMENT & GUIDANCE SERVICE, New York, NY, 1976-77

Rehabilitation Counselor

* Managed programs of New York State rehabilitation clients

    - Provided evaluation and counseling services to adults with all disabilities

    - Developed all services for deaf clients

    - Administered in-service training for staff

CROTCHED MOUNTAIN CENTER, Greenfield, NH, 1970-74

Occupational Therapist

* Evaluated clients' physical and emotional needs; devised individualized programs for all ages, all disabilities

    - Supervised all therapy aides, assistants and students

    - Was instrumental in establishing departmental staff meetings between school and rehabilitation center

    - Served as acting director of department in 1974

    - Developed pioneer therapeutic horseback riding program for 40 students

    - As Secretary-General for Northeast Wheelchair Games was responsible for housing, meals and qualifying events for over 120 participants

OTHER EMPLOYMENT:

NEW YORK UNIVERSITY

Adjunct Instructor

Sign language for graduate students in School of Education and adults from School of Continuing Education (1975-78)

Sign Language Interpreter

Deaf graduate students (1975-76)

EDUCATION: New York University
MA - 1976, Deafness rehabilitation

    Awarded full fellowship

Utica College of Syracuse University
BS - 1970, Occupational Therapy

PROFESSIONAL CERTIFICATIONS:

Rehabilitation Counselor, Certified Rehabilitation Counselor
National Registry of Interpreters for the Deaf, Sign Language
    Interpreter, C.S.C.

AFFILIATIONS:

American Deafness & Rehabilitation Association (Chairperson, 1977-78)
American Society for Training and Development

JOSHUA HARRIS · 220-01 124th Road · Laurelton, NY 11413

Business: (212) 978-4515   Home: (212) 580-9950

OBJECTIVE: SECURITY MANAGEMENT

SUMMARY: Ten years experience as an officer with award-winning record in crime prevention and apprehension of perpetrators in New York City subways. Worked in both uniform and plainclothes divisions. High conviction record. Established community relations which effectively reduced neighborhood crimes. Business experience includes training and motivating personnel.

HIGHLIGHTS OF POLICE WORK:

(See Page 2 for Business Experience)

1968-78   NEW YORK CITY TRANSIT POLICE DEPARTMENT

Plainclothes Patrol   (1976-78)

* Initiated and conducted training programs for employees of New York Telephone Company in self-protection from robbery and assault in Grand Concourse Station

    - Approximately 100 employees attended each of three seminars in Telephone Company offices

    - Resulted in demonstrably appreciable rate of reduction of platform crimes, especially on paydays

* Investigated numerous robbery and assault complaints

    - Resulted in 25 to 30 arrests

    - Supplied District Attorney's office and grand jury with hard evidence resulting in conviction of perpetrators

    - Testified successfully in court

* Worked closely with community organizations to decrease neighborhood crime

    - Strategy of coordinating patrol patterns with self-protective measures created dramatic drop in robbery and assault offenses

Uniform Patrol   (1968-76)

* Responsible for revenue protection in mid-town Manhattan (protection of coin booths)

* Rode subway patrol; was responsible for apprehension of approximately 75 robbery suspects over period of service

* Practiced crime prevention on one-to-one basis by warning individuals of incorrect self-protective measures on subway platforms and on trains

* Was awarded decorations for distinguished police duty

    - Received 3 Meritorious Service Awards
              2 Distinguished Service Awards
              2 Honorable Mentions
              2 Letters of Merit

BUSINESS EXPERIENCE:

1978 to Present	O-M OFFICE SERVICES/SUPPLIES COMPANY New York, NY

<u>Senior Buyer</u>

* Purchase all office supplies and equipment at wholesale for resale at retail
  .
    - Maintain correspondence by mail and telephone with manufacturers
    - Administer bid procedure for quantity and large ticket items
* Supervise staff of four employees

1964-68	CBS TELEVISION New York, NY

<u>Purchasing Expeditor</u>

* Responsible for accurate processing of all purchase orders and timely delivery of equipment and supplies
* Communicated with vendors; maintained liaison between vendors and departmental purchasing authorities
* Followed through on all purchase orders; handled problems smoothly
* Trained three additional expeditors

EDUCATION:

Modesto Junior College, Modesto, CA
1963 - Associate in Accounting

MILITARY:

U.S. Air Force; Honorable discharge with rank of Airman 2/c
1961-1965

THELMA L. CUMMINGS   ·   175 West 73rd Street, #8G   ·   New York, N.Y. 10025

WORK 212-960-2137   HOME 212-496-4142

OBJECTIVE	HOSPITAL ADMINISTRATOR
	Managerial/administrative position at the departmental level or in core administration
SUMMARY	M.P.A. degree and four years experience in health care administration. Prepare and review budgets up to $500,000. Adept at trouble-shooting and formulating systems to solve operational problems. Extensive personnel experience including ability to supervise, motivate and counsel employees

HEALTH CARE ADMINISTRATION EXPERIENCE

1978 to Present   ST. JOSEPH'S HOSPITAL CENTER, New York, N.Y.
Administrative Manager, Emergency Services Department (1979-Present)

Administer all aspects of Emergency Department including line supervision of clerical staff of 21. Prepare budget and review expenditures; formulate and interpret departmental policies for all personnel; purchase and maintain equipment; M.D. staffing of Screening Clinic

* Reduced projected overtime requirements by 40% annually through institution of relief position with staggered hours; cut overtime costs and improved staff morale

* Department came within budget in 1980 for first time in three years due to: careful budget preparation based on actual spending adjusted for projected growth and inflation; monthly review of expenditures; investigation of unusual expenses

* Upgraded levels of supervisory personnel in order to clarify lines of authority and improve accountability for clerical performance

* Conceived and implemented weekly multi-disciplinary conference for review of problems and recommendation of appropriate actions, significantly improving both communication and staff cooperation

1977 - 1978   MONTESSORI HOSPITAL AND MEDICAL CENTER OF BROOKLYN, Brooklyn, N.Y.
Manager/Personnel Grants

Organized and administered operations of CETA on-the-job training program for 34 employees including orientation, counselling and partial supervision; assured conformity with governmental regulations and effective liaison with outside agencies; initiated and maintained all data systems.

* Hospital grossed more than $65,000 in nine months due to careful program implementation and monitoring

* Compiled and wrote CETA Manual; clarified and systematized Hospital's responsibilities for participation and reimbursement; provided continuity for program administration

* Participated in Personnel employment and wage/salary activities; e.g., communicated with union hiring hall, screened applicants, conducted salary surveys, and wrote job descriptions

1977   NEW YORK HOSPITAL, New York, N.Y.
                 Administrative Resident

                 Rotated through Hospital departments; line responsibility as
                 Administrator-on-Call; completed special projects as assigned.

                 * Successfully coordinated and collected Medicaid and Blue
                    Cross surveys required for reimbursement in 1/12 normal
                    time; resulted in recommendation for employment at MHMCB

                 * Proposed systematization of photocopying operations and
                    equipment for projected savings of 30%; data generated
                    from this study was used to help equip new hospital under
                    construction

BUSINESS AND PUBLIC SERVICE EXPERIENCE

1977   DAVID DONLAN FOR COUNTY EXECUTIVE (political campaign), Garden City, N.Y.
                 Office Manager/Bookkeeper

                 Set up systems for cash flow and fiscal operations; prepared
                 financial statements for submission to Board of Elections;
                 arranged meetings with community and political leaders.

1975   PILOT FABRICS CORPORATION, New York, N.Y.
                 Assistant Convertor/Shipping Supervisor

                 Assisted in directing conversion of raw goods to finished textiles;
                 liaison and trouble-shooter to assure on-schedule activity of mills,
                 dyers, and truckers; and effective communications with customers.

1972-1973   UNITED WAY OF GREATER NEW YORK, New York, N.Y.
                 Fund Raiser

                 Organized and assisted campaign committees and groups; arranged
                 promotional, educational, and fund-raising events.

EDUCATION   NEW YORK UNIVERSITY, GRADUATE SCHOOL OF PUBLIC ADMINISTRATION, New York, N.Y.
                 1977 - M.P.A., Health Policy, Planning and Administration (4.0 cum. avg.)

                 NEW YORK UNIVERSITY, WASHINGTON SQUARE COLLEGE, New York, N.Y.
                 1971 - B.A., Religion (Founders' Day Honors Certificate; 3.9 cum. avg.)

                 VASSAR COLLEGE, Poughkeepsie, N.Y.
                 1966 - 1968, 64 credits towards B.S., Religion & Biology (Dean's List)

                 Additional Professional Study:

                 1978 - Grants Writing Seminar, The North Group of Falls Church, VA
                 1974 - Group Dynamics in Human Relations, New School for Social Research

AFFILIATIONS   American Public Health Association
                 American Hospital Association

HELEN SCOFIELD
25 Hill Street
Boston, Massachusetts   02105
(617) 266-2575

OBJECTIVE: FOOD SERVICE MANAGEMENT

SUMMARY: Three years experience in institutional food service and
                dietary consultation. Strong skills in supervision, menu
                planning, food preparation, forecasts and cost control.
                Ability to plan nutritious meals within budget, including
                dietetic and vegetarian dishes.

PROFESSIONAL HIGHLIGHTS:

Aug 1980   HARVARD UNIVERSITY DINING SERVICES
  to   Cambridge, Massachusetts
Present
                Dining Services Supervisor

                *   Supervise 35 persons in operation of college residence
                     dining hall

                *   Write monthly marketing newsletter directed to dining
                     service consumers

                *   Prepare data in forecasting orders, menu planning and
                     inventory control for computer system

                *   Upgraded nutritional value of meals for 500 college
                     students

                *   Developed menu cycle, lowering food cost and boosting
                     profits for unit

                *   Established sanitation schedule

Sep 1979   BUREAU OF SCHOOL FOOD SERVICES OF BOARD OF EDUCATION
  to   White Plains, New York
Aug 1980
                School Lunch Manager

                *   Supervised food service staff in four public schools

                *   Redesigned forms for evaluating employee performance

                *   Responsible for menu planning, food preparation service,
                     scheduling, purchasing, inventory, payroll and sanitation.

                *   Designed food preference questionnaire (adopted and used
                     by 19 schools)

School Lunch Manager (Cont'd)

*   Set up nutrition committee to promote nutrition education
    and to obtain feedback from students, faculty and parents

EDUCATION: Hunter College, New York, N. Y.
                1978 - B.S., Foods and Nutrition

                Additional Courses:
                    Vegetarian Cookery, Yoga Institute, New York, N. Y.
                    Educational Writing, Pace University, White Plains, N. Y.

AFFILIATIONS: American Home Economics Association
                American Dietetic Association

VILMA COVINAS
25 Locust Street
New York, New York 10040
(212) 304-6090

OBJECTIVE: **EXECUTIVE POSITION AS NURSING ADMINISTRATOR OR DIRECTOR OF OPERATING ROOM/RECOVERY ROOM SERVICES**

SUMMARY: Eighteen years progressive leadership and administrative experience in a large, technologically advanced operating and recovery room complex. Strong background in planning, organizing, coordinating, directing and evaluating patient care programs, management and operational systems, orientation and staff development programs, as well as facilities expansion and renovation. Experienced in developing and analyzing patient scheduling, staffing and management information systems. Skilled in budgetary and fiscal management, with responsibility for administering $10 million budget. Expert in labor relations and contract administration. Well-versed in interdisciplinary project management, problem solving and communications. Knowledgeable of regulatory standards, medico-legal considerations, quality assurance and cost reimbursement processes.

EXPERIENCE: **FLOWER FIFTH AVENUE HOSPITAL,** New York, New York

1963
to
Present

Assistant Director of Nursing, O.R./R.R. Division (1978 – Present)

Manage delivery of safe and effective patient care in 35 Operating Rooms and 28-bed Recovery Rooms, requiring supervision of 225 professional and auxiliary nursing personnel and coordination with appropriate medical and hospital services.

- Responsible for strategic planning, implementation, coordination and evaluation of patient care programs and network of management and operational systems.

    — Instituted nine new clinical programs in 1982 alone

    — Organized ambulatory surgery program

    — Devised synchronized system for O.R. scheduling and bed reservation

    — Planned and operationalized O.R./R.R. transport system

    — Designed and implemented O.R.-C.S.S. case cart exchange system, including standardization and cataloging of all instrument sets

    — Instituted system to expedite blood reservation and delivery for O.R.

- Establish and maintain effective staffing patterns, recruitment, retention, staff development and labor relations programs.

    — Devised formula for determining staffing requirements, with target of professional nursing staff providing intra- and post-operative care

    — Developed and implemented orientation programs for nursing staff, residents, medical and nursing students

    — Initiated the clinical preceptor and specialty rotation programs

    — Reduced staff turnover rate from 10% to 1% by providing for expeditious fulfillment of vacancies and establishing atmosphere conducive to high morale and retention

    — Co-conducted Philippine recruitment resulting in hiring of 100 nurses

- Develop and implement policies and procedures; monitor compliance.

  - Wrote and compiled specialty procedure/policy manuals for O.R., R.R., Cystoscopy, Endoscopy, Hyperbaric Chamber, and Ambulatory Surgery

  - Wrote job description for all categories of divisional personnel

  - Initiated and maintained surgeons' preference card system

  - Developed and implemented risk management/quality assurance programs

  - Directed activities relative to three successful JCAH inspections

- Project, prepare and monitor capital and operating budget ($10 million) for ten cost centers; established O.R./R.R. charging system.

  - Administer materials handling and cost containment program

  - Negotiated contracts for procurement of high-usage/expenditure items

  - Initiated standardization and development of perpetual suture inventory system, with consolidation of back-up and ordering through C.S.S.

  - Initiated inventory system for grafts, implants and orthopedic prostheses

  - Initiated program for preventive maintenance and repair of specialized equipment

  - Formalized mechanism for processing new program/product requests with budgetary impact

- Develop effective system for maintaining clinical and administrative records and reports.

  - Designed and implemented patient operative records

  - Devised statistical system for reporting caseload and utilization

  - Participated in development of computerized management information system, in conjunction with systems analysts, computer consultants and programmers

- Plan, organize and coordinate facilities expansion and renovation.

  - Participated in planning, functional programming and establishment of current O.R./R.R. facility, including selection/installation of equipment, as well as reorganization and expansion of staffing system

  - Coordinated renovation of ambulatory surgery and endoscopy suites

  - Planned for expansion of current R.R. facility

  - Participated on hospital advisory committee, ambulatory and surgical working groups in planning new hospital, including nationwide on-site survey of major tertiary care hospitals

- Represent the nursing department in hospital and community activities.

  - Participated on Medical Board Committees on Surgery, Medical Standards, Infection Control and Disaster Planning, as well as various hospital project management teams and task forces

  - Represented the hospital on the New York City Health and Hospital Corporation—Emergency Medical Services Hyperbaric Advisory Council

Nurse Coordinator, Operating Room/Recovery Room Division (1977-1978)
35 Operating Rooms and 28-Bed Recovery Rooms

Clinical Supervisor, Gaisman Surgical Suite (13 Rooms) (1975-1977)

VILMA COVINAS/3

Asst. Supervisor, Administration & Staffing, O.R./R.R. (1970-1975)

Asst. Supervisor, Inservice Education, O.R. (1966-1970)
Started as Staff Nurse in 1963 and promoted to Assistant Head Nurse in 1965, then to Head Nurse in 1966

1962-1963   **ENGLEWOOD HOSPITAL,** New Jersey
Staff Nurse, Operating and Recovery Room

1960-1962   **MARGARET HAGUE MATERNITY HOSPITAL,** Jersey City, N.J.
Exchange Visitor, Labor and Delivery/Operating Room Units

1959-1960   **UNIVERSITY OF THE EAST MEDICAL CENTER,** Manila, Philippines
Staff Nurse, Surgical Unit

EDUCATION: **COLUMBIA UNIVERSITY, TEACHERS COLLEGE,** New York, NY
1970—Master of Arts in Nursing Service Administration

UNIVERSITY OF THE PHILIPPINES, COLLEGE OF NURSING, Manila, Philippines
1959 B.S., Nursing (College Scholar, 2 semesters; Entrance Scholar)

Completed numerous career-oriented continuing education courses sponsored by AORN, American College of Surgeons, American Society of Anesthesiologists, American Management Associations, Ethicon, AMSCO, etc.

LICENSURE: Professional nurse licensure in New York and New Jersey.

CERTIFICATION: Professional Achievement in O.R. Nursing Practice, 1979-1984 (AORN)

AFFILIATIONS: American Nurses Association and New York State Nurses Association

Association of Operating Room Nurses, Inc.: Various offices held in New York City Chapter, including President, Vice President, Secretary and Board Member; chairman of various committees; Chapter Delegate to AORN Congress 13 years (Delegate Chairman two years); Test Pool Item Writer, AORN Certification Examination; Chapter Liaison to National AORN Research Committee, 1981 to present

Advisory Council of National AORN Committee for Collaboration with Industry

Medical-Surgical Industry Product Development/Evaluation Panels

Philippine Nurses Association of New York, Inc., President, 1982-84

PRESENTATIONS: "Documentation of Patient Care in the O.R."; AORN Conference, New York, NY, 1982

"O.R. Scheduling"; AORN Conference, New York, NY, 1981

"Surgery, Then What? Patterns of Disfigurement"; AORN Regional Workshop, New York, NY, 1981

"Developing the Operating Room Module for a Hospital Disaster Plan"; 25th National AORN Congress, New Orleans, LA, 1978

"Ethical, Moral, and Legal Aspects of Organ Homotransplantation"; American Association of Critical Care Nurses Seminar, New York, NY, 1972

"Hazards of Ethylene Oxide Sterilization," AORN-NCE Regional Institute, New York, NY 1975

"Developing, Implementing, and Evaluating Nursing Care Plans for Patients in Surgery"; AORN, NYC Chapter Workshop, 1973

PENNY MORGAN

210-20 Village Road, Apt. 80A
Parkway Village
Jamaica, NY 11435

Home: (212) 591-9791
or (212) 723-7244
Business: (212) 592-4180

OBJECTIVE: <u>SENIOR CHILD CARE COUNSELOR</u>

SUMMARY: Highly experienced in counseling/consultation with adolescents in institutional setting designed on campus plan, or in a group home setting. Firm though sympathetic toward personal problems. Expert in motivating youngsters to complete education and aspire to vocational independence. Capable administrator, achieving satisfactory results within limited budget.

HIGHLIGHTS OF PROFESSIONAL EXPERIENCE:

1976 to
Present

ST. JOSEPH'S CHILDREN'S SERVICES, Brooklyn, NY
<u>Senior Child Care Worker</u>

* Manage household, administer budget, supervise staff

* Care for physical, emotional and spiritual needs of adolescent residents, aged 14 to 18; give support and affection

   - Consult on goal orientation; emphasize religion as a positive force in their lives; help them see parents as positive role-models; establish idea of organized and productive living (budgeting time and money for short- and long-range planning); how to help their younger siblings

   - Motivated at least 12 residents to return to school full time

   - Motivated at least three to overcome alcoholic problems

* Provide alternate activities - take them to plays; involve them in drama classes

* Motivate residents to learn vocational trades; become self-reliant and self-supporting rather than rely on welfare for support

   - One recent resident completed course in pattern-making; is now lucratively employed

* Interact with community as agency representative; interpret policies and principles of agency

1970-75

LEAKE & WATTS CHILDREN'S HOME, Yonkers, NY
<u>Senior Child Care Worker</u>

* Duties similar to those at St. Joseph's

1969-75

IRVING TRUST COMPANY, New York, NY
<u>Bank Clerk</u>

1941-68

GEORGE F. HUGGINS & CO., LTD., Trinidad, WI
<u>Shipping/Insurance Clerk</u>

EDUCATION: Oxford and Cambridge Senior School Certificate

LICENSES/CERTIFICATES:

University of North Carolina
- 1979-80, Group Child Care Consultant, School of Social Work
- General Certificate, Child Care Work
Swedish Institute, Stockholm, Sweden
- General Practices, Emotionally Disturbed and Handicapped Children

Information Systems

GARY GRAY · 86-11 94th Ave. · Jackson Hts., NY 11372 · (212) 672-6606

POSITION: <u>COMPUTER PROGRAMMER</u>

          HARDWARE: IBM 3033, IBM 360/22, IBM 370/168, AMDAHL 470/V6 1403 Printer, 2540R Reader, 2311 Disk Drive, 2415 Tape Drive, Digital Decwriter II, Datamedia Elite CRT, PDP 11/40 minicomputer, Singer ten, Prime minicomputer, Nixdorft minicomputer

          SOFTWARE: COBOL, ASSEMBLER (BAL), ASSEMBLER (DMF-II); working knowledge of PRG II, PL-1, BASIC, FORTRAN, IBM/OS, Teleprocessing, Hardware Systems and Systems Analysis

EXPERIENCE:

Current   BASIC RESEARCH AND DEVELOPMENT, Long Island, NY
<u>Minicomputer Assembler Programming/Data Processing Coordinator</u>
(Report directly to Senior V.P. in charge of Engineering)

* Designed and implemented customized data entry programs for clients including a major New York utility

* Assist Chief Systems Analyst in design of upcoming projects

  - Set up computerized library control system for use in and out of house

  - Worked on the development of softwear for users with turnkey expectations

  - Attended regular meetings with D.P. personnel at utilities companies to assess their softwear needs

1980   HARDACH TRAVEL SERVICE, New York, NY
<u>Mini-Computer Operator</u> (On-line system)

* Directed department responsible for computation and issuance of invoices, credit and debit statements

* Issued international airline tickets on Nova system connected to Sabre system

* Developed accounting program in COBOL; saves company 500 work-hours annually

* Worked independently; set own schedule and work hours

1979   SMITH, BARNEY, HARRIS, UPHAM & COMPANY, New York, NY
<u>Lead Operator - Data Entry</u>

* Responsible for verification of work of 40-member computer staff

* Within four months, achieved speed levels which surpassed all others in department

GARY GRAY/2

1974-1979   1001 DISCOUNT STORES, DBA EA DISCOUNT, Richmond Hill, NY
              <u>Manager</u>

* Increased annual revenues from zero base of $500,000 per store in six year period

* Installed NCR electronic digital cash registers in both branches

(Worked while attending school)

EDUCATION: BARUCH COLLEGE, New York, NY
              1980 - Certificate: Computer Programming and Systems
                                            Design

              NEW YORK UNIVERSITY, New York, NY
              1/80-5/80 - COBOL

              QUEENSBOROUGH COMMUNITY COLLEGE, Queens, NY
              1975-76 - Course concentration: Business Administration

              YORK COLLEGE, CUNY, New York, NY
              1973-75 - Course concentration: Music Composition

              Working knowledge of Spanish

PERSONAL: Willing to relocate; free to travel

ROY CHURNUTT
40 Maple Road
Princeton, New Jersey 08540
(609) 921-2329

OBJECTIVE: To apply my expertise in computer programming, mathematical analysis
and problem solving to new and challenging projects.

SUMMARY: More than 20 years participation in government-funded research toward
developing a new source of energy through controlled thermonuclear
fusion. Expert in scientific computer programming and mathematical
analysis. Designer of mathematical models for problem interpretation
and solution. Author and contributor to published technical papers.

KNOWLEDGE OF AND EXPERIENCE IN:

- FORTRAN, PL/1

- Interactive computer systems: CDC Cyber 172 (NOS)
                                vm370, DEC PDP 10
                                NMFECC at Livermore, CA

- Batch systems on IBM 360/91, CDC Cyber 172

- Libraries and packages: IMSL, SSP, SORT, PERT

PROFESSIONAL EXPERIENCE:

1960 to   PLASMA PHYSICS LABORATORY, PRINCETON UNIVERSITY, Princeton, NJ
Present
              Scientific Computer Programmer/Mathematical Analyst

* Member of support team for government-funded controlled thermonuclear fusion research

* Analyze raw output from a data acquisition system connected to a
  large fusion machine

* Write and run FORTRAN programs to solve differential equations,
  make numerical approximations and produce graphic output

* Interpret problem, establish method of solution and translate
  data to computer language for intermediate and final analysis

  - Interact with physicists and engineers

  - Produce necessary documentation for programs

  - Meet deadlines for material to be included in papers published
    in technical journals and/or presented at conferences by senior
    researchers

1957-60   UNIVERSITY OF WISCONSIN

              Graduate Teaching Assistant

* Taught mathematics to undergraduate students

1956-57   RAND CORPORATION, Santa Monica, CA

              Programmer/Analyst

* Checked out and wrote programs in the Air Force's SAGE computer
  system on the IBM ANFSQ/7

1952   U.S. NAVY (NEW YORK NAVAL SHIPYARD), Brooklyn, NY

               <u>Physicist</u>

               * Conducted photometric tests of lighting devices prior to purchase by
                 U.S. Navy

MILITARY: UNITED STATES ARMY, Guided Missile Equipment (Radar)
               12/53 - 9/55 (Honorably discharged)

EDUCATION: University of Wisconsin
               1957-60 - Post-graduate work toward PhD in Mathematics

               University of Wisconsin
               1956 - MS, Mathematics

               City College of New York
               1952 - BS, Physics

LANGUAGES: Read some French, German and Spanish

RECOGNITION IN PUBLICATIONS (Partial List):

1980   - T.L. Chu and Y.C. Lee: "Energy Confinement Comparison of
                 Ohmically Heated Stellarators to Tokamaks"

1979   - S. Suckewer and H. Fishman: "Conditions for Soft X-Ray Lasing
                 Action in a Confined Plasma Column"

1979   - J. Sredniawski, S.S. Medley and H. Fishman: "Vaccuum System
                 Transient Simulator User's Manual for PPLCC Cyber System"

1975   - S. von Goeler et al: "Thermal X-Ray Spectra and Impurities in
                 the ST-Tokamak" (Nuclear Fusion)

1974   - M. Porkolab: "Theory of Parametric Instability Near the Lower
                 Hybrid Frequency" (Physics of Fluids)

1972   - M. Porkolab: "Magnetic Instabilities in a Magnetic Field and
                 Possible Applications to Heating of Plasmas" (Nuclear Fusion)

1970   - M. Porkolab and R.P.H. Chang: "Non-Linear Decay and Instability
                 of a Non-Uniform Finite Amplitude Plasma Wave" (Physics of Fluids)

1962   - J. Dawson and C. Oberman: "High Frequency Conductivity and the
                 Emission and Absorption Coefficients of a Fully Ionized Plasma"
                 (Physics of Fluids)

1957   - H. Fishman: "Numerical Integration Constants" (MTAC)
                 Tables reprinted in Handbook of Mathematical Functions, U.S.
                 Department of Commerce, 1964

CHARLES KISER . 115-05 76th Avenue . Kew Gardens, NY 11418 . (212) 847-0413

OBJECTIVE: PROGRAMMER/SYSTEMS ANALYST

HARDWARE: IBM S/370, S/360; Assorted Peripherals

SOFTWARE: Fortran, Cobol, GPSS, SPSS, STATPACK

EDUCATION: MBA, Operations Research, 1980
Baruch College, Queens, NY
Thesis: "Bimatrix Game Theory"

BA, Computer Science, 1975
Queens College, Queens, NY
Dean's List, 1974, 1975

Regents Scholarship, 1971
Bronx High School of Science, Bronx, NY

IBM Course in ANSI Cobol

EXPERIENCE:

1978 to
Present

BARUCH COLLEGE, New York, NY   (9/80-Present)
Research Assistant, Educational Computer Center

* Troubleshoot, define and resolve problems regarding new and
  existing programs in Fortran, Cobol, SPSS, GPSS and any
  intervening software needs

* Facilitate debugging of programs; review logic sequence
  and flowcharting; analyze SPSS output

Research Assistant, Statistics Laboratory   (9/79-6/80)

* Assisted in applied mathematical and statistical problem
  solving; programmed for IBM S/370

Research Assistant, Academic Computer Center   (9/78-6/79)

* Wrote Cobol programs to analyze other Cobol programs

1977 to
1978

U.S. DEPARTMENT OF HEALTH, EDUCATION & WELFARE, Flushing, NY
Claims Adjuster Trainee

* Charged with judgmental decisions for recipients of social
  security benefits on basis of submitted evidence

* Researched 15-volume para-legal library to arrive at
  decisions and compute benefit rates

1975 to
1976

CT CORPORATION SYSTEMS, New York, NY
Programmer Trainee

* Wrote and documented Cobol programs

1973 to
1974

INTERPUBLIC GROUP OF COMPANIES, New York, NY

* Bursted and decollated computer output into report form
  IBM S/360

* Assisted computer operators: mounted tapes, typed responses
  on operator console, cleaned tapes, used card sorter

BERNARD LENAPE
135-31 112th Street . South Ozone Park, NY 11420 . (212) 529-8203

OBJECTIVE: SENIOR COMPUTER OPERATOR

HARDWARE: IBM 360/30   RCA SPECTRA 70/35
BURROUGHS B3500 and 4800   HONEYWELL 100 Series

OTHER SKILLS: Keypunch, Unit Record Equipment, Adding Machine, Manual
and Electric Typewriter, Record-Keeping

EDUCATION: Elizabeth Seton College, Yonkers, NY
1980 - AAS, Business Administration

Borough of Manhattan Community College, New York, NY
1971-73 - Liberal Arts/Data Processing

Northeast Region Education Center, New York, NY
1970 - RCA Computer Systems Certificate in TOS/TDOS

Institute of Computer Technology, New York, NY
1969 - Certificate in IBM Punched Card Data Processing
1964 - Certificate in ABM Keypunch and IBM Keypunch

EXPERIENCE:

1977 to   BOWERY SAVINGS BANK, New York, NY
Present   Computer Operator

* Run bank applications on daily cycle; create tape and turnover
  log sheet
  - Use online thrift system (B4800)

* Debug COBOL programs
  - Compile, test and execute (if program has bug, take memory
    dump and send back to programming)

* Fill in as lead operator during vacations and absences

1972-1977   AMERICAN INSTITUTE OF CERTIFIED PUBLIC ACCOUNTANTS, New York, NY
Lead Computer Operator (1975-1977)
Computer Operator (1972-1975)

* Used B3500 online accounting system
  - Updated membership records, including names and addresses
  - Maintained records on publications
  - Ran all accounting applications

* Balanced reports (located errors when reports were out of balance);
  debugged COBOL, RPG and FORTRAN programs

1972   SOCIETY OF AUTOMOTIVE ENGINEERS, New York, NY
Computer Operator

* Ran entire computer operation on IBM 360/30; designed in-house
  job request form

1969-1972   BOROUGH OF MANHATTAN COMMUNITY COLLEGE, New York, NY
Computer Operator

* Trained students in operation of IBM 360/30, RCA SPECTRA 70/35
  and keypunch machines; supervised student aides; tutored students
  in COBOL programming (BASIC) in basic and advanced applications;
  evaluated performance

* Compiled and debugged COBOL, ALP, RPG, BAL programs for administration and students; maintained tape library

* Given opportunity to experiment with system to determine extent
  of applications available

JAMES LERO
90 East Compo Road   Westport, CT 06880   (203) 226-4014

OBJECTIVE: INFORMATION SYSTEMS MANAGEMENT

SUMMARY: More than 10 years data processing experience in both management and technical areas, with emphasis on systems analysis, troubleshooting and design. Strong background in proposal preparation and presentation.

PROFESSIONAL
EXPERIENCE: DATA COMPUTING, INC., Darian, CT
President

1977
to
Present

* Contract with diverse industry client base to identify, analyze and solve corporate MIS problems of varying magnitudes

* Representative assignments and clients:

  - North American Reinsurance Co.--Managed loss fund accounting system project to permit reserve fund control of potential liabilities

    . Supervised staff of programmers through completion of project after defining functional requirements and providing an approved system documentation

  - Citicorp Industrial Credit--Designed, coded, tested and documented series of on-line finance programs for automatic processing of leasing agreements from proposal through booking stages

    . Programs were written in COBOL using Command CICS and accessing an IDMS data base

  - Marine Midland Bank--Designed, coded and tested most of on-line print programs for international money transfer system

    . Program browsed a data base for completed transactions, generated contracts and confirmations for pre-printed forms, and then routed documents to appropriate printers

  - Drexel Burnham--Designed and programmed Alpha Sort Key Generation system after bidding successfully against several other firms

    . System consisted of COBOL module and four BAL sub-routines that generated sort key by scanning several name and address fields

  - Blue Cross/Blue Shield--Acted as troubleshooter during system testing of batch COBOL medical claims system

    . Researched problem reports generated by testing group and made necessary program modifications

  - U.S. Trust Co.--Modified stock transfer system to conform to Canadian banking regulations

    . System written in BAL using Macro CICS, including numerous user-written macros

  - Currently producing turnkey practice microcomputer software package using most sophisticated data base package in existence as nucleus of management system for psychiatrists and psychologists

TOUCHE ROSS, New York, NY
Systems Analyst

1976
to
1977

* Implemented a Macro CICS data entry system with responsibility for writing all on-line COBOL and BAL programs to collect billing entry and print proof listing on entering branch's printer

    - Maintained CICS control tables for entire development system

SONY, INC., New York, NY
Senior Programmer/Analyst

1975
to
1976

* Evaluated user requests for system modifications and worked with programming staff to implement same

    - Consulted with user to develop program specifications and related operations documentation

    - Wrote batch and CICS Macro COBOL programs for in-house accounts receivable system

METROPOLITAN LIFE INSURANCE COMPANY, New York, NY
Programmer/Analyst

1973
to
1975

* Designed batch COBOL system to collect data for company's Psychological Testing Service, and programmed major portion of it

    - Researched existing 360/20 card system and consulted with user to determine desired enhancements

* Supervised correlation studies on effectiveness of testing system evaluating sales representatives

    - Managed research, discussion, negotiation, presentation, approval, programming and testing of entire system

* Promoted from Programmer Trainee after three months on job

MANAGISTICS, INC., New York, NY
Computer Payroll (Manager)

1970
to
1972

* Authorized printing of payroll checks after validating client input data

    - Dealt directly with clients regarding use of standard input documents and correction of errors arising from previous payroll runs

EDUCATION

QUEENS COLLEGE, SUNY, Queens, NY
1971 - B.A., Anthropology

NEW YORK UNIVERSITY, New York, NY
Intensive 37A Assembler; Advanced 370 Assembler; OSLVS Supervisor
Services & Macros; Introduction to Microcomputers; CICS/VS Macro Programming

CAPABILITIES

Languages: COBOL; 370 Assembler; RPG; Z80 Assembler; Basic Teleprocessing
             Packages; CICS/VS Macro & Command
Data Bases: IMS; IDMS; MDBS (Z80 Microcomputer version)
Timesharing Packages: TSO (with SPF); CMS; On-line Librarian; ICCF
On-line Debugging Packages: EDF; Intertest (On-line Software International)
Hardware: IBM 370; 3030 series; 4330 series, North Star Horizon

Legal

ROWENA SCOTT, Esq.
111-46 96th Drive
Forest Hills, NY 11375

Home: (212) 793-2063   Business: (212) 840-8151

GOAL

Corporate Counsel or equivalent level business position

BACKGROUND

Associate Counsel   MANDELBAUM & SCHWEIGER, Esqs.
1979 to Present   New York, NY

- Prepared agreements and corporate documents, commercial and
  personal real estate transactions, litigation, some estate
  work in general practice with emphasis on corporate, commercial and international business law

Associate Counsel/Assistant Corporate Secretary   SEIKO WATCH COMPANY, INC.
1966 to 1979   Jackson Heights, NY

INTERNATIONAL   - Handled all matters related to international marketing, manufac-
RELATIONS   turing and intercorpate relationships

                 - Negotiated and prepared contracts and distribution agreements

                 - Set up and later divested operation in American Samoa, including
                   all negotiations with Samoan government, U.S. Departments of
                   Commerce and Interior

                 - Represented company in problems involving customs and tariffs

RESEARCH/   - Established and was member of patent policy committee to study
DEVELOPMENT   development of new products and improvements to determine whether
                   to file patent applications

                 - Screened ideas for new products submitted to company; negotiated
                   with inventors and prepared legal documents for contractual
                   arrangements

LICENSING/   - Initiated in-house patent licensing, trademark licensing
PROTECTION
                 - Supervised preparation of and managed litigation in infringement
                   matters

CORPORATE   - Approved all press releases and advertising
COMMUNICATIONS/
GOVERNMENT   - Conducted media interviews; assisted CEO in conducting others
RELATIONS
                 - Assisted CEO in public appearances on problems of multi-national
                   corporations and corporate case history

                 - Wrote speeches and articles for CEO

                 - Maintained contact with legislators, administrative and trade
                   agencies on national and local levels in all matters affecting
                   watch industry

                 - Represented company in legislative and administrative hearings

JOINT   - Performed all legal work in connection with joint ventures and
VENTURES   establishment of subsidiaries, both in United States and abroad

                 - Negotiated all agreements, including shareholders' agreements

ROWENA SCOTT/2

MARKETING	° Studied competition (in cooperation with marketing survey specialists) on matters of product quality and brand image, dealer and consumer acceptance
ASSISTANT SECRETARY	° Served as officer of parent corporation and various subsidiary and affiliated corporations
	° Attended all meetings of Board of Directors
REAL ESTATE	° Negotiated real estate transactions including leases, property sales and sale/leaseback contracts; prepared legal documents
EMPLOYEE RELATIONS	° Negotiated and prepared employment contracts; interacted with all departments in personnel relations
	° Represented company's legal position in contact with human rights agencies
	° Maintained legal aid service for employees
	° Served as Director of Bulova Credit Union
GOVERNMENT CONTROLS AND REGULATIONS	° Monitored compliance with trade regulations, including anti-trust, FTC and Wage/Price Control
LITIGATION	° Represented company in proceedings and hearings before administrative agencies, e.g. Human Rights Commission and Environmental Protection Agency
	° Supervised counsel in multi-million dollar litigation (anti-trust, contracts and general business problems); handled some of own trial work
INSURANCE	° Handled all legal matters related to insurance, including directors' and officers' liability

Associate Counsel, Managing Attorney   GARY PACKWOOD, Esq.
1965 to 1966   Woodbury, NY

Associate Counsel   HART & IRVIN, Esqs.
1960 to 1965   Long Island City, NY

° Full range of trial practice: all aspects of pleading and practice, client interview, negotiation of settlements, pre-trial, appeals

EDUCATION

Brooklyn Law School, Brooklyn, NY
1959 - LLB

Hunter College, New York, NY
1954 - BA, Political Science

BAR STATUS

Admitted to practice in New York State, U.S. Eastern and Southern District Courts, U.S. Customs Court

BRUCE BONDURANT
35 Nob Hill Avenue
Bridgeport, CT 06610

Home: (203) 335-9077

OBJECTIVE: To employ my tax, legal and business experience in a position with
growth potential in a corporate legal department or a law firm.

SUMMARY: - More than two and one-half years general legal experience involving
real estate contracts and titles, estate planning and administration,
personal injury litigation and criminal law.

- Experienced in analyzing matters involving personal income taxation.

- Contributed, by invitation, material for 1979 edition, Connecticut
Practice Book, Kaye and Effron, West Publishing Company.

Admitted to the Connecticut Bar and United States District Court for
the District of Connecticut - 1978.

EXPERIENCE:

June/79 to   STEWART S. KLEIN, Attorney-at-Law, Bridgeport, CT
Present
Associate Attorney

* Interview, advise and represent clients in matters pertaining to
civil and criminal litigation, collections and domestic relations.

* Draft real estate contracts and leases; negotiate real estate sales/
purchase agreements; conduct title searches.

* Research and prepare pleadings and memoranda.

* Generate new business for firm.

January/78   FRANK A. GRIFFITH, Attorney-at-Law, Darien, CT
to June/79
Associate Attorney

* Worked on matters pertaining to personal income taxation, estate
planning and administration; prepared wills.

* Prepared real estate contracts.

* Generated new business; represented clients in criminal, civil and
probate court; researched and prepared pleadings and memoranda.

May/77 to   LAWSON & GRIFFITH, Attorneys-at-Law, Darien, CT
January/78
Legal Assistant

* Conducted title searches, prepared contracts, pleadings and wills;
interviewed clients and performed legal research.

* Joined Frank A. Griffith upon dissolution of partnership.

1973-1974   TAX MAN, INC., Cambridge, MA

Income Tax Consultant

* Interviewed and advised clients on matters relating to personal
income taxes; prepared tax returns of varying complexity.

* Clients included students, employed and self-employed individuals.

BRUCE BONDURANT/2

ADDITIONAL EXPERIENCE (while attending school) - 1975 to 1977

        UNIVERSITY OF LOUISVILLE, SCHOOL OF LAW
        Louisville, KY

        <u>Research Assistant</u>

* Researched questions pertaining to estate law, commercial law and domestic relations.

* Performed legal research of issues involving criminal law and procedure and constitutional law.

* Selected by law professors for this job during last three semesters before graduation.

        GEORGE MUNSING, Attorney-at-Law
        Bridgeport, CT

        <u>Legal Clerk</u>

* Conducted legal research, answered court calendars, performed title searches and prepared pleadings.

        FAIRFIELD COUNTY LEGAL SERVICES
        Bridgeport, CT

        <u>Legal Assistant</u>

* Researched and prepared memoranda for cases involving indigent clients.

EDUCATION:

        University of Louisville School of Law, Louisville, KY
        1977 - Juris Doctor

        Boston University College of Business Administration, Boston, MA
        1974 - BS, Business Administration/Economics, Dean's List

        Member, Society for Advancement of Management
        Representative to Student Government

MEMBER:

        Connecticut Bar Association
        American Bar Association
        ABA Section of Real Property, Probate and Trust Law
        ABA Young Lawyer's Section
        Stamford-Darien Bar Association
        Greater Bridgeport Bar Association

PERSONAL:

        Married, no children. Date of birth: May 25, 1952.

DIANE LOVENDAHL
304 Brooklyn Avenue
Brooklyn, NY 11213
(212) 493-6053

OBJECTIVE: LABOR RELATIONS ATTORNEY

SUMMARY: Experienced and deeply interested in EEO and other personnel
             considerations with demonstrated ability to arrive at equitable
             solutions through intense investigative and interpretative
             procedures. Proven expertise in drafting, developing and
             amending pension plans; drafting and developing language for
             group annuity contracts and research/analysis of federal
             regulations from point of view of employee/management relations.
             Effective in communication; perceptive and sensitive to socio/job-
             related problems. Work well under pressure.

EDUCATION: University of Akron School of Law, Akron, OH
             1977 - Juris Doctor

             Brooklyn College, Brooklyn, NY
             1974 - BA, Political Science/English, Economics

RELEVANT EXPERIENCE:

1977-1979   NORTH AMERICAN PHILLIPS CORPORATION, New York, NY
             Labor Relations/EEO Department

    * Prepared and handled employment discrimination cases

       - Mounted full investigation of each case; interviewed supervisors,
          department managers and other employees

       - Examined personnel records and documents; researched applicable
          areas of law; filed briefs and affidavits with appropriate State
          Administrative Hearings and Appellate Review Boards

    * Charged with responsibility for writing affirmative action plans,
       assisting personnel managers during on-site audits by government
       agents and acting as consultant in re Federal Maternity Act, Age
       Discrimination in Employment Act and effects of 1978 ADEA Amendments
       on Company Benefit and Pension Plans

    * Effected reversal of unfavorable charge by compliance officer during
       one on-site audit, based on alleged violation of Equal Pay Act in
       regard to female employees (one of several such instances)

       - Researched problem; represented company at hearing; produced
          documents and records showing that female employees requested
          certain jobs requiring less facility in English

       - Designed program to instruct non-English-speaking employees in
          English to provide position upgrading and chances for promotion

       - Instituted craft-apprenticeship programs for women

       - Company was awarded government contract; affirmative action
          program was approved

    * Designed and implemented techniques for maintaining personnel records

Fall 1976	SUMMIT COURT PRE-TRIAL RELEASE PROJECT, Akron, OH <u>Legal Intern</u>

* Performed interviewing research and counseling; made recommendations

SUMMIT COUNTY PROSECUTOR'S OFFICE, Consumer Fraud Division, Akron, OH
<u>Investigator</u>

* Investigated consumer complaints; prepared detailed reports

Spring
1976

SUMMIT COUNTY LEGAL AID SOCIETY, Akron, OH
<u>Interviewer/Researcher</u>

* Worked in Family Law, General and Housing Divisions; interviewed petitioners, researched relevant matters

* Assisted in writing briefs, filing motions and affidavits

Fall
1975

APPELLATE REVIEW OFFICE, University of Akron, Akron, OH
<u>Staff Member</u>

* Performed research; wrote briefs

Summer
1973

NEW YORK CITY DEPARTMENT OF CONSUMER AFFAIRS, New York, NY
<u>Volunteer Complaint Counselor</u>

OTHER EXPERIENCE:

1979 to
Present

BOWNICK, INC., Brooklyn, NY (Family-owned enterprise)
<u>Assistant Manager</u>

* Supervise operations and personnel; enforce company policies and procedures

* Provide on-the-job training for employees; process weekly payroll and unemployment insurance claims; maintain excellent employee relations

* Resolve customer relations problems

PROFESSIONAL AFFILIATIONS:

Association for Black Women Attorneys
Bedford-Stuyvesant Lawyers Association
Council of New York Law Associates

MARILYN GARBER   .   344 West 52nd Street, #9R   .   New York, NY 10023   .   (212) 873-6320

OBJECTIVE: Seeking position in social service agency in which I may utilize my
              legal education and experience as well as my experience in social
              service situations

SUMMARY: Knowledgeable about legal aspects of community-oriented services and
              institutions. Experienced in counseling in a variety of situations
              including drug abuse, mental health, prisoner welfare, retarded adults
              and income maintenance for public assistance applicants.

EDUCATION: Yeshiva University, Benjamin Cardozo School of Law, New York, NY
              1981 - JD

              Cornell University, College of Arts and Sciences, Ithaca, NY
              1977 - BA, History (Dean's List) New York State Regents Scholarship

EXPERIENCE:

Summer   OFFICE OF THE DISTRICT ATTORNEY, KING'S COUNTY, Brooklyn, NY
1980   Intern (Eugene Gold, District Attorney)

              * Assigned to aid Assistant District Attorneys in investigations, Supreme
                Court, Criminal Court and Sex Crimes bureaus

                - Researched legal issues, drafted motions and bills, wrote memoranda
                  of law, helped prepare cases for trial, contacted and interviewed
                  witnesses and complainants

              * Participated in research/writing of Methods of Obtaining Physical
                Evidence from the Defendant (published Fall, 1980)

Fall   FAMILY COURT, BRONX COURT HOUSE (Hon. Gertrude Mainzer), Bronx, NY
1979   Judicial Clerkship

              Took notes of trial testimony; did legal research; summarized and catalogued
              current domestic relations case law

              BENJAMIN CARDOZO SCHOOL OF LAW, New York, NY
              Law Library Assistant

              * Assisted students in use of library, microfilm and microfiche

Summer   HOFFINGER, FRIEDLAND & ROTH, Attorneys at Law, New York, NY
1979   Legal Assistant

              * Researched and wrote memoranda regarding criminal, matrimonial and health
                 law; drafted and served motions

1977-1978   TOMPKINS COUNTY DEPARTMENT OF SOCIAL SERVICES, Ithaca, NY
              Social Welfare Examiner

              * Interviewed public assistance applicants; determined welfare, food stamp
                 and medicare eligibility; supervised income maintenance for 100-household
                 caseload

1975-1977   THERAPIST/YOUTH WORKER/COUNSELOR, Ithaca, NY (While attending school)

              Crisis Counselor, Mainline Drug Center - walk-in and phone-in

              Youth Worker, Ithaca Youth Bureau - coordinated street theatre group

              Therapist, Tompkins County Mental Health Clinic - couseled jail inmates
              and long-term clinic patients

Aide, Meadow House Center for Retarded Adults - directed dance movement in music

INTERESTS: Singing, sewing, dancing, cooking

PROFESSIONAL AFFILIATIONS:

New York Women's Bar Association
American Bar Association
Rochester Folk Art Guild (clothing design)

Marketing

ROBERTO SEPULVEDA
150 East 40th Street, Apt. 7-J
New York, NY 10020
Home: (212) 687-9000 Ext. 250   Business: (212) 997-8738

OBJECTIVE: INTERNATIONAL BOOK PUBLISHING LINE MANAGEMENT

A line management position in international book publishing with
general management responsibilities

SUMMARY: More than twenty years experience in sales management and administration in domestic and international book publishing with major
publishing houses. Heavy experience in hiring, training and motivating successful salesmen, new market development, advertising
and promotion.

EXPERIENCE: OPTIMUM INTERNATIONAL BOOK COMPANY, New York, NY

1968-1983   Group Marketing Director - Asia (Based in Tokyo 1975-1983)

* Responsible for sales of all book company products

* Hired, trained, motivated and supervised sales and promotion
  staff of 30 people

* Supervised local sales managers and representatives; coordinated
  sales activities in offices in Tokyo, New Delhi, Singapore, Kara-
  chi, Hong Kong, Bangkok, Manila, Jakarta and Nairobi

* Created and established sales promotion and advertising campaigns
  for Asia and East Africa; calculated and established budgets and
  expenses

* Became first known U.S. publishing representative to open negotiations with Mainland China; sales there increased from $0 in
  1976 to $500,000 in 1979

* Analyzed potential new markets and established new sales territories in Hong Kong/Taiwan, Thailand/Burma, East Africa, Indone-
  sia and Korea

* Increased sales by average of 20% annually since assuming sales
  management position

Manager of Editorial Optimum LatinaAmericana
(Based in Bogota, Colombia, 1974-1975)

* Responsible for sales and distribution of Spanish language books
  throughout South America, except Brazil; for the Caribbean and
  Central America

* Supervised and coordinated 60 warehouse personnel, salesmen,
  editors and order service people

* Supervised publishing of 40 university level Spanish language
  textbooks

* Attained annual sales of $2 million during both years as Manager

Continued

OPTIMUM INTERNATIONAL BOOK COMPANY (Continued)

<u>Manager International Book Co.</u> (Based in Singapore 1970-1973)

*   Set up sales and distribution center, which was responsible for
    sale of all book company products to Asian, East African
    and some Middle Eastern countries

*   As sales manager, also directed and coordinated efforts of ten
    sales representatives for these areas

*   Achieved 25% increase in sales in each of four years in position

<u>Sales Manager/Export</u> (Based in New York 1969-1970)

*   Hired, trained and supervised 12 resident sales representatives
    to sell to markets primarily in Asia, Africa and Middle East

*   Planned, organized and conducted sales meetings

*   Directed promotion and advertising from New York into those
    export areas

*   Established credit and pricing policies in export market covering
    45 countries and 600 accounts

*   Increased sales volume by 15%

1962-1968   JOHN WILEY & SONS, New York, NY
            <u>Sales Manager - Mexico</u> (1966-1968)
            <u>Sales Representative - Northern California</u> (1962-1965)

1958-1962   ALLYN & BACON INC., Boston, MA
            <u>Regional Sales Manager - College Division</u> (1961-1962)
            <u>Sales Representative - Northern California</u> (1958-1960)

1954-1958   THE MENNEN COMPANY, San Francisco, CA
            <u>Sales Representative</u>

1951-1954   COLGATE-PALMOLIVE COMPANY, St. Louis, MO
            <u>Sales Representative</u>

EDUCATION:

            St. Louis University, St. Louis, MO
            1951 - BA, Political Science - History

LANGUAGES:

            Fluent Spanish
            Speak Japanese

LUTHER BURNS · 300 East 63rd Street, 25C · New York, NY 10016 · (212) 532-3707

OBJECTIVE: <u>DIRECTOR OF SALES/MERCHANDISING - FASHION INDUSTRY</u>

SUMMARY: Ten years experience in successful buying and selling of fashions for men and women at wholesale and retail. Highly knowledgeable of European designs for the American market with proven ability to forecast trends and educate customers to changes in styles. Experienced at working with designers to create selling collections. Have traveled to Italy and France several times a year to study collections and make astute purchases.

PROFESSIONAL HIGHLIGHTS:

1976-1980 RAFAEL FASHIONS, New York, NY
<u>Sales/Merchandising Manager</u> (1978-1980)

* Supervised five-person sales force in developing major accounts for men's and women's fashions ($10 million annual sales)

* Instigated and implemented intensive customer relations program to improve company's position with store buyers

* Worked with designers to create sales-oriented designs

  - Established procedures for controlling design expense

* Accurately projected sales/volume to exercise control over fabric purchases

  - Reduced fabric inventory through program of special cuttings and sales to selected outlets for piece goods

* Effected increase in profit/cost ratio through increase in markup

* Established advertising program in cooperation with stores

* Improved coordination of fabric delivery to factory and finished orders to stores

* Exercised quality control over line design, manufacturing and overall company performance

<u>Merchandise Manager</u> (1977-1978)

* Supervised three people handling key accounts in establishing quality control of designer lines and factory performance

* Acted for company in liaison with manufacturers of piece goods in Italy to exercise control over manufacturing and distribution

* Instigated and implemented records systems for piece goods to coordinate delivery with projected date of manufacture of finished product

* Worked with pattern cutters, technicians and production personnel to ensure excellence of product and on-time readiness of sample line for showing to buyers

* Worked closely with owner/designer to create saleable product at good price for most favorable profit/cost factor

Continued

RAFAEL FASHIONS (Continued)

Salesman (1976-1977)

* Opened and developed major accounts with high-ticket stores (Saks, Neiman-Marcus, I. Magnin and Bloomingdale's)

* Responsible for increase in volume from $2.5 million to $8 million

* Guided clients in merchandise selection; projected sales for more effective production

1974-1975   BARNEY SAMPSON, New York, NY
             Salesman

* Opened and developed major accounts doubling sales volume to $3 million

    - Brought in Bonwit Teller, Saks and Bergdorf-Goodman

* Educated customers to styling and design of European clothing

* Studied collections in Europe and selected parts of collections for the American market

1970-1974   TYRONE MEN'S APPAREL, Cedarhurst, NY
             Salesman

(Started as stockboy while in high school and emerged as top salesman while in college)

* Learned men's European clothing business at retail level giving me opportunity to judge customers' tastes and reaction to style and style changes

EDUCATION: Hofstra University, New York, NY
             1974 - History/Political Science

             Speak Italian

ARTHUR BERTUZZI . 66-25 100th Street . Forest Hills, N.Y. 11375

(212) 897-7311

SALES MANAGEMENT (TEXTILES)

1976-Present   President, SPECIAL IMPRESSIONS
Flushing, New York

* Achieved $800,000 average annual sales

* Supervised manufacture of T-shirts, including selling, financing, marketing, and establishing overhead

* Reporting to me at the Lindenhurst Plant were:

  1) Production Manager
  2) Shipping Manager
  3) Bookkeeping Department
  4) Accountant
  5) 5 Salesmen
  6) 50 Employees of the cutting and sewing
     department

* Improved working relationships with mills and cut &
  sew staff, resulting in reduced cost of manufacturing
  by approximately 10%

* Developed working relationships with wholesale distributors, chain stores, department stores, media sales
  promotion situations, sales reps, individually owned
  T-shirt retailers, and boutiques

* Managed and extended credit to customers when warranted

* Promoted independent contractor reciprocation

* Liquidated company July, 1979

1975-1976   Sales Manager, GOTHAM KNITTING MACHINERY
Glendale, New York

* Handled in-house sales

* Gained 35-40 new accounts, at an average billing of $50,000 each

* Maintained gross sales of $5 Million

* Delegated work to 4-5 salesmen worldwide

* Traveled to mills throughout country in order to evaluate
  machinery needs and update and service existing system

* Established long-lasting customers through good will and public relations

* Worked part-time during senior year in college

* Resigned from firm to go into business for myself

EDUCATION

BS (Sociology/Psychology), Queens College   1975

Far Rockaway High School   1970
   Dean's List, 2 years
   Student advisor to school newspaper, The Phoenix

SPECIAL INTERESTS

Languages: French--read/speak;   Spanish--read

Member, New York City Chamber of Commerce Board

1975-Present:

   Basketball Coach for last four years, Forest Hills Jewish Center
   Basketball League for 17 year olds

PERSONAL

Age: 27   Married   Will Travel
                                                          Own Car

MARLENE PARKS . 725 Ocean Parkway, Apt. 1C . Brooklyn, NY 11218

(212) 941-9759   (212) 870-8210

OBJECTIVE: To employ my expertise in clinical chemistry in a position as a technical representative for a pharmaceuticals or laboratory equipment manufacturer

SUMMARY: More than ten years experience as a graduate biochemist with in-depth knowledge of clinical laboratory procedures and equipment. Proven capability in establishing and implementing work-flow processes for expedited, integrated hospital record-keeping. Specialist in accurate testing techniques.

PRIMARY
INSTRUMENTS
USED:

Gamma Counting Spectrometer	Auto Analyzer
Flame Photometer	Micro-Centrifugal Analyzer
Atomic absorption	Blood gas machine
Micro Sampler Spectrophotometer	

HIGHLIGHTS OF EXPERIENCE:

1970 to
Present

ST. LUKE'S HOSPITAL, New York, NY

Laboratory Technologist

* Developed and established standards for accuracy of hospital tests and quality control of special procedures

* Assisted with development and implementation of successful installation of Gamma Counter for use in radioimmunoassay procedures

    - Trained staff, established standards for use of Gamma Counter

* Perform standard and special clinical tests including analyses of whole blood serum, fluids and urine, using both manual and automated methods

* Trained and supervise staff of five technicians; maintain good relationship with co-workers; distribute daily workload in high pressure atmosphere

* Trouble-shoot equipment and serve as consultant on new procedures

* Drug identification tests

* Member of IV team

1969-70

ELIZABETH SEATON'S HOSPITAL, Cochabamba, Bolivia

Biochemist

* Established and implemented laboratory procedures in new hospital

* Assisted in introduction of new manual methods; set up laboratory equipment and prepared reagents

* Performed routine tests in hematology, chemistry, urine, bacteriology and serology and blood bank

1968-69   MINISTRY OF PUBLIC HEALTH-CENTRAL LABORATORY, Cochabamba, Bolivia

               Biochemist Trainee

               * Worked under supervision of group leader

               * Performed routine detailed tests in hematology, serology, para-
                 sitology, bacteriology

Concurrent: FARMACIA COCHABAMBA, Cochabamba, Bolivia

               Pharmacist Trainee

               * Organized and filled prescriptions

               * Prepared special compounds not available from manufacturer:
                 tablets, suppositories, suspensions, solutions and lotions

EDUCATION: University of St. Simon, Cochabamba, Bolivia
               1970 - Degree in Biochemistry/Pharmacy
                      (Annual Best Student Award with 4.0 grade average throughout
                      five-year program)

               Hunter College, New York, NY
               1965 - Course in Histology

               The American Institute, Cochabamba, Bolivia
               1963 - Graduated among five top students

CERTIFIED: Biochemist and Pharmacist
               Laboratory Technologist

LANGUAGES: Trilingual: Spanish/English/German
               Working knowledge of Italian

STEPHEN FURMAN
150 West End Avenue
New York, New York 10023
Home: (212) 873-6512   Messages: (212) 787-4900

OBJECTIVE: INFORMATION INDUSTRY: MARKETING REPRESENTATIVE

SUMMARY: Seven years of sales and merchandising experience, including technical products. Consistent track record of sales volume increases. Trained sales team. Willing to travel extensively if necessary. Have completed Lockheed Information System's basic course in DIALOG and Radio Shack's TRS-80 Mini-computer course.

EXPERIENCE:

1979
to 1980

ALEXANDER'S DEPARTMENT STORE, INC.
NEW YORK, NY

Assistant Buyer, Appliance Department

* Purchased appliances for retail chain; $7 million annual appliance volume

* Assisted with store merchandising to create additional departmental traffic for 15 stores

* Follow-up on delivery of merchandise

* Monitor distribution of goods to various stores

* Check competitive retailers for comparative pricing

* Act as troubleshooter in solving store management problems pertaining to appliances

1971
to 1979

Assistant Manager of Radio and Television

Promoted to Manager of Calculator Department

* Responsible for operation of calculator department

* Tripled the department's sales from $125,000 to $500,000 during period of sharp price competition

* Increased sales volume each year as manager

* Trained commission team with high morale and low turnover

* Sold (personally) over 15,000 calculators during an eight year period

* Made recommendations to buyers on merchandise selection

* Sold programmable calculators to end "users" including business and technically oriented customers (priced as high as $500)

EDUCATION: DeWitt Clinton High School, New York, NY
               1966 - High School Diploma

               American International College, Springfield, MA
               1971 - BA, History

               Additional Skills and Interests:

                   Logic Seminar   Mechanics
                   Philosophy   Statistics
                   Communications   Financial Research - gold,
                                            foreign currency markets

PERSONAL: Wish to be based in New York, but will travel.

BARRY ROGERS · 25-25 Parsons Boulevard · Whitestone, NY 11357 · (212) 445-5300

OBJECTIVE: SALES/TECHNICAL REPRESENTATIVE

SUMMARY: Experienced as wholesale and retail salesperson, buyer and technician. Extensive knowledge of photographic market, product lines and product maintenance. Excellent sales track record. Familiar with sales, promotion, merchandising and forecasting of market trends.

EXPERIENCE:

1980 to   L.J. CRANSTON CORPORATION, New York, NY
Present   (Rep organization for manufacturers of photographic equipment)

Manufacturers' Representative

* Represent the following manufacturers in Connecticut and Westchester County, NY

    - Holson: photo albums
    - M.W. Carr: photo frames
    - Amphoto: photographic books
    - Harwood: movie and video lighting equipment
    - Taprell Loomis: picture folders

* Opened up 35 to 40 new accounts, increasing sales volume by $100,000

* In first year, sold $300,000 in supplies and equipment

1977 to   ALEXANDER'S DEPARTMENT STORES, New York, NY
1980   Assistant Buyer

* Purchased photographic products and equipment for 15 camera departments with $7 million combined annual volume

* Researched and evaluated new products; identified and defined changing trends in consumer preference

* Analyzed sales figures; planned advertising and sales promotions

* Conducted weekly personal visits to stores to check inventory; supervised display and merchandising

* Extensive vendor contact

1972 to   ALEXANDER'S DEPARTMENT STORES, Rego Park, NY
1977   Camera Department Manager

* Managed camera and calculator departments; supervised and motivated staff of 19

* Purchased bulk of camera department inventory; monitored stock levels

* Advised management on changes in customer preferences and buying trends

ALEXANDER'S DEPARTMENT STORES (Continued)

Book and Stationery Department Manager 1973-1977

* Managed staff of 9
* Purchased and merchandised 95% of all books and stationery; made all merchandising and ordering decisions
* Showed consistent 10% seasonal increase in sales; demonstrated success in targeting merchandise to the needs of the community

Camera Sales Clerk 1972-1973

* Sold cameras and accessories to retail customers

1963 to 1969   HOFSTRA UNIVERSITY, Hempstead, NY

Audio/Visual Technician/Photographer/Darkroom Technician

1969 to 1972   Elementary School Teacher

EDUCATION: Hofstra University, Hempstead, NY
              1966 - BA, English/History
              1973 - MS, Education

EXTRA CURRICULAR ACTIVITIES:

        Hofstra University - Photo Club, Campus Newspaper,
                             Yearbook and Radio Station

        Member of Fresh Meadows Camera Club, NY

EARL ORR

150 Lark Court   (404) 953-0705 (home)
Marietta, Georgia 30067   (404) 266-8259 (office)

EXPERIENCE   TRAVELERS INSURANCE CO.   October 1968 to Present

Regional Assistant Vice President/Marketing Operations Officer
Southeast Region Atlanta, Georgia 12/79 to Present

Management responsibility for General Managers of regional branch
offices; areas of supervision include marketing, underwriting,
claims handling, and administrative support.
Directly accountable for results in seven of region's 13 branch offices;
offices produce $125 million in revenues, require operating budget of
approximately $20 million, and employ 750 people.

* Youngest in company to hold position of Market Operations Officer.

* Initiated management actions necessary to change and upgrade
  ineffective leadership in critical branch offices.

* Maximizedrevenue opportunities through successful producer
  management actions.

* Minimized expense deterioration by developing and implementing
  needed expense control actions.

* Analyzed product and pricing needs, state by state, and worked
  successfully with technical staff to achieve desired filings,
  particularly in commercial lines.

* Effectively represented assigned offices in the annual negotiations
  with Regional Headquarters.

Regional Assistant Vice President/Management Services
Southeast Region Atlanta, Georgia 12/77 to 12/79

Responsible for all administrative support functions including budgeting,
expense control, credit and collections, internal audit, manual and
computer processing operations, employee relations, training and
development, purchasing and real estate.
Provided support to 13 branch offices in 11 southeastern states;
offices produced $225 million in revenues, required operating budget
of approximately $30 million, and employed 1300 people.

* Established decentralized regional operation; management had been centralized prior to 12/77.

* Selected as top region in 1978 and 1979 from an overall administrative support perspective.

* Directly responsible for the corporate wide implementation of a more effective compensation program.

* Developed and implemented computerized monitor and control system for all regional training and developmental activities.

Manager/Administrative Operations
White Plains Service Office White Plains, New York 10/68 to 12/77

Comprehensive management responsibility for Financial Services, Administrative Operations and Personnel.
Prepared, allocated and distributed office operating budget in excess of one million dollars.
Directed personnel in collections, data processing, filing, mail, supply, telecommunications, and typing departments.
Supervised all employment activities; included recruiting, screening, and testing for staff of 120.

* Consistently exceeded assigned productivity standards.

* Functioned as in-house Management Consultant for General Manager.

* Reduced outstanding receivables from $100,000 monthly to only $1,500 without any adverse effect on sales.

* Created a formal orientation program for new employees.

EDUCATION   MASTER OF BUSINESS ADMINISTRATION 1972 Iona College
             Major in Organizational Behavior
             Graduated Cum Laude

             BACHELOR OF SCIENCE 1968 University of Bridgeport
             Major in Marketing
             Attended on athletic scholarship

REFERENCES   Provided upon request.

R.D. GRANEY · 35 East 46th Street · New York, NY 10016 · (212) 889-9920

OBJECTIVE: MANUFACTURING/MARKETING COORDINATOR

SUMMARY: More than five years' experience in competitive design and marketing of brand-name clothing for boys and girls. Highly expert in close coordination of marketing and manufacturing divisions. Demonstrated excellence in supervision of design staff and management of showroom. Possess conceptual acuity in interpreting buyer ideas into saleable designs.

EXPERIENCE:

1978 to Present

PERKY PRINT TEXTILES, INC., New York, NY

Corporate Design Director/Showroom Manager (1/80 to Present)

* Direct design and merchandising of domestic and international line of children's wear with corporate volume of $60 million

* Maintain close and constant communication with marketing executives in establishing achievement of marketing plans

* Coordinate manufacturing and marketing divisions for most effective production of seasonal and standard merchandise

* Manage New York office including showroom, design department and all administrative functions for international division

* Maintain retail-client relations in the field in determination of local and regional taste and demand

* Instigate use of available machinery to produce new lines

* Company maintaining strong market position in recessional climate

* Also carried full responsibilities of Senior Design and Merchandising Coordinator (see below)

Senior Design and Merchandise Coordinator (7/78-12/79)

* Researched market for merchandise mix and capacity for introduction of Perky Print products in particular stores and/or locales

* Established and implemented systems to improve design, color and fabrics of line

Design and Merchandise Coordinator (1/78-7/78)

* Dealt directly with national chain store accounts in development of private label lines

* Established input into models and colors from results of market research

* Designed children's garments for mass production for private label accounts

* Designed line of children's clothing (models, colors, fabrics) for Infants to Girls 7-14, Boys 8-16

7/77-12/77 COLONIAL CORPORATION OF AMERICA, New York, NY

<u>Consultant</u>

* Set up coordinates program for line of boys' and youths' garments from conception to final production
* Structured division based on the development processes of the program for private label sales to J.C. Penney and K-Mart
* Participated in design of men's knit and woven shirt line
* Conducted market research for colors, models, stripes and plaid formations

10/74-6/77 GARAN, INC., New York, NY

<u>Head Designer - Girls' 7-14 Division</u> (7/75-6/77)

* Designed and merchandised Garanimal line
* Designed four collections annually (400,000 dozen - $35 million in retail sales)
* Improved coordination between design, production planning and manufacturing divisions
* Developed new size specifications to increase marketability
* Expanded previously minimal girls' line through development of more feminine silhouettes

<u>Associate Designer - Girls' 7-14 Division</u> (10/74-7/75)

* Assisted head designer in all areas listed above

EDUCATION: Fashion Institute of Technology, New York, NY
1973 - AAS, Major: Apparel Design; Specialization: Children's Wear

CERTIFICATIONS:

Dale Carnegie Institute: Dale Carnegie Personal Development Course Diploma, July, 1977

MICHAEL REMINGTON, 2 Franklyn Avenue, East Brunswick, NJ 08816 · (201) 238-6201

OBJECTIVE   SALES/MARKETING or DIVISION MANAGEMENT

SUMMARY   Record of significant contributions to profit levels and productivity in
every position held. Capable leader and motivator with broad overview
of sales and marketing. Adept at market analysis and conceptualization.
Able product spokesman.

PROFESSIONAL ACHIEVEMENTS

1974-1981   FEARON CORPORATION, Piscataway, NJ
Vice President, Fearon Tool Group Division (1980-81)

* Control sales, marketing, P&L, inventory and purchasing for five tool
  lines with annual sales of $22 million and staff of 250

  - Developed and managed nationwide sales organization of
    92 manufacturers' rep firms, 10 direct sales managers
    and 35 inter-office personnel

* Established sales incentive program resulting in 13% increase in
  annual sales and previously unparalleled gross profit levels

* Reorganized marketing and creative departments, resulting in
  increased efficiency and improved market analysis

* Through analysis of item costs, market and competition, increased
  gross profit share of three assumed lines by 10% in one year

* Resolved marketing difficulties through reorganization to encourage
  total market penetration

* Expanded merchandising productivity almost 200% through analysis and
  redesign of merchandising aids after studying competitive aids and
  consumer acceptance

* Established new product concept and conducted market tests; supervised design, pricing, item selection and selling program

Vice President, Delco Division (1977-80)

* Directed division with annual sales of $13 million; oversaw inventory,
  quality control, sales and marketing of two tool lines

  - Managed 45 rep firms, 5 direct sales managers and
    20 inter-office personnel

* Established and organized national advertising campaign to penetrate
  all markets

* Increased gross profit share 5% through market analysis and reformu-
  lation of marketing program

* Improved product quality and expanded all categories for favorable
  competition with domestic tool manufacturers, raising sales by 25%

National Sales Manager, Delco Division (1976-77)

* Directed sales force of 45 rep organizations

* Upgraded Delco image from small import to top-quality line, per-
  mitting favorable competition with domestic manufacturers; formulized
  and marketed Pro-Mate as secondary line

MICHAEL REMINGTON/2

Western Regional Sales Manager, Delco Division (1974-76)

* Directed 8 rep organizations throughout 12 states

* Ranked number one in regional sales during 1974 and 1975; sales volumes more than doubled between 1974 and 1976

* Originated merchandising aids and pricing structure ideas which were adopted by home office for implementation throughout company

1968-1974   ALBERTO CULVER COMPANY, New York, NY
District Sales Manager (1972-74)

* Supervised one assistant and 10 salespeople working throughout seven northwestern states

* Awarded President's Cup for highest district sales increase in 1972; in 1973, scored within top third of total districts in company

* Ranked number one district salesman between 1972 and 1974

* First manager in company to hire saleswoman to represent women's health and beauty products

Assistant District Sales Manager (1970-72)

* Supervised five salespeople and headed Len Dawson (Kansas City Chiefs quarterback) promotion program

Sales (1968-70)

* Represented company among drug wholesalers, food trade, mass merchandisers and rack jobbers in Kansas City, Missouri

1964-1968   SHEAFFER PEN COMPANY, Fort Madison, IN

Sales

* Called on retailers and wholesalers in Oklahoma, Kansas and Missouri

EDUCATION   BA, Business - Northeast Missouri State University

Professional Seminars:
    Dale Carnegie Sales/Management Program
    American Management Associations

PROFESSIONAL AFFILIATIONS

American Management Associations
National Association of Service Merchandisers
General Merchandise Distributors Conference
Automotive Service Industries Association
Automotive Warehouse Distributors Association

Willing to relocate and free to travel

PETER CHEUNG
32 Burton School Avenue
Westport, Ct 06880
(203) 226-7721

OBJECTIVE: To employ my expertise and experience in international marketing in a senior management position for a manufacturer of industrial or consumer goods

SUMMARY:
— More than 20 years experience in international marketing between Asia and USA-Europe, including industrial and farm equipment and consumer goods

— Thirteen years as manager for consumer goods exporter in Hong Kong

— Expert in locating markets in Asia, negotiating contracts and expediting shipping details and government documentation

— Completely fluent in English, Mandarin Chinese, Shanghai and Cantonese

— Have MBA in International Business

— Intimate knowledge of entire East Asian marketplace with specific knowledge of China

BUSINESS HIGHLIGHTS:

1975 to
Present

C.K. CHAN CO.,INC.
Westport, CT

President

• Have developed market for tannery equipment, chemicals and raw materials in Taiwan, Hong Kong, Bangkok, Singapore and Malaysia

• Conduct market analysis surveys through personal contact with buyers and agents and on-site exploration in trading countries

• Negotiate contracts with suppliers and buyers

• Exploring markets in China proper; negotiations proceeding

• Maintain financial intelligence through correspondence and personal investigation relevant to exchange rates and credit requirements

• Maintain excellent customer service relations through correspondence and in-plant visits

• Transact shipping details: letters of credit, freight forwarding, customs clearances and delivery verification

| 1971 to 1975 | **SHANGHAI TRADING CORPORATION** |
| | New York, NY |

Vice-President/Executive Manager

- Charged with responsibility for shipment of materials to Vietnam and Cambodia under US Government Aid Program

  - Machinery shipped included: textile fabrication machinery, tractors and tractor-drawn implements for small farms

  - Tools included: digging and chopping tools for farmers; hand tools for factory and construction workers

  - Raw materials included: farm chemicals and fertilizers, plastics for use in manufacturing

  - Full range of consumer products

- Directed all export procedures and processing of US Government documents

| 1958 to 1971 | **WELLMING TRADING CO., LTD.** |
| | Hong Kong |

Export Manager

- Exported products manufactured in Hong Kong to importers in United States, England, West Germany, Belgium, Italy and France

  - Products included men's and women's garments, gift items, costume jewelry and toys

- Analyzed markets, negotiated sales, maintained customer relations through correspondence and personal visits and processed shipping documents

EDUCATION:

Hong Kong University
1963 — MBA, International Business

Regional College, Hong Kong
1958 — BA, Philosophy

Able and willing to travel extensively

STACY HALL
42 Knot Road
Tenafly, NJ 07670
(201) 567-6987

OBJECTIVE: ADVERTISING ACCOUNT EXECUTIVE

SUMMARY: Ten years' experience in advertising with direct client contact throughout, three years in account management. Demonstrated expertise in budget management. Creative copywriter on variety of industrial, consumer and corporate campaigns including print ads, direct mail, and collateral material. Proven ability to supervise production, assist in new business development, and maintain excellent client relations with all levels of management.

Clients included Conrac Corporation, Maserati Automobiles, McGraw-Hill Publications Company, North American Philips Corporation, Thomas J. Lipton Company, "21" Brands, U.S. Industries, Xerox Corporation and Zeiss-Ikon.

EXPERIENCE:

1976-1979 DOBBS ADVERTISING COMPANY, INC., New York, NY
Account Executive (1976-1979)

* Successfully planned and administrated advertising and promotion for several clients, in many cases maximizing limited funds through knowledge of media and production (i.e. utilizing free media publicity to support insertions, negotiating most advantageous rate structures and getting the most efficiency from production expenditures)

* Conceived, developed, and directed advertising and promotion programs for numerous industrial and consumer accounts

* Planned and supervised selection and purchase of print and broadcast media

* Wrote or directed copy on all accounts handled

Copy Director (1976-1978)

* Created concepts and wrote copy for print and broadcast media as well as collateral, sales material, direct mail literature, and publicity releases

* Supervised all in-house and free lance copywriting

* Served as client contact on several accounts

* Recommended media schedules

Highlights

* During tenure as account supervisor and head writer, one account experienced 20% sales increases on numerous products

* Developed print ad for leading surveying equipment manufacturer that completely repositioned client in the market, increased sales, and influenced the "look" of future advertising in publication in which it appeared

* Created and directed a campaign which reaffirmed client, the Bank of Toms River, as the number one bank based in Ocean County, NJ

1971-1976 MULLER JORDAN HERRICK/N.J., Inc., Fort Lee, NJ and New York, NY (Formerly Richard James Associates)
Copywriter and Assistant Account Executive

* Conceived and wrote advertising and promotion copy for print ads and collateral material for industrial and consumer accounts

* Served as account executive for numerous clients

* Planned and purchased media

Highlights

* Created a coupon-response newspaper campaign for retail tire dealer; as a result, client had to restaff and reorganize to handle increased business

* Produced print ad for new account that generated more inquiries from the first insertion than had been achieved by former agency's year-long campaign

1969-1971 KALMAR ADVERTISING, INC., Englewood Cliffs, NJ
Copywriter

* Wrote advertising and promotional copy for consumer and industrial accounts

* Served as copy contact

* Recommended and purchased print and broadcast media

* Developed numerous public relations programs for clients

1968-1969 PRENTICE-HALL, INC., Englewood Cliffs, NJ
Assistant Production Editor

* Planned and coordinated book production from manuscript to completed bound book

* Copyedited and supervised same

* Acted as liaison with authors, suppliers and internal personnel

* Checked galleys, page proofs, blueprints

* Generated advertising copy for book jackets

EDUCATION: Fairleigh Dickinson University, Teaneck, NJ
1968 - Bachelor of Science

LANGUAGE: French

JOHN POWELL . 154 East 49th Street . New York, NY 10011 . (212) 684-8820

OBJECTIVE: <u>CORPORATE ADVERTISING DIRECTOR</u>

SUMMARY: Proven track record in creating and developing comprehensive advertising campaigns, with special emphasis on sales promotion materials, direct response advertising and direct mail. Experienced in negotiation for cooperative advertising. Ability to design and coordinate trade show activities. Highly skilled in all production techniques, creative direction, account management and media selection.

PROFESSIONAL HIGHLIGHTS:

1980 to Present
MKP, INC., New York, NY (Graphics Studio)
<u>Manager</u>

* Direct, coordinate and exercise quality control of production activities

    - Four creative departments: Design, Art, Typesetting and Color Proofing

Clients include: United Technologies, Hearst Publications, Union Carbide

1978 to 1980
INTERSIGHT DESIGN, INC., New York, NY (Packaging Design)
<u>Art Director</u>

* Charged with responsibility for studio production and final art for product packaging

* Selected and coordinated outside services: typesetting, photography/retouching, printing, color proofing

* Knowledgeable about product packaging and marketing

Clients include: Bristol Myers, Pilsbury, Mennen, Hoescht

1975-1978
THE WENK ORGANIZATION, INC., New York, NY (Advertising Agency)
<u>Creative Director/Account Executive</u>

* Managed, directed and supervised creative production

    - Specified and purchased outside support services: typography, photography, printing, mailing lists and media

    - Provided creative concept and direction to 15-member staff including in-house and freelance artists; supervised and personally designed and produced material; edited and wrote copy and headlines

* Assumed management of media department

    - Upgraded department operation through initiation of improved production/traffic systems and contract negotiations

    - Handled an increase in media sales of approximately 200% without additional staff

    - Developed media budgets with most effective allocation for radio, print and some TV

Continued

THE WENK ORGANIZATION, INC. (Continued)

* Managed direct response and coupon advertising campaigns
  - Developed campaigns for various clients; targeted audiences; suggested appropriate media; made account presentations
  - Followed through with total production after client approval
* In-depth experience in direct mail
  - Targeted audiences based on specific criteria
  - Researched list companies; purchased lists for test markets and full scale efforts
  - Designed printed material to be mailed, including personalized letters
  - Monitored responses and fulfillment of campaigns ranging from 5,000-piece test market to half-million piece general mailing

Clients included: Chase Manhattan Bank, Mego Toys, New School, Parsons School of Design, New American Library

1973-1975   THE TYPE FACTORY, New York, NY (Advertising and Graphic Design Studio)

* Directed all creative activities: print campaigns, catalogs, trade show exhibits and sales promotional material

Clients included: R.R. Bowker Company, Library Bureau Division of Sperry, New Process Steel

1973   OTTINO/SOLOMON, INC., New York, NY (Design and Typography Studio)

* As Studio Manager/Designer, was responsible for production including concept, design, type direction, boardwork and process lettering

1968-1970   BOROGRAPHICS, INC., New York, NY (Design and Typography Studio)

* Instituted, directed and promoted growth and operation of full-service graphics and typography studio

EDUCATION   John Jay College, New York, NY - Marketing Major

Served apprenticeship in graphics in several art and graphics studios in New York and Los Angeles

GEORGE HALKIADES . 100-55 77 Drive . Forest Hills, NY 11375 . (212) 896-3275

OBJECTIVE: <u>MANAGEMENT - RETAIL OPERATIONS</u>
To apply my experience and expertise in retail management, organization and merchandising in a position with growth potential to general management/executive management level

SUMMARY: More than ten years experience in retail/customer service management with four years definitive experience in full management responsibility and accountability. Skilled in selection of merchandise to attract local customers, merchandising and cost control. Creative in traffic-stopping displays and promotion with keen eye to profitability. Excellent in customer and employee relations.

HIGHLIGHTS OF PROFESSIONAL EXPERIENCE:

Current MAXI-DISCOUNT DRUGS, Richmond Hill, NY
<u>Manager</u>

* Solved problem of confusion over price changes by proposing price-coding system to be circulated to managers of eight stores in chain

  - Proposal adopted by general management has developed into orderly presentation of imminent price changes on merchandise to allow all store managers a method to put changes into effect simultaneously

* Developed creative merchandising plan for Christmas sales

  - Proposed codification of Christmas display set-up to enable local managers to effect same or similar merchandising displays

  - Personally supervised set-up for five of the eight stores

  - Through grouping of Christmas items for easy access, merchandise is moving well in every store in chain with profitable outlook anticipated

1973-1980 F.W. WOOLWORTH COMPANY
<u>Manager - Rego Park, NY</u>

* Developed, instigated and maintained fluid merchandising policy to meet the demands of a changing neighborhood

  - Stocked merchandise to attract different ethnic groups

  - Improved profit picture to turn around operation which was scheduled for closing

* Recommended removal of lunch/fountain operation which was losing money through poor sales and high maintenance costs

  - Instituted expansion of horticultural, shoe and hosiery departments which produced large increases for the year (25% to 50%)

* Initiated merchants' committee of 40 local store managers to install special Christmas lighting to improve night traffic, which had declined considerably over four-year period

  - Night business showed large increase over previous year with minimal cost to all concerned

(Continued)

F.W. WOOLWORTH (Continued)

Manager - Rye, NY (1977-1978)

* Hired dynamic individual to replace retiring operator of lunch fountain that had been steadily losing sales over long period

  - Lengthened hours of operation; hired additional, competent help

* Developed reputation of being "the place to eat" in Rye, especially at breakfast; sales took upward turn and increased dramatically

Positions of Increasing Responsibility - Various Stores (1973-1977)

* Was accepted into Management Trainee program, which included training in merchandising, office procedures, lunch operations and overall management of store

* Was steadily promoted to Assistant Manager, Advanced Assistant Manager and Specialized Assistant Manager prior to official appointment as Manager of Rye store

1969-1973   GLATT TRAVEL, Hicksville, NY
             Tour Coordinator

* Managed arrangements for world-wide tours of 20-30 people

  - Scheduled tours; booked members into hotels; dealt directly with carriers for most timely and economical travel accomodations

* Interacted with people at all levels on a one-to-one basis

* Booked in excess of $20,000 per year in general and customized tours

EDUCATION:

Queens College, Flushing, NY
1969 - Majored in History

SPECIAL INTERESTS:

Reading, stamp collecting, sports events

BETTY AMES • 24-54 Lancaster Avenue Jamaica, New York, NY 11432 • (212) 521-7240

OBJECTIVE: Product management position utilizing diversified marketing
              experience and strong analytical skills

EXPERIENCE: STATLER-MORRISON, INC., New York, NY
1980   <u>Account Executive</u>
to   Supervised marketing and advertising of two major accounts:
1981
                          HAIRCARE, INC.

        *   Developed and implemented $10 million advertising budget

        *   Created new product "Le monde" and new color line
            "Corsage D'Amour," increasing both market share and
            profitability

        *   Supervised research, media, creative and production
            staffs

        *   Designed media plans for placement of print and network
            advertising

        *   Developed all necessary production estimates and cost
            analyses for advertising campaigns

        *   Prepared and presented product strategy statements to
            senior management

                          STILL SPIRITS, INC.

        *   Prepared and implemented $3 million advertising budget

        *   Planned, positioned and launched major new product
            "Bourbon Royal" in response to market need, including
            packaging, pricing and merchandising

        *   Developed promotional packages, point-of-purchase
            displays and sales force incentive programs

              SIMMONS AND STERNS INC., New York, NY
1978   <u>Senior Research Analyst</u>
to
1980   *   Formulated and implemented quantitative questionnaire to
            forecast marketing trends

        *   Prepared and presented marketing recommendations to
            clients, based on survey feelings

        *   Predicted potential market share for new product entries
            based on qualitative and quantitative analyses of con-
            sumer response

	CHESEBROUGH POND'S INC., Greenwich, CT
Summer	Research Analyst
1977	

* Conducted design testing for product packaging

* Developed and prepared commercial evaluation reports

EDUCATION:

UNIVERSITY OF PENNSYLVANIA, Wharton School
1978 - BS, Marketing
1978 - BA, Psychology

* Dean's List, 1976 - 1978

HARVARD UNIVERSITY, Graduate Program in Clinical Psychology
1977 - Study of Small Group Communication

PERSONAL:

* President, Juvenile Diabetes Foundation

* Extensive travel throughout Europe and Middle East

WAYNE PENDERGRAFT . 4121 Seaview Avenue . Brooklyn, NY 11203 . (212) 469-4725

OBJECTIVE: SALES/SALES MANAGEMENT

SUMMARY: Five years experience in sales and production management with
               effective, low-key approach to promotion of business appreciation.
               Demonstrated expertise in staff motivation for quality production
               of product in highly competitive industry. Strong ability to
               establish and maintain excellent customer relations in turn-around
               of company image. Fully knowledgeable about account management
               from point of initial contact to impact on bottom-line profitability.

EXPERIENCE:

1976-1980   ALL PURPOSE IDENTIFICATION, LTD., Kingston, Jamaica
               Sales Manager

* Charged with effecting turn-around of company that was losing
  sales and revenue due to poor image

* Established and maintained excellent customer relations program

  - Heeded customer complaints on product quality and took steps
    to institute major quality control system

  - Negotiated contracts to ensure adherence to orders by the
    customer and delivery by company

* Directed activities of five salesmen in promotion of identification
  badges

  - Motivated, routed and monitored staff efforts; established
    incentive system for surpassing set quotas

  - Traveled with each salesman on periodic basis to assess per-
    formance and customer acceptance of personality and sales
    presentation; offered suggestions for improvement where needed

* Instituted and systemetized sales call program to ensure regular
  visits by representatives with positive service attitude

  - Customers responded through increased orders

* Administered collection process

  - Worked with slow-pay customers to establish reasonable base
    for time payments

  - Improved collections by 45%

* Opened several new major accounts

* Improved overall sales volume by 35% each year

* Set incremental pricing policy to cover constantly rising costs
  of imported materials

  - Sold policy to customers who agreed to abide by it

* Developed effective advertising campaign with ads in local
  papers and on radio; wrote all copy

(continued)

ALL PURPOSE IDENTIFICATION, LTD. (continued)

Production Manager

Charged with re-establishing rapport with customers with serious complaints on quality òf product

* Called on each dissastified customer; ascertained problem customer was having with product and/or company performance

* Quietly persuaded each customer to "bear with us" and that as new Production Manager I would take necessary steps to improve quality and delivery times

   - Initiated, established and maintained systems for improving quality of product and high degree of quality control on a continuing basis

   - Initiated, established and maintained shipping systems to ensure on-time delivery to customers

   - Program resulted in keeping the accounts in-house and receiving larger and more frequent orders and referrals to new customers

* Increased productivity and efficiency of production staff

   - Set clear standards of performance in regard to punctuality and responsibility

   - Established incentive program for adherence to rules

   - Attracted higher quality of personnel to work in plant

* Improved performance, again, resulted in increased sales volume and better customer relations

1975-76	GOODYEAR TIRE, LTD., Kingston, Jamaica Sales Manager (while attending school)

* Directed activities of three salesmen; set sales quotas and performance standards

* Personally opened 12-15 new accounts (local firms and gas stations)

EDUCATION:	College of Art, Science and Technology, Kingston, Jamaica Personnel Management
	Jamaica School of Business, Kingston, Jamaica Accounting
SKILLS:	Knowledge of laminating and pouching machinery, embosser, Polaroid Land ID-2 and 4-way ID cameras

JANICE WHITE
205 Bushnell Avenue, Hartford, CT 06103
Home: (203) 522-2193   Office: (203) 241-4202

OBJECTIVE   SENIOR BUYER FOR AGGRESSIVE, MULTI-STORE RETAIL OPERATION

SUMMARY   Highly motivated buyer with four years domestic and import experience in
             various retail furniture departments. Strong color and design sense with
             ability to identify market winners. Creative and effective merchandiser;
             good advertising and budgeting skills. Nation's youngest casegoods buyer.

EXPERIENCE   STERN AND COMPANY, Hartford, CT
             Buyer, Bedroom, Dining Room, Occasional and Lifestyle Furniture

1979 to   * Purchase for and manage $2 million inventory throughout eight stores
Present   representing average of $22 million in annual revenues
              - Supervise all aspects of retailing from product purchasing
                through merchandising to floor presentation
              - Hire, train and supervise assistant buyer and sales staff of eight
              - Formulate and administer departmental objectives; prepare
                long-range plans

             * Increased volume of Lifestyle Department from $200,000 to $800,000 in
               one year (Ranked #1 Lifestyle Buyer for all Stern and Company stores)

             * Personally selected program for importing profitable, high-volume
               line of European chairs, with assistance of head marketing
               representative for the Stern and Company
              - Visited nine Italian factories to assure best product and value,
                with goal of achieving additional $3 million in sales

             * Organized cooperative publicity venture with Museum of Modern Folk
               Art in conjunction with marketing effort for new casegoods line
              - Worked up seminar/slide show conducted by museum director of collection
                on which product line was based, and which attracted 50 potential
                customers

             * Promoted from Assistant Buyer to Buyer after only three months on job

1978 to   W & J SLOANE, New York, NY
1979   Assistant Buyer

             * Assisted buyer for bedroom and dining room, mattresses and sleep sofas,
               and contemporary and occasional furniture departments

             * Promoted from Trainee Assistant Buyer after only four months on job, as
               part of University of Massachusetts Internship program

1977   W & J SLOANE, San Francisco, CA
             Floater (summer, junior college year)

             * Assigned to various departments: Advertising, Accounts Payable and
               Accounts Receivable, Personnel, Decorating Studio, Executive offices

1975   STERN'S DEPARTMENT STORE, Boothbay Harbor, ME
             Salesperson, Women's Specialty Operation (summer, freshman college year)

1975   CLOTHES CORNER, Acton, MA
             Salesperson, Women's Discount Operation (between high school and college)

EDUCATION   UNIVERSITY OF MASSACHUSETTS, Amherst, MA
             1979 - BS, Retail Merchandising

INTERESTS   Photography, Sailing

DAVID BENCKE . 300 East 93rd Street . New York, NY 10028 . (212) 737-6620

OBJECTIVE: <u>MEDIA SALES - PRINT/BROADCASTING</u>

SUMMARY: Results-oriented salesman with proven ability for productive effort.
             Broad background in self-education through employment in different
             types of industries as well as extensive travel throughout United
             States, the Caribbean, Latin America and Europe. Excellent verbal
             skills. Proficient in French. Strong in interpersonal relations.

RELEVANT EXPERIENCE:

1980   TREND NEWSPAPERS, INC., Boston, MA
             <u>Account Executive</u>

             * Serviced established accounts; contacted and sold new accounts

             * Presented prestige concept of publication to prospects; assisted
                clients in ad design and composition

             * Worked with clients in establishing new format for ads when publica-
                tion changed size from tabloid to magazine

             * Maintained excellent customer relations with established accounts
                through reinforcement of magazine concept

             * Brought in two important accounts in first week

Concurrent   TIME/LIFE LIBRARIES, INC., Boston, MA
             <u>Telephone Sales Representative</u>

             * Developed sales of Home Improvement Series through phone contact
                with people in their homes

                - Established nineteen new accounts in four days (200 calls,
                   50 pitches - working four hours per day)

1979   BARNES & NOBLE BOOKSTORE, Boston, MA
(Christmas   <u>Sales Clerk</u>
Season)
             * Maintained company policy of instant and courteous assistance to
                customers; set up displays for best attraction; helped with inventory

OTHER EXPERIENCE:

1979   73 MAGAZINE, INC., Peterborough, NH
             <u>Book Production Assistant</u>

             * Edited manuscripts and other copy; proofread and corrected galleys;
                selected type; produced rough pasteups; participated in research

1972-1978   SUMMERTIME AND PART-TIME JOBS WHILE GOING TO SCHOOL

             - Lumber Industry, Missoula, MT - sawmill assistant
             - Management Consulting Firm, Durham, NH - groundskeeper
             - Construction Industry, Lee, NH - swimming pool installation
             - Laundry Industry, Portsmouth, NH - delivery driver
             - Prescott Park Arts Festival, Portsmouth, NH - art instructor
             - Also: crewed on 65 ft. ketch; housepainter, Alaska; landscape
                   gardener; grape harvester in France

EDUCATION: UNIVERSITY OF NEW HAMPSHIRE, Durham, NH
             1978 - BA, English; Minor: French
             ALLIANCE FRANCAISE, Paris, France
             1976 - French

RUSSELL CARTER • 2-20-4 KUDAN KITA, CHIYODA-KU • TOKYO 102, JAPAN

Home Phone: (011-81-03) 262-3412

OBJECTIVE: **MAGAZINE PUBLISHING MARKETING CONSULTANT**
SALES MANAGEMENT

SUMMARY: More than 20 years of high productivity in sales, sales management and marketing for major magazine/book publisher. Demonstrated expertise in direction of Far East operations with in-depth knowledge of Australasian business practices and procedures. Highly successful track record in creation, training and motivation of sales force. Proven ability to generate exceptional increases in circulation and advertising sales.

HIGHLIGHTS OF EXPERIENCE

1957 - 1980 UNIVERSAL INDUSTRIES, INC., New York, NY

UNIVERSAL PUBLICATIONS CORPORATION, Tokyo, Japan
Director of Asia Pacific Operations (1978-1980)

Directed all business operations in Japan, Australia, Singapore, the Philippines, Taiwan, Hong Kong and South Korea; supervised space sales and circulation for 28 publications; investigated and researched business and joint-venture potential throughout Asian and Australian markets

- Managed definitive sales effort resulting in 21% ($500,000) increase in advertising space during first year in Japan

  – Supervised staff of 20 sales, promotion and clerical personnel; conducted regular motivational meetings to establish and examine strategies for deeper market penetration

  – Accompanied Japanese salesmen in calls on customers and prospects in direct sales presentations to top management; traveled throughout Asian and Australian territories to work with independent sales representatives in Hong Kong, Melbourne and Sydney

- Investigated, researched and drew up presentations of potential acquisition or joint venture investments for corporate consideration

  – Met with scores of other publishers, entrepreneurs, writers and correspondents throughout Asia to assess publishing ideas

  – Determined value of and recommended four new Asian ventures worthy of presentation (two are pending, two others tabled for future reference)

  – Interfaced with executives of two major Asian joint ventures: Nikkei Universal, Tokyo; *The American Industrial Report,* Hong Kong (monthly publication directed to People's Republic of China)

- Met periodically with Japanese counterparts to advise them on promotion tactics, circulation development and advertising sales strategies; advised Hong Kong group on special projects (personal efforts helped Japanese associates generate $100,000 in current new business)

- Facilitated closer cooperation between corporate office in New York and Far Eastern/Australian representatives (was first person from Universal management Australian representatives had seen in seven years)

  – Assessed problems in Australia; instituted new procedures resulting in $100,000 new business.

Continued

UNIVERSAL PUBLICATIONS CORPORATION (Continued)

- — Advised corporate management on advertising/promotion programs for *Business Week*'s new Asian Edition (programs covered both advertising and circulation strategies)

- — Successfully assisted and advised Hong Kong representatives on special *Business Week* sections featuring Korea and Taiwan

- — Instrumental in contributing to sales increases in Hong Kong, Singapore, Melbourne and Sydney

- Explored circulation problems and opportunities throughout Asia in relation to all 28 Universal magazines with particular emphasis on *Business Week*

- — Consulted with customers, sales organizations, distributors and air freight companies; improved delivery service through elimination of shipping bottlenecks

- Selected by United Nations, Geneva, to participate in Singapore seminar (1979); discussed advertising, sales promotion and research with export management

UNIVERSAL (BUSINESS MONTH), Houston, TX
Account Manager (1960-1978)

- Successfully sold both product and corporate advertising campaigns in tough, competitive market including South Texas, Louisiana and Mississippi

- — Demonstrated outstanding achievement in face of strong competitors — *Fortune, Forbes, Wall Street Journal, Time, Newsweek, U.S. News and World Report*

UNIVERSAL PUBLICATIONS COMPANY, Houston and Dallas, TX
Advertising Sales Representative (1957-1960)

- Sold space in as many as 28 different publications covering such fields as power, construction, electronics, aviation, computers, mining and electric utilities

- — Uncovered technical equipment manufacturers serving specific industries (presented them with marketing data to aid them in marketing their products)

EDUCATION: University of Illinois, Urbana, IL (Attended on merit scholarship)
1957 - BS, Journalism, Advertising
Member of Alpha Delta Sigma (Advertising Fraternity); Illini Marketing Club

PROFESSIONAL AFFILIATIONS:

Tokyo: American Chamber of Commerce in Japan (Served on China Trade Committee; directed Publication Advertising Committee)
Foreign Correspondents Club of Tokyo
Forum for Corporate Communications
Tokyo American Club
Pacific Area Travel Association

Hong Kong: Hong Kong Press Club
American Chamber of Commerce in Hong Kong (Served on China Trade Committee)

Other: Chamber of Commerce, Houston, Texas
Houston Advertising Federation
Business and Professional Advertising Association
Houston Illini Club (University of Illinois alumni); President four years

ESTHER BURNS   300 Adelphi Street   Brooklyn, NY 11205   (212) 795-1657

OBJECTIVE: BROADCAST MEDIA BUYER

SUMMARY: Experienced buyer in both national and local radio and TV. Skilled in negotiations, client relations, planning and market analysis

HIGHLIGHTS:

1979 to Present

ZEA MARKETING COMMUNICATIONS, New York, NY
Media Director

* Planned and selected media campaigns in agency with billings of 3 million annually. Client list included:

            - FSC Corporation
            - ABC-FM owned stations
            - Fall's Poultry
            - Handleman's Garden Center

* Participate in all phases of planning, including client contact, negotiations with media and payment of affidavits

* Successfully negotiate client/media relations:

    - Obtain favorable rates for clients
    - Convince well-known media personalities to endorse client services
    - Secure favorable positioning of announcements during prime time at no extra cost

* Planned and administer all details of $40 thousand Yellow Page budget for a national telecommunications client

* Established in-house specialty trade research library which ensures speed and accuracy of information delivery to client companies

* Perform continuing and ongoing liaison between agency, media and clients, resulting in excellent rapport and improved service

1976-1979

FOOTE CONE AND BELDING, New York, NY
Broadcast Buyer

Client list included:

            - Bristol Meyers
            - Noxell Lestoil
            - Frito-Lay
            - Campbell Soup Company

* Monitored rate, affiliate and programming changes

* Negotiated favorable radio and television rates and buys

* Developed improved reporting system to provide clients with faster GRP information; (system was adopted by buying group and remains in current use); this significantly improved client relations

* Worked closely with clients to coordinate contests and merchandising promotions

    - Coordinated 40+ stations for Long & Silky promotion

* Established format for facilitating the provision of aircheck and GRP information to clients; "sold" new procedure to both stations and clients, cementing client/agency relations

* Organized contract book and monitored buys for clients and agency

* Charged with approval of make-goods and spot preemptions

(Continued)

FOOTE CONE AND BELDING (Continued)

Estimator Print/Broadcast

* Coordinated buys and issued media estimates which contained:

    - Total gross dollars spent
    - Number of stations used
    - Total GRPs
    - Length of announcements
    - Scheduled flight dates

* Issued discrepancy reports; maintained continuing rapport between station reps and billing department

* Organized various computer reports and distributed finished estimates to clients

1975   KENYON AND ECKHARDT, New York, NY
Accounts Payable Clerk

* Disbursed payments and processed vouchers

1972-1974   WILLIAM ESTY ADVERTISING, INC., New York, NY
Print Estimator

* Coordinated planners' insertion orders and compiled print estimates through use of Standard Rate and Data books

* Checked tearsheets; made lineage adjustments; facilitated payment of invoices

* Handled rebates, short rates and compiled final lineage reports

EDUCATION: Junior College of Albany
             Business Marketing

JOSEPH WANG
822 North Sixth Street
Brooklyn, NY   11211
Home: (212) 387-5420 Business: (212) 763-9571

OBJECTIVE: SALES/MARKETING - CABLE TV/TV SYNDICATION
To employ my time sales/marketing experience in a
position with growth potential in the industry

SUMMARY: Extensive experience in broadcasting industry as
account executive in sales and service of major
accounts. Successful track record in acquiring
direct accounts as well as additional business through
advertising agencies. Adept in creation of advertising campaigns to sell sponsor's product. Worked
extensively with TGI, Simmons and Scarborough market
research.

PROFESSIONAL
HIGHLIGHTS: WYZO/AMERICAN GENERAL, New York, NY
   1976 to   Account Executive
   Present
                 *   Beginning at zero base, created list of accounts
                      with annual billing of $250,000

                 *   Presented marketing studies and created campaign
                      that brought Berdorf-Goodman to the use of radio
                      advertising for the first time

                      - Designed special Columbus Day coat sale
                         promotion (proved more successful than sponsor
                         had anticipated)

                      - Consulted with Berdorf-Goodman executives;
                         advised on buying time on other radio stations
                         in New York, Chicago and Philadelphia

                 *   Deal with account people at all levels of
                      advertising management both in client and agency
                      contact

                 *   Communicate promotional ideas to retailers
                      utilizing radio/in-store promotion tie-ins

                      - Created successful radio campaign and
                         commercial for La Mode Fashion; designed
                         co-op campaign for Minolta, Polaroid and
                         Goodyear; developed major campaign for Macy's
                         Shoe Department

* Established major cooperative advertising programs between manufacturers and dealers
* Design marketing research to position station demographics (specifically to the 18-34 age group)
* Developed and presented marketing research to Westinghouse
  - Resulted in first buy of a contemporary radio station

1974 to 1976

KRMI RADIO, Oakland, CA
Account Executive

* Beginning at zero base, developed account list with $100,000 annual billing
* Designed marketing research and evaluated merchandising concepts for client use
* Worked with clients in determining marketing problems; provided successful promotional ideas

1973 to 1974

KRAC RADIO, Alameda, CA
Account Executive

* Handled all record industry accounts and major advertising agencies in San Francisco Bay area
  - Increased billing by 120%

1972 to 1973

JACK WODELL & ASSOCIATES (Advertising Agency)
San Francisco, CA
Mailroom Supervisor

EDUCATION:

UCLA, Los Angeles, CA
1972 - Graduate courses in Marketing and Advertising

University of Denver, Denver, CO
1972 - BA, History, Political Science

Golden Gate University, San Francisco, CA
1973-1974 - Marketing courses

SANDRA NURENBERG . 400 East 77th Street, Apt. 2625 . New York, NY 10162 . (212) 734-2648

OBJECTIVE: TRAVEL SALES/SALES PROMOTION

To apply my broad knowledge of and experience in the travel
industry to a position in sales or sales promotion with a solid
energetic operation in the travel field.

SUMMARY: Wholly knowledgeable of the travel industry. Experience includes
positions in sales and sales promotion in varied phases of the
industry. Have lived, worked and traveled in Europe, Latin America,
Asia, Africa and 40 of the 50 United States (including Alaska and
Hawaii), providing priceless first-hand knowledge about much of
the world.

RELEVANT EXPERIENCE:

1979-1983   INTERNATIONAL WOMEN'S CLUB OF COPENHAGEN, Copenhagen, Denmark
President

* Founded the organization in 1977; founded club magazine in 1978

* Responsible for all financial affairs of the organization; raised
  in excess of $300,000 for philanthropic purposes

* Worked with embassies, tourist offices and airlines to arrange
  monthly programs and philanthropic projects throughout the world

* Organized and arranged all tours throughout Scandinavia and
  Eastern Europe

* Chaired meetings of 10-member board and monthly meetings for 250
  general members; addressed various organizations and associations
  regarding functions of Club

* Sold 90% of all advertising to, and received donations from,
  major international corporations and organizations

* Coordinated editing, proofreading and layout of magazines with
  staff and printers

* Wrote press releases for use on TV and radio and in magazines
  and newspapers

1977-1979   AMERICAN WOMEN'S CLUB IN DENMARK, Copenhagan, Denmark
President

* Functions similar to those performed with International Women's Club

* Worked with universities and foundations in Denmark and United
  States to further club's scholarship program

* As a member of Danish-American 1976 Bicentennial Committee, coordinated activities with Danish Foreign Affairs Office

* Personally presented club's book to the Queen of Denmark prior
  to her departure for the United States to attend Bicentennial

* Raised funds for and assisted in planning of Bicentennial student
  group tour of United States, including housing

1974-1975   ECOLE SUPERIEURE D'AFFAIRES ET de SECRETARIAT, Brussels, Belgium
Business English Lecturer

* Taught American business techniques from letter composition to
  filing systems to 80 women students from 16 countries

* Gave private consultations to individual students and to interested employers

1972-1973	BELTZ WORLD TOURS, San Francisco, CA

Travel Consultant

* Met with retail accounts and individual clients and formulated plans and made arrangements for transportation, hotel accommodations and tours for business and pleasure

* Sold Asian travel packages including cruises and steamship lines

* Top sales representative for three consecutive months with fewest cancellations

* Travelled extensively to Europe and Latin America; coordinated tours with competitive travel agencies

1971-1972   JAPAN EXTERNAL TRADE ORGANIZATION, Chicago, IL
Administrative Assistant

* Supervised Chicago showrooms and displays

* Arranged special promotions and exhibits for trade shows, state fairs and exhibitions in the Midwest promoting Japanese products

* Hired personnel to work special exhibits

* Worked with management of various hotels in setting up conferences, banquets and receptions

* Created, administered and arranged for public reaction questionnaires to be given out to people viewing products and exhibits

* Worked special assignments in Tokyo, Osaka and Vienna

1969-1971   NORTHWEST ORIENT AIRLINES, Chicago, IL
Reservation Sales/Service Agent

* Processed reservations and tickets for domestic and international flights; maintained passenger manifests

* Handled cancellations; investigated passenger complaints

1964-1969   HERTZ CORPORATION, Chicago, IL
Station Manager

* Supervised 12 employees

* Coordinated all office procedures including processing monthly accounts, acquisition of office supplies and equipment with the main office

EDUCATION: Northwestern University, Evanston, IL
1966-67: Liberal Arts/European History

Loyola University, Chicago, IL
1967-68: Liberal Arts/European History

Florence Utt Business School, Indianapolis, IN
1963-64: Business Administration

LANGUAGES: Danish, German, French (read and write)

LEAH GARST
1182 Hancock Street
Washington, D. C. 20008
(202) 345-7787

OBJECTIVE: ORGANIZATIONAL FUND-RAISER

To apply my experience in fund-raising to a position for a recognized non-profit organization, or foundation, or a privately-endowed educational institution, possibly entailing some travel.

SUMMARY: More than seven years experience in direct fund-raising. Demonstrated expertise working with governmental and non-governmental agencies. Traveled extensively in Europe, Latin America and the United States.

EXPERIENCE: EPICURES CLUB OF NICE, FRANCE

1973 to
1980

<u>President/Founder</u>

Responsible for all financial affairs; raised $300,000+ for philanthropic purposes.
Worked with embassies, tourist offices and airlines to arrange monthly programs and philanthropic projects throughout the world; organized and arranged all tours.
Addressed various organizations regarding Club functions.
Wrote press releases for use on TV and radio and in magazines and newspapers.

HELEN TOURS, Aspen, Colorado

1971 to
1973

<u>Travel Consultant</u>

Top sales representative for two consecutive years with fewest cancellations.
Traveled extensively throughout Europe and Latin America; coordinated tours with competitive travel agencies.

EDUCATION: Vassar College, Poughkeepsie, New York
BA Literature/History 1971

LANGUAGES: Fluent in French, German, Italian and Spanish

REFERENCES: Provided upon request.

Operations

KENNETH CANNON   2403 Needham Street, Brooklyn, NY 11235   (212) 646-7522

OBJECTIVE: INVENTORY CONTROL MANAGER
              To employ my expertise in inventory control with a multi-national
              corporation in a position with growth potential to Operations Manager

SUMMARY: More than five years experience in inventory control and production
              planning. Strong ability to gain confidence and cooperation of produc-
              tion management to alleviate inventory problems. Knowledgeable about
              BASIC and COBOL languages and the use of computers. Multilingual,
              fluent in Swedish, Polish and Russian, with working knowledge of
              German and Norwegian.

EXPERIENCE HIGHLIGHTS:

1979 to   WHALEDENT INTERNATIONAL (Dental Products)
Present   New York, NY

              Production Controller/Planner

              * Charged with the detail planning and release of work orders to four
                 production departments in accordance with Master Schedule

                 - Plan material requirements

                 - Requisition purchases

                 - Interface with production supervisor and materials manager

              * Improved planning system through use of MRP principles; introduced
                 use of more efficient instruments for shop floor control

              * Pinpointed inventory management problems through use of ABC analysis
                 in estimation of excess inventory

1976-79   THORN LIGHTING DIVISION AB (Subsidiary of Thorn Electrical Ind., London)
              Stockholm, Sweden

              Inventory Control/Purchasing Supervisor

              * Charged with responsibility for purchasing $5-$6 million/year of
                 lighting equipment, reporting directly to financial controller

              * Established inventory levels for four regional warehouses

                 - Implemented and assisted in designing control system

                 - Decreased value of inventory with 40% (approximately $250,000)
                   savings per year

                 - Increased inventory turnover and service level

              * Controlled procedures for Purchasing Department

                 - Set up and followed yearly supplies budget

                 - Purchased products from Thorn's factories in England

              * Worked with Data Division to computerize order processing procedures
                 with subsequent savings in manpower

                 - Implemented ABC Analysis

                 - Member of select management team to implement integrated MIS

              (Parent company has annual gross of one billion pounds sterling)

1974-76   SIEMENS AB, Stockholm, Sweden (Subsidiary Siemens AG, West Germany)

<u>Inventory Control Planner - Lighting Fixtures Division</u>

* Charged with planning for sales and manufacturing, setting inventory levels for six regional warehouses and planning for future production based on marketing forecasts and production capacity

* Established inventory control system through use of computer reports

* Implemented Master Production Schedule for local factory

* Generated sales statistics for marketing and sales departments

* Promoted from office clerk within six months of employment in recognition of my analytical ability and studies

    - Worked full time while attending school

(Parent company is sixth largest in world in its field with annual gross of approximately $16 billion)

EDUCATION: Stockholm University, Stockholm, Sweden
1978 - B.A., Business Administration

Quantitative Methods for Business Decisions
- Marketing/Management

MEMBER: American Production-Inventory Control Society

BRUCE FREEMAN
720 Ocean Parkway
Brooklyn, New York 11218

Home: (212) 436-9928   Office: (212) 689-7523

OBJECTIVE: SENIOR MANAGEMENT - CONSUMER PRODUCTS

SUMMARY: - More than 17 years of bottom line responsibility in manufacturing,
                    marketing and merchandising consumer products

                  - Creative and innovative in product management encompassing purchase
                    of raw materials, design, production, merchandising and sales

                  - Aggressive and energetic salesman with discerning ability to analyze
                    market trends and forecast consumer demands

                  - Strong motivator of merchandising team, able to spark imagination
                    and productivity

                  - Capable of producing quality merchandise in competitive market with
                    excellent cost/profit ratio

CAREER HIGHLIGHTS:

1967 to   SHAPIRO & SON CORPORATION, New York, NY
Present   Vice President, Director of Purchasing and Production   (1973-1980)

                  * Developed cost reduction apparatus and profit improvement systems
                    and set annual production budget

                       - Implemented and tightened procedures effecting increase in
                         percentage of net profit

                       - Researched and managed installation of computer system components
                         facilitating sophisticated forecasting of piece goods requirements,
                         production scheduling and sales volume

                  * Created new products and designs, some of which remain as staples in
                    company's line

                  * Controlled sales of special promotions to major retailers, national
                    chains and catalog houses

                       - Maintained close and active contact with top buyers

                       - Created products for specific promotions; negotiated sales;
                         worked up sales proposals for account executives

                       - Realized $3.5 million in "plus" sales from three orders

                  * Devised system for merchandising discontinued styles, turning projected
                    losses into net profits exceeding $250,000

                  * Established more effectual control system over packaging and dis-
                    tribution to more than 3,000 outlets, reducing claim rate to less
                    than ½ per cent

SHAPIRO & SON CORPORATION (Cont'd.)

* Improved control systems of record keeping, retention scheduling and perpetual inventory

* Developed recruitment and training programs; heightened employee interest through education of company services and products

Production Manager   (1970-1973)

* Responsible for planning, scheduling and coordinating production for all factories employing more than 700 people

    - Purchased raw materials, scheduled production cycles in relation to marketing trends, consumer demand and seasonal aspects

* Effected ten per cent cost reduction through restructure of converting department procedures and in-house printing of greige goods

* Controlled activity of outside contractors

Purchasing Manager - Raw Materials   (1969-1970)

* Negotiated contracts with mills involving $12 to $15 million

    - Established and administered systems resulting in 5% economies

    Scheduled current and future orders of greige goods and printed materials to coincide with production requirements, thereby reducing warehouse inventory costs

Purchasing Agent - Piece Goods   (1967-1969)

* Effective handling of this department was directly responsible for assignment to positions of greater accountibility

Prior   GREYWOOD KNITWEAR INDUSTRIES, New York, NY

Production Manager

* Hired as Assistant to Production Manager; promoted after two years to Production Manager

* Was responsible for purchase of raw materials, plant scheduling in a cut-and-sew operation, sales and production forecasting and liaison with factory management

EDUCATION   Queens College
                  1963 - BS, Math/Science

PERSONAL   Free to relocate

ETHEL BURKS
300 East 24th Street, 4RW
New York City 10009

Home 212-477-6525
Work 212-751-6216

OBJECTIVE   OFFICE MANAGEMENT

SUMMARY   Departmental manager with ten years corporate administrative background. Experienced in purchasing, budget forecasting, salary planning and personnel evaluation. Expert at anticipating problems and effecting their resolution. Excellent writing and production skills. Knowledge of telecommunications and word processing.

EXPERIENCE   MEDICARE DIVISION OF HUMANA, INC., New York, NY
               Manager, Secretarial Services (1982 - Present)

1980   * Supervise 13 secretaries and typists in completion and daily up-
to   dating of all medical records and tests for 17,000 patient base
Present
                  - Prepare all correspondence to parent company and physician
                     clientele

                  - Responsible for departmental budget forecasting, salary planning
                     and personnel evaluation

               * Trained and supervised five additional typists to accommodate
                  dramatically increased workload over four-month period

                  - Created and implemented double shifts to assure completion of
                     extra work volume on time and without sacrifice of quality;
                     appointed interim supervisors for both shifts

               Executive Administrative Assistant (1980-1982)

               * As right hand to company CEO, responsible for coordination of
                  executive office functions

                  - Assisted President with confidential matters affecting all company
                     activity and managed office during his absences; scheduled meetings
                     and appointments

                  - Maintained ongoing contact with nationwide sales force; monitored
                     activities of managers reporting to President and prepared schedules
                     and recommendations for his consideration

                  - Prepared executive correspondence and composed internal adminis-
                     trative correspondence; composed and distributed minutes and other
                     pertinent documents; prepared legal forms, statistical reports and
                     contracts

               * Developed methods to streamline office repair and maintenance functions
                 affecting comfort and efficiency of 100 employees

3M COMPANY, New York, NY
Publicity Assistant

1976
to
1980

* Composed product and news releases, feature stories and quarterly reports; supervised printing and photography and coordinated national mailings to consumer and trade media

* Made arrangements for press events; researched and selected sites, designed press kits and invitations, monitored responses and prepared guest lists

CORE COMMUNICATIONS IN HEALTH, INC., New York, NY
Script Coordinator/Assistant Director of
Program Development

1973
to
1976

* As first employee in new organization, assisted in start-up and office management, including purchase of all supplies

* Assisted in creating and updating library of audiovisual education programs; researched and edited program material

* Typeset and assisted in design of educational print materials

EDUCATION

QUEENS COLLEGE, Queens, NY
1973 Baccalaureate Degree, English, Writing

- Phi Beta Kappa and magna cum laude
- Honors in English and Creative Writing
- John Golden Award for Creative Writing, 1972
- Fiction Editor, College literary magazine

Professional Programs:

Buffalo University Seminar in "Management Tools"
Katherine Gibbs Entree Program
Betty Owen Word Processing Program
Dale Carnegie Public Speaking Course

SALVATORE ORAZIO . 21 Pine Street . Cresskill, NJ 07626 . 201-568-8770

OBJECTIVE   <u>OPERATIONS MANAGEMENT</u>

SUMMARY   Operations specialist with excellent track record in coordination of
             sales and production. Adept at analysis and reformulation of systems
             to increase profits. Able to establish effective rapport with superiors,
             colleagues and subordinates. Hands-on knowledge of computer services.

ACHIEVEMENTS IN OPERATIONS MANAGEMENT

             BURLINGTON INDUSTRIAL FABRICS, Rockleigh, NJ
             <u>Administrative Supervisor, Inventory & Reconciliations</u> (1980-1981)
             <u>Sales Coordinator</u> (1980)
             <u>Planning Coordinator</u> (1973-1979)
             <u>Production Planning Manager, Assistant Planner</u> (1972-1973)

Sales/   During period of 15-fold sales expansion, balanced plant production with
Production   sales requirements while overseeing planning, scheduling, sales and cus-
Coordination tomer service, distribution and R&D functions

             Increased sales 25%-50% by improving liaison between sales and production

             * Instituted control sheets with daily updates for individual salesmen
             * Developed easy-to-read open contract status record book to aid control,
               scheduling and sales
             * Initiated operations to accommodate on-the-spot requests

Production   Increased sales and production 25% through careful production scheduling
Planning   and close liaison with sales department

             * Allowed for new business in production scheduling
             * Assured customer satisfaction through communication with sales on load
               conditions and possible substitute orders during heavy load periods
             * Instituted daily flow of inventory contracts and coordinated saleable
               inventory with sales manager

Contracts   Institute measures resulting in same-day service for rush orders and
Adminis-   quicker processing of entire order volume
tration
             Decreased composition and transmittal period for typed contracts by 50%

             * Established capability for telephone credit approval on rush orders
             * Set priorities for transmittal of contractions and corrections between
               northern and southern offices, improving liaison

             Developed capability for daily processing of sales notes, cutting four
             to six days from original procedure; set up system eventually taken
             over by clerical staff

Inventory   Through timely purchases of greige goods, saved $40,000 and maintained
Control/   better control of inventory
Purchasing
             Increased efficiency of inventory process, decreasing time required by
             66% while effecting one of division's best audited inventories on record

Computer   Worked closely with programmers to set up weekly computerized status
Operations/ reports on contracts, inventory available for sale, and case listings
Records
             Set priorities for computer services; developed accurate manual and
             computerized records

SALVATORE ORAZIO/2

H.W. LOUD MACHINE WORKS, INC., Pomona, CA
(Div. of Menasco Manufacturing Co.)
<u>Supervisor</u> (1970-1971)
<u>Material & Systems Control Supervisor</u> (1965-1970)
<u>Scheduling & Records Supervisor</u> (1956-1964)

Personnel
Training

Eased overload conditions and increased output by 50%-66% by cross-training personnel in purchasing, traffic, stock, shipping and receiving

Production
Planning

Coordinated purchasing, outside production and production liaison with Montebello and Burbank plants; supervised production control office

Increased work flow control, eliminated over-issuance of plant and outside production work orders, and promoted planning flexibility

* Created simple, accurate location control system for thousands of components in process

Upgraded production coordination

* Instituted system for establishing assembly priorities
* Created procedures for nightly status reports on all components of open orders

Computer
Operations

Developed accurate shop load computer reporting system; worked with outside consultant, computer programmer and in-house personnel to set up input and completion data

BURLINGTON INDUSTRIES, New York, NY and Teterboro, NJ
<u>Assistant Department Head, Office Services</u> (1954-1956)
<u>Warehouse Supervisor</u> (1948-1954)

Office
Services
Management

Coordinated and supervised 15-member staff responsible for office moves and services; prepared budgets; directed outside contractors

Developed system for timely delivery of mail between five major New York City office buildings

Warehouse
Supervision

Set up inexpensive and effective location control system for thousands of piece goods in process

EDUCATION

<u>Professional Courses and Seminars</u>

AMERICAN MANAGEMENT ASSOCIATIONS, New York, NY

Various 8-10 week courses in Supervisory Management, Planning, Organization, Standards and Appraisals, Communication, Motivation, Decision Making

Free to travel

ALAN TOULOUSE   150 East 71st Street   New York, NY 10021   (212) 838-7777

OBJECTIVE: GENERAL MANAGEMENT/OPERATIONS

SUMMARY: More than nine years experience in day-to-day administration at management
level in import/distribution industry. Highly expert at initiating and
implementing systems, including data processing, for inventory and cash
control. Capable of startup of major installations including warehousing
from point of site selection to full operation. Excellent in recruitment
and supervision of personnel and in customer relations.

HIGHLIGHTS OF EXPERIENCE:

1977 to   INTERCO PARTS CORPORATION, Syosset, NY
Present   General Manager

Charged with startup of parts distribution business in 1977; administer
all phases of business (accounting, inventory control, data processing
and enhancement of management information capability of computer operation)

- Achieved growth to $6 million/year

* Participated in preparation and administration of annual budget

* Installed and implemented in-house computer to perform inventory
control, accounts receivable, sales and product analysis

* Created and implemented warehouse operating procedures with internal
controls (current 13-man staff); established and maintain paper-flow
procedures and internal audit control

1971-77   GEON INTERCONTINENTAL CORPORATION, Woodbury, NY
General Manager-Operations, Woodbury, NY (1976-77)

Had direct responsibility for data processing and transition to in-house
EDP capability for company now at $38 million level

* Served as project leader for installation of IBM System 3 computer

- Participated in system design; wrote operating manual, trained
operators

- Scheduled procurement of hardware and software

- Eighteen-month project (IBM estimate) delivered on-line in seven
months

* Administered New York headquarters with staff of 80 in the office;
130 at warehouses

Concurrent: General Manager-Operations, Richmond, VA/Los Angeles, CA (1975-77)

Had control over two warehouses (280,000 sq. ft.) with 130 personnel
and over $20 million/year in sales

* Controlled budget; daily operation and planning (except sales);
warehousing; customer service; data collection/transmittal;
union negotiations

* Reduced expenses by 30-40% overall through efficient management of
employees and information

- Instituted uniform training program to strengthen first-line and
middle management

* Carried over expense control systems from Richmond operation to Los
Angeles warehouse with same success

* Recalled to New York to head up computer project

Continued

General Manager, Richmond Warehouse, Richmond, VA (6/75-12/75)

Line responsibility for $10 million profit center

* Administered all operations (except sales)

* Instituted cost accounting system to control expense; reduced operating expenses by 40% while maintaining sales level and improving order turn-around time

Assistant to President, Woodbury, NY (1973-75)

Member of "Office of the President"

* Maintained liaison between administration and department managers

* Helped prepare and controlled budget; implemented corporate policies and procedures

* Appointed project manager in movement of warehouse from New York to Virginia

    - Located site; negotiated for purchase; negotiated favorable contract for construction; supervised recruitment of personnel; developed and implemented warehousing procedures

* Assisted in union contract negotiations

Manager, Data Entry, Woodbury, NY (1972-73)

* Supervised staff of 32 data entry operators feeding to outside service bureau

* Helped establish and implement inventory control system for 102 wholly-owned branches

* Developed data reporting systems (sales analysis, stock status and forecasting) in concert with other department managers and service bureau

Customer Service Manager, Woodbury, NY (1971-72)

* Established goodwill and maintained clientele during period of extreme competition

    - Resolved customer complaints; reduced response time from 8-10 weeks to two weeks

    - Established returns authorization and other procedures for issuance of credits to customers

EDUCATION: New York University, New York, NY (On scholarship)
1971 - MA, Latin American History

SUNY, Buffalo, NY
1970 - BA, History (Dean's List)

National Honor Society and Dean's List at Jamaica (NY) High School

American Management Association: Writing of Administrative Manuals
Digital Equipment Corporation: Concepts of Computer Programming
Programming in DIBOL

LANGUAGES: Spanish

EMILE BERGSON, 220 West 76th Street, New York, N.Y. 10020   (212) 761-2571

OBJECTIVE   SENIOR LEVEL OPERATIONS MANAGEMENT

SUMMARY   Twelve years direct management responsibility in proposal management, cost estimating, contract administration, scheduling and cost control, quality assurance, engineering, and technical and new product development. Expertise in domestic and international technical and commercial operations including air pollution control systems, fuel cell and solar energy devices, semiconductors, ceramics and catalytic materials.

Principal customer industries: electric utilities; petrochemical; pulp and paper; combustion equipment; coal; and federal, state and local governments.

Published in numerous technical journals; author of various device-oriented patents.

EXPERIENCE   FLAKT, INC., Old Greenwich, CT (American Group company of AB Svenska Flaktfabriken, Stockholm, Sweden)   Annual Revenues: $40 million

1980
to
Present

Director of Pre-Contract Operations
* Direct all Proposal Management, Applications Engineering, Cost Estimating, Project Planning and Sales Support
* Develop and implement technical, pricing and commercial strategies for proposals
* Manage all pre-contract negotiations (bid approximately $300 million, capturing approximately $70 million)
* Convinced management of need for series of procedures manuals; authored Proposal Management and Cost Estimating Operations manuals

1975
to
1980

UOP AIR CORRECTION DIVISION, Norwalk, CT
Manager of Project Services (1978-1980)
* Created department to serve as support group to Project Management, at request of management
* Directed activities related to Cost Engineering, Scheduling (Multi-level, CPM), Contract Administration (Contract Interpreting, Claims Preparation and Negotiation) and Project Administration
* Authored company Project Control manual
* Formulated division Cost Code of Accounts, remedying lack of adequate cost definition seriously hampering cost control efforts

Manager of Quality Assurance (1977-1978)
* Created Quality Assurance department at request of management
* Formulated and directed total division quality program including Planning, Inspections and Reliability
* Created division Operations Auditing Program for identifying and solving systematic organization and procedural problems, encompassing all departments
* Formulated Quality Cost Monitoring Program to identify and eliminate significant and recurring avoidable costs (Resulted in 70% reduction of such costs associated with Engineering, Manufacturing and Construction)
* Authored division Quality Assurance Manual

Manager of Engineering (1976-1977)
* Directed all Engineering activities of department of approximately 100 engineers and 60 drafters
* Managed entire company product line of Flue Gas Desulfurization Systems, Electrical Precipitators and Multi-cyclone Collectors
* Reorganized department from Functional Organization to Matrix Management organization, to better utilize limited manpower resources; productivity increased by 26% as a result
* Authored and developed Engineering Drafting Manuals

Manager of Precipitator Technology (1975-1976)
* Created department to eliminate performance liability situations
* Directed field diagnostic studies and corrective action programs
* Invented and developed proprietary designs for new ancillary product lines, now marketed (Sales approximately $15 million)
* Conducted world-wide survey, including site visits to Europe, Asia and Australia, evaluated licensing potential for a rigid frame-type precipitator (In lieu of licensing, recommended proprietary design field tested in 1981)
* Invented, developed and marketed new products

1970
to
1974

UOP CORPORATE RESEARCH CENTER, Des Plaines, IL
Research Administrator
* Served as Air Correction Liaison with Corporate Research, directing field studies and developing annual division R&D programs
* Administered and directed research projects in auto emission control, energy conversion and materials development
* Nine patents issued

EDUCATION

CITY UNIVERSITY OF NEW YORK, New York, NY
1970 - Ph.D., Physics
1967 - M.A., Physics
1964 - B.A., Physical Sciences

UOP Management Development Program
AMA seminar on Project Planning and Control
American Society for Quality Control seminar "Managing for Quality"
Lincoln Electric Company seminar on Welding
EPA seminar on Gaseous Emission Control
Working knowledge of French and Hebrew

HONORS

Guest speaker at ASME regional conference, "Air Pollution Engineering"
Guest speaker at ASQC Energy Division annual conference
President of employees' Federal Credit Union
Recipient of company award for Outstanding Support of.Sales

ARTHUR RINEHART . 1050 Maple Avenue . Bronx, NY 10475 . (212) 994-2770

OBJECTIVE: **EXPORT MANAGER/INTERNATIONAL TRADE SPECIALIST**

To obtain a position as export manager for energetic, high-volume exporter of consumer or industrial goods or services.

SUMMARY: Broadly experienced in all phases of export and domestic operations. Demonstrated expertise in new market development, sales forecasting, budgeting, inventory control, warehousing and shipping. Knowledgeable about medical and publishing industries specifically.

EXPERIENCE:

1968 to Present

NORTHWESTERN PUBLISHING COMPANY, Brooklyn, NY
Export Manager, Eastern Division   (1979-Present)
   ($15 million annual revenues)

Operations Manager   (1968-1979)

* Charged with full responsibility for developing marketing strategies, operations management and the management of combined sales and support staff of 17 for this major branch

MARKETING: * Expanded foreign sales from base of $150,000 (1968) to $3 million (1979)

* Research and analyze potential markets; project forecasts on which sales are based

* Travel extensively Puerto Rico, Mexico, Central and South America and Africa studying educational systems and determining potential textbook markets

   - Initiate contacts and work out agreements with distributors to promote and distribute products

   - Work out all sales contracts including sales conditions, credit terms, banking, discounts and promotion

* Most recently selected and set up marketing/distribution organizations in Liberia and Nigeria as well as South America

OPERATIONS: * Prepare annual transportation and distribution budgets (in excess of $1.25 million/year)

* Determine quarterly sales needs; prepare appropriate stock requisitions

* Coordinate physical inventory (two million units monthly)

* Establish agreements with warehousing concerns for consolidation with other publishers for overseas shipments

* Organize special Container/Consolidation Programs with major airlines at reduced rates

* Work closely with U. S. Postal Service in simplifying mail classification and requirements for mailing to foreign countries

* Was instrumental in getting the limit of Custom Free Import Entry amount increased from $250 to $500

* Develop major sales promotions for teachers and educational groups through direct mail and specially designed seminars and workshops

ARTHUR RINEHART/2

1962-1968   NATIONAL SURGICAL SUPPLY, INC., Westchester, NY
               (Major manufacturer of surgical instruments - $25 million
                annual sales)

               Assistant Service Manager

               * Responsible for all customer service aspects including problem
                 solving and handling of customer complaints of highly technical
                 nature

               * Instructed members of medical profession in proper methods of
                 maintenance, sterilization and application of instruments

               * Personally inspected repaired instruments to ensure quality
                 control

               * Supervised technical and secretarial staff

1960-1962   STUDENT'S TUTORING INSTITUTE, Larchmont, NY

               Instructor

               * Taught Italian and Spanish to businessmen, doctors and
                 lawyers on individual and group basis

EDUCATION: Instituto Magistrale Lucrezia Della Valle, Cosenza, Italy
               BA, Secondary Education/Foreign Languages

               Hunter College, Bronx, NY
               42 credits in English, History, Marketing, Spanish, Italian

AFFILIATIONS: Tri-State Traffic Management Association (Secretary)

               Bronx-Westchester Traffic Club

               Latin American Chamber of Commerce

               Modern Language Association

LANGUAGES: Fluent Italian; Excellent Spanish; Working knowledge of French
               and Portugese

ERNEST CAWLEY • 125 Forest Lane • Radnor, PA 19087 • (215) 293-0151

OBJECTIVE: To establish, develop, and direct an export division or subsidiary for a manufacturer new to exporting.

SUMMARY:
— Astute evaluator of foreign market potential for USA manufactured consumer products

— Proven organizer of export activities for manufacturers without previous overseas sales experience

— Strong connections with worldwide business community through extensive travel and personal contact

— Broad experience in corporate development and financing, investment analysis, venture capital, and business management

BUSINESS HIGHLIGHTS:

1976 to Present

TREMONT INTERNATIONAL
Bryn Mawr, PA

Founder and Managing Director

- Develop export sales for "new-to-export" USA manufacturers; successful sales in more than 100 countries on 5 continents

  — Thoroughly research the industry, product, competition, and client manufacturer, including definitive profitability assessment of potential overseas markets

  — Make convincing presentation to acquire client manufacturers' export distribution or representation rights

  — Expertly handle all export procedures from creating the sales through distribution, transportation, and collection

  — Effectively represent dozens of client companies concurrently

- Personally generate export business and develop overseas markets

  — Sell diverse lines of products (mainly consumer), including safety and security equipment, laser-engraved prestige advertising specialties and corporate awards and gifts, specialty housewares and hardware, building materials and interior architectural products; micro-electronic ceramic sub-assemblies

  — Process more than 100 pieces of correspondence per week, plus telexes, cables, and overseas telephone calls

  — Participate in trade shows and exhibits in market countries

- Established export activities for two corporations and currently serve on their Boards of Directors

ERNEST CAWLEY/2

1970 to 1976	HORNBLOWER & WEEKS, HEMPHILL NOYES & CO. Bala Cynwyd, PA

Account Executive

- Managed portfolios of my individual and institutional accounts

- Consistently produced high profit margin business for the firm; responsible for millions of dollars in investments

- Consulted with and did exhaustive investment analysis research for my clients in matters of investment banking, venture capital, and corporate development

- Selected to this nationwide firm's Management Advisory Board (1972) in recognition of consistent professionalism and competence

1960 to 1970	NEWBURGER & CO. Philadelphia, PA

General Partner (1966 to 1970)

- Among my investment banking responsibilities, structured and raised venture capital for two manufacturing corporations and was co-founder of each; continued the activities below

Investment Analyst (1960 to 1966)

- Managed investment portfolios for my own clients and the firm's investment advisory clients; investment analysis; created venture capital plus merger and acquisition opportunities

- Restructured research department to reflect current methods and practice

- Wrote regular research reports on attractive investment opportunities and edited the monthly bulletin

1959 to 1960	SHEARSON, HAMMILL & CO. New York, NY

Investment Analyst

- Researched and analyzed investment potential in securities of publicly owned corporations, with emphasis on electronics, aerospace, airline, shipbuilding, and other industries of similar scope; consulted on investment banking and merger and acquisition proposals

MILITARY: U.S. Army and U.S. Army Reserve, 1957 to 1965
Captain, Finance Corps — Finance Regional Accounting Officer

EDUCATION: Wharton Graduate School, MBA 1958 — Finance and Investments, Real Estate
University of Texas, BBA 1957 — Finance and Banking

MEMBER: International Trade Development Association, Greater Philadelphia Region
President, 1977-1978; Director, 1978-present

Manufacturers & Agents National Association (MANA)

Main Line Chamber of Commerce

EDWARD BARTLESVILLE
20 Lincoln Plaza • New York, NY 10023

Home: (212) 247-9827   Office: (614) 475-5070

OBJECTIVE: **SENIOR MANAGEMENT IN AGGRESSIVE RETAIL ORGANIZATION**

SUMMARY: Ten years retail management experience with rapid and consistent record of growth and advancement. Conceptual and creative approach to marketing and merchandising. Sound long- and short-range planning skills. Astute motivator with ability to identify and maximize talent of subordinates.

PROFESSIONAL EXPERIENCE:

1982
to
Present

FEDERATED STORES CORPORATION, Columbus, OH
Director of Merchandise Marketing

- Advise top management regarding incorporation of innovative marketing strategies and concepts for all six divisions of $600 million corporation

- Develop marketing programs to reposition corporation as necessary
  — Created 120-store test to analyze customer buying patterns for purposes of maximizing inventory investment
  (testing validated program implementation in all 489 stores)
  — Initiated and implemented merchandise line plan to fully develop previously non-formalized corporate policy
  (concept to be layered into organization as basis for focusing merchandise purchase in second and third quarters of 1983)

1976
to
1982

SAKS FIFTH AVENUE, New York, NY
Senior Vice President   **General Merchandise Manager, Sportswear and Intimate Apparel (1980-1982)**

- As member of Executive Committee and Management Board, participated fully in all marketing and merchandising decisions for $500 million organization

- Generated 22% volume increase ($102 million to $125 million) and 1.2% gross margin increase (46.3% to 47.5%) through restructuring and redefinition of planning, merchandising, marketing, merchandise distribution, and training and development operations
  — Trained, developed and managed five divisional merchandise managers and 21 buyers to achieve their professional goals, as well as company objectives

SAKS FIFTH AVENUE
Vice President   **Divisional Merchandise Manager,**
                                                         Intimate Apparel (1979-1980)

- Supervised planning, management, merchandising and marketing operations of $25 million business to achieve annual gross margin objective

- Improved division profit ranking from tenth to first (out of 17 divisions) by broadening customer base, reorganizing resource structure and developing effective marketing strategies

- Generated 26% sales volume increase ($20 million to $25 million) and 2.1% gross margin increase (49.0% to 51.1%)

Divisional Vice President   **Managing Director Branch Store,**
                                                         Fairlane Mall, Detroit, MI (1978-1979)

- Assumed total responsibility for start-up and opening of individual store
  — Led and managed all areas (merchandising, operations, personnel and inter-community relations) to achieve sales volume and profit objectives

  — Trained, developed and managed Assistant Managing Director, six operational Department Managers, 13 merchandising Department Managers

  — Established environment of full employee input preparatory to store opening, keeping motivation and morale at optimum levels

- Generated $14 million in sales volume and 2.6% pre-tax profit during first year of operation

Divisional Merchandise Manager   **Men's Clothing, Boys' Clothing and**
                                                         Furnishings divisions (1976-1978)

1973
to   **BLOOMINGDALE'S, New York, NY**
1976   **Group Manager**   **Men's Sportswear and**
                                                         Designer Sportswear (1975-1976)

- Promoted from two Buyer positions after starting as Staff Assistant to Divisional Merchandise Manager in 1973

EDUCATION: **SOUTHERN METHODIST UNIVERSITY**
                 1973 — M.B.A., Major: Marketing

                 1972 — B.A., Major: History; Minor: Economics
                         Dean's List, eight semesters
                         Sigma Phi Epsilon Fraternity

HECTOR LOPEZ
7720 Cowne Court
Nokesville, VA 22123
(703) 594-9570

OBJECTIVE: **GENERAL MANAGEMENT — BUILDING TRADES INDUSTRY**

SUMMARY: Twenty years experience in top level management with definitive expertise in creative marketing and sales techniques in the building trades industry. Proven ability to penetrate new markets through establishment and implementation of successful marketing strategies and initiating and maintaining highly effective distribution systems. Outstanding achievement record in start-up and growth situations.

HIGHLIGHTS OF EXPERIENCE:

1972 to Present

ONDULINE, U.S.A., INC. (Subsidiary of Media General, Inc.) Fredericksburg, VA

Senior Vice-President

Charged with responsibility for start-up of company in the United States, dealing with specialized building materials items

- Developed initial market analysis that led to company's establishment

- Initiated, established and implemented marketing strategies; hired and trained field and office personnel; set corporate and financial policies (still in force)

- Directed company's sales effort from zero base in 1972 to $8.1 million in 1979

  - Establisned markets by selling product through most levels of distribution

  - Generate high volume through wholesale building supply and retail home centers, OEM and agricultural cooperatives

  - Instituted Select Distribution System to permit increased distributor responsibility for product marketing

  - Increased sales volume to extent that construction of $10 million U.S. manufacturing installation was justified

  - Established record of not losing a single distributor during eight-year period

  - Personally field-trained salesmen and developed sales education program

- Developed and direct advertising programs whose success has caused budget increase from $30,000 in 1972 to $600,000 in 1979

  - Achieved product recognition in the industry by trade name

- Won "Drummer Award" for 1975 by Building Supply News in two categories: Unique Educational Literature; Dealer Promotional Literature

- Elevated to Senior Vice-President following acquisition by Media General of 100% of stock of French parent company

  - Immediately assigned additional responsibility of starting up new product line for the residential market and managing full test marketing campaign (still in progress)

HECTOR LOPEZ/2

1970 - 1972 INTERNATIONAL BOARD SALES, New York, NY

National Sales Manager

- Established marketing arm for European-based plastic laminate manufacturer
  - Redesigned line for U.S. market; reduced line to 40 items
  - Developed copper-clad laminates for decorative purposes (first time in United States)
- Started sales through home centers and retail stores; developed network of manufacturers' representatives for furniture, tabletop and dinette makers to expand market
  - Sales increased from zero base to $1 million in two years
- Assigned additional responsibility to sale of imported products in plywood and furniture divisions (increased sales to $4 million)

1967 - 1970 BUDD COMPANY POLYCHEM DIVISION, New York, NY

Regional Salesman

- Assigned failing territory; effected turnaround with increase in sales from $300,000 to $800,000 in first two years
  - More than tripled sales to large customers including Otis Elevator, Stuart-Warner and Republic Aircraft
- Initiated blanket order system with distributors, locking in both company and buyer on a year-by-year basis (resulted in elimination of competition and improved service)

1966 - 1967 ITEK CORPORATION, New York, NY

Salesman

- Made comprehensive studies of needs of large corporation for in-house printing plants; demonstrated specific savings in cost through use of Itek plate-maker for offset work
  - Made formal presentations to corporate management, documenting accrued savings from purchase of capital items costing from $12,000 to $18,000
  - Success ratio of 80% including such major firms as Booz-Hamilton, Gray Advertising, General Dynamics, Hooker Chemical and Edison Electric Institute

1961 - 1965 JOHNS MANVILLE SALES CORPORATION, New York, NY

Territory Salesman

- Assigned most of New England after service as a trainee and inside sales coordinator, and developer of customer relations
- Increased sales from $17,000 to $100,000 in two years (territory had been neglected for several years)
- Received special award for formal presentation to City of Hartford introducing improved line of general building products

EDUCATION: Villanova University, Villanova, PA
1960 — BS, Economics/Pre-Law—Marketing

JUSTINE SHIPLEY   107 HUDSON STREET   HOBOKEN, N.J. 07030   (201) 795-9573

OBJECTIVE: **ADMINISTRATIVE MANAGEMENT**
Seeking management level position in corporate administration with potential for advancement to line management.

SUMMARY: Strong administrator in large volume operation with follow-through ability in implementing company policies and programs. Expert in departmental organization for maximum efficiency at minimum cost. Results-oriented salesperson with conceptual marketing acuity. Proven capacity for discharging increasing responsibility and accountability.

CAREER HIGHLIGHTS:

1973-80   *AMERICAN EXPRESS COMPANY,* New York, N.Y.

Administrator — Retail Sales   (1978-80)
- Directed flow of detail in operation of credit card retail sales contract negotiations throughout United States

  — Managed agreements, advertising & operational budgets, advertising addendum program, discount re-evaluation programs, sales presentations, repetitive sales activity

  — Administered charge account solicitation and promotional mailing campaigns throughout United States

- Wrote retail section of cardmember newsletter and president's letter in addition to a variety of departmental communications

- Represented department at conventions, meetings and other events locally and throughout United States; prepared agendas

Senior Administrative Secretary   (1976-78)
- Coordinated and supervised input from offices reporting to Vice President - Domestic Sales; directed activities to subordinate staff

Secretary to Director — Lodging Sales   (1974-76)

Secretary/Back-Up Assistant — Manager Domestic Sales   (1973-74)

1972-73   *PATROLMEN'S BENEVOLENT ASSOCIATION,* New York, N.Y.

Executive/Personal and Confidential Secretary to President
- Maintained current intelligence on political & police activities; assisted Public Relations Manager; prepared releases for news media

1969-72   *MERRILL LYNCH, PIERCE, FENNER & SMITH,* New York, N.Y.

Secretary
- Prepared Turnpike & Tunnel & Bridge Association reports, financial statements and prospectus reports

1969   *AMERICAN EXPORT ISBRANDTSEN LINES*

Assistant to Manager — Bill of Lading Department
- Directed functions of office personnel; maintained teletype procedures for overseas communications

1968-69   *CASTELO & SONS, SHIP SERVICING CO., INC.,* Hoboken, N.J.

Assistant to Payroll Supervisor/Secretary
- Prepared manual payroll; posted A/P and A/R journals

LANGUAGE: Bilingual — Spanish-English

EDUCATION: New York University — Courses in Business Administration & Personnel

JAMES CYRUS

250 E. 76th Street, New York, NY 10021   (212) 879-6216

OBJECTIVE: Construction Superintendent, with enough growth opportunity to permit advancement to project manager, and ultimately to General Project Manager.

EXPERIENCE: 1975 to   JPD Construction Company
Present   New York, N.Y.

Construction Superintendent (1978-Present)

--Order materials; deal directly with suppliers; schedule payments for sub-contractors

--Supervise electrical, painting, carpentry, masonry, HVAC, flooring, hardware and final cleanup trades

--Deliver all materials to job sites; prepare billing and payroll reports

Accomplishments

* Organized front office; realigned unorganized stacks of blueprints by specific jobs

* Served as Acting General Project Manager for one month in boss's absence

* Originated uniform manner of processing each job from point of sale to final billing; recommended new equipment for field and front office

* Purchased trade manuals at own expense to improve job knowledge

Foreman's Assistant; Estimator; Salesman (1975,1977)

--Started as laborer in 1975; promoted to carpenter's helper; learned estimating at night school; promoted to estimator (time out for military)

1970 to   Laborer, Zerep Construction Company
1974   New York, N.Y.

--Drove company truck; assisted in demolition work; acted as mason's helper, carpenter's helper

EDUCATION: Music and Art High School, New York, N.Y.; graduated 1974

Attended Institute of Design and Construction, 1977

Military: USMC, 1975-1977; separated with rank of Lance Corporal; honorable discharge

Demolition and Construction Specialist; demolition instructor; completed Basic Combat Engineer School and refresher course; instructed officers in basic land mine warfare

JUAN S. GEISLER   975 East 44th Street, Brooklyn, NY 11234   212-645-7133

OBJECTIVE   BUILDING MANAGEMENT of PRESTIGIOUS OFFICE BUILDING or CORPORATE HEADQUARTERS

SUMMARY   Extensive experience in commercial building management, supervision and ad-
             ministration. Excellent track record in energy conservation, cost-effective
             maintenance and minimization of down time for all systems. Able to motivate
             engineering and maintenance staffs and contractors to produce work of high
             quality. Work effectively under pressure. Solid understanding of technical
             details and problems.

EXPERIENCE

1977 to   DAKOTA REALTY INC., New York, NY
Present   Managing agents for six commercial buildings including 720 Fifth Avenue
             (ICC Building) and 445 Park Avenue (MCA-Universal Pictures)

             Vice President-Director of Operations (1981-Present)

             * Charged with administration of all six buildings
               - Recruit, train and supervise personnel responsible for on-site
                 operations and Supervisor of Operations overseeing all six sites
               - Approve interior design, decorating, signage and maintenance
                 and service contracts
               - Supervise energy management
               - Interface with owners and principals; assist brokers with leasing details
               - Oversee all electrical billing and surveys

             * Saved thousands of dollars on selection of fire safety system through
               utilization of existing resources
               - Carefully analyzed all contractor bids and received variances
                 that eliminated the need to install expensive equipment

             * On a regular basis, assure reconstruction of office space for new tenants
               within critically limited time schedules
               - Through careful planning, maintain revenue level and
                 promote good landlord-tenant relationship

             * Interface with City bureaucratic agencies, including Fire Department
               and Departments of Buildings, Air Resources & Environmental Protection,
               and Sidewalks & Highways

             Supervisor of Operations (1980-1981)

             * Oversaw daily operations of six office buildings
               - Analyzed and solved emergencies
               - Supervised six employees and trained new personnel
               - Oversaw all construction, maintenance and repair work
               - Acted as Purchasing Agent

             * Set up schedule for periodic checking of all systems to assure
               interruption-free service

             Building Manager - 445 Park Avenue (1978-1980)

             * Upgraded productivity of maintenance and engineering staffs, resulting in
               improvement in occupancy rate from 65% to 95% and promotion of building
               as company show place

             * Instituted major energy management program that cut steam usage in half
               and resulted in:
               - Letter of commendation to landlord from the City
               - Three attempts by Con Edison to control revenue losses by
                 installing new meters

JUAN S. GEISLER/2

<u>Building Superintendent & Engineer - 720 Fifth Avenue</u> (1977-1978)

* Established excellent reputation for building security by instituting tenant file and ID card security system

* Operated 300-ton electrical drive centrifugal air condition, heating systems and all other building systems

* Supervised six-person staff

1973 to   WILLIAMS REAL ESTATE, New York, NY
1977   <u>Building Superintendant</u>

* Decreased energy consumption by improving efficiency of boiler and installing flourescent lighting

* Acted on brokers' behalf showing space to future tenants

1971 to   BROWN BROTHERS HARRIMAN, New York, NY
1973   <u>Manager, Air Conditioning Section</u>

* Planned and implemented preventive maintenance program to reduce purchases of major parts, down time and service costs

MILITARY SERVICE

1966 to   US AIR FORCE
1970   Honorably Discharged as Staff Sergeant

* Awarded commendation medal for meritorious service

EDUCATION   Kingsborough Community College, Brooklyn, NY
              1974-1975 Liberal Arts Courses

              New York City Community College, Voorhees Campus
              1974   Environmental Science Courses
              <u>Coursework for professional advancement:</u>

              Building Owners and Managers Institute: Real Estate Property Administrator
              Apex Technical Institute: Certificate in Theory of Thermodynamics;
                  courses in Commercial HVAC, Blueprint Reading, Drafting

CERTIFICATIONS AND LICENSES

              Certified Fire Safety Director
              Licensed Sprinkler Operator
              Licensed in Standpipe Maintenance
              Licensed as #6 Oil Burner Operator

AFFILIATION

              Building Owners' and Managers' Association

GREG MAXWELL
157 Charing Cross Road
Tucson, Arizona 85713
(602) 771-2510

OBJECTIVE: Security administrator or related management
position.

EXPERIENCE: HAMPTON HILLS COMMUNITY ASSOCIATION, Tucson, AZ
Security Director

1979   *   Supervise approximately 30 security officers
to   and guard personnel at a four-season re-
Present   creation community

- Implement and evaluate all security
programs

- Manage personnel

- Act as liaison with federal, state and
local officials

- Plan and approve all budgets

FEDERAL BUREAU OF INVESTIGATION, Washington, DC
Special Agent (Retired)

1951   *   Responsible for extensive investigative,
to   training and supervisory level positions
1979   covering all investigative matters and
operations

- Planned, organized and directed investigative staff and interfaced harmoniously
and effectively with executives at all
levels

- Commended for excellence in performance
on numerous occasions

MILITARY: U.S. Navy 1944-1946 (Honorable Discharge)

EDUCATION: Seton Hall University - Graduated with B.S.
Degree in 1950.

ORGANIZATIONS: Society of Former Special Agents of the Federal
Bureau of Investigation

Interstate Law Enforcement Association

International Association of Chiefs of Police

Research & Development

MATTHEW SILVERMAN . 45-59 65th St. . Woodside, NY 11377 . (212) 786-3576

OBJECTIVE: <u>INDUSTRIAL MANUFACTURING ENGINEER</u>

Responsible production development opportunity with growth-oriented electronics manufacturer.

SUMMARY: Eight years experience in all phases of electronics manufacturing engineering. Expertise in set-up and planning for entire production process. Capable of reducing costs while simultaneously increasing quality and output. Familiar with development and introduction of new designs. Effective supervisor of engineering staff.

RELEVANT EXPERIENCE:

1979-Present   GBC CLOSED CIRCUITS TV CORPORATION, New York, NY

<u>Technician</u>

* Repair, control, adjust, modify and test equipment used in manufacture of closed circuit television systems; equipment includes:

  - B/W and color TV receivers   - Video and RF TV cameras
    and monitors   - Total darkness TV cameras
  - Video switchers   - Amplifiers and Distributors
  - Video/audio minisystems   - Intercoms and talk-a-phones
  - B/W VTR   - Lenses

* Was recently invited by Company President to tour new production line. As a result of visit:

  - Pinpointed defect in adjustment during initial product run of latest design; modification resulted in major quality improvement at no cost

  - Suggested use of specialized tool, which immediately reduced total assembly time by 5%

  - Advised manufacturing department of change in electronic thermal "cooking" procedures, which could, if adopted, reduce processing time by more than 75%

1973-1978   KOZITSKY TV MANUFACTURER, Leningrad, USSR

<u>Chief Manufacturing Engineer</u> (1975-1978)

* Conceived, planned and organized total structure of new department; planned shop layout and assembly production line; established testing and adjustment procedures; organized work flow and determined equipment and manpower requirements; wrote production manuals

* Successfully solved technical problems in production

  - Production increased from ten to 1,200 units per day over three-year period

  - Overall production costs were reduced by 15% in one year

(continued)

KOZITSKY TV MANUFACTURER (continued)

- Improved quality was achieved in manufacture of color TV sets, radio receivers, tape recorders, and other products

* Directly supervised ten engineers and 12 technicians in department of firm with 1,600 employees

* Through "state of the art" production techniques, was able to reduce number of employees required from 50, in initial tests, to 15, in large scale production

* Developed technique for producing new model equipment by utilizing same production used in producing older models

* Evaluated prospective engineers for other departments

* Served as assistant plant manager; monitored four production lines; supervised experimental shop where new models were conceived

Senior Engineer - Experimental Section (1974-1975)

* Responsible for design, assembly and testing of experimental TV models and radio receivers

* Supervised two assistant engineers

Engineer - Experimental Section (1973-1974)

* Participated in experimental assembly, control tuning and testing of electronic equipment

EDUCATION: Leningrad Institute of Mechanical-Electronic Engineering
Leningrad, USSR
1973 - MS, Radio-Electronic Engineering

Advanced training in Manufacturing and Production Technology (150 hours)

LANGUAGES: Fluent English (Native Russian)

VISA STATUS: Permanent resident with intent to apply for citizenship

PETER TAGORE
720 Lenox Road
Brooklyn, New York 11203

Home: (212) 469-5971
Message: (212) 270-9630

OBJECTIVE: <u>PRODUCTION ENGINEER/PROJECT ENGINEER</u>
To apply my skills and experience to a position as a planning and
production engineer in a machine shop, fabrication shop, or foundry;
a construction site manager's position to manage turnkey projects
in piping, structurals or machinery installation and commissioning.

SUMMARY: Highly experienced as site manager, works manager and operations
manager in directing the performance of turnkey contracts, projects, machine shop and fabrication shop operations and inspections.

RELEVANT EXPERIENCE:

1976-80   UNIQUE BUILDERS, LTD.
<u>Operations Manager</u> (350 Employees)   Cuttack, India

* In overall charge of Rourkela works and site in Rourkela steel plant, to direct
   and coordinate the complete operations of turnkey contracts in piping, fabrication
   erection and commissioning of heavy structurals and equipment

   - Supervised design-to-completion (turnkey) construction of air line and
      oxygen line for plant expansion in Rourkela steel plant

   - Designed and supervised fabrication and commissioning of ferro-alloy
      addition system in steel melting shop

   - Developed door frames and door bodies with improved sealing for coke ovens

* Directed and coordinated sales, contract negotiations, planning, procurement,
   and sales promotion

* Directed, coordinated and motivated personnel in all phases of manufacturing
   process including design, layout, foundry, machine shop, fabrication, fitting,
   assembly, final erection and commissioning and office management

* Maintained quality control of projects from inception through shakedown;
   provided advisory and practical assistance in the solving of problems
   occurring subsequent to shakedown

1975-76   EAST INDIA ENGINEERING COMPANY
<u>Projects Manager</u> (300 Employees)   Rourkela, India

* Responsible for the management of mini steel project involving labor management, materials management, project planning, supervision and inspection in
   all phases of manufacture, construction and commissioning including office
   administration

* Introduced and implemented partial sub-contracting system for labor at a saving
   of 25% on labor costs, eliminating the problem of providing labor facilities
   (housing, transportation, etc.) on project sites; introduced sub-contracting
   for projects reducing capital investment by 50%

* Supervised and coordinated activities of 300 employees

(continued)

EAST INDIA ENGINEERING COMPANY (continued)

1974-75
Project Engineer

* Responsible for the supervision and inspection in all shops of manufacture, erection and commissioning; also responsible for stores inventory and manpower planning for the economy and time schedule of the project

* Introduced and implemented incentive-bonus system for bringing projects in on time with 20% increase in on-time execution of contracts

    - More efficient allotment of manpower resulted in savings of 20% in labor costs

    - Improved raw materials inventory; reduced waste and saved 5% in materials cost

1972-74   PRABHAT IRON FOUNDRY & METAL INDUSTRIES
Planning Engineer   Rourkela, India

* Directed department responsible for job planning for machine and fabrication shops

    - Supervised procurement of raw materials, tools and consummables for both shops, and of tools required by inspectors; supervised inspection and quality control

* Introduced incentive-bonus system for more efficient utilization of manpower resulting in 10% increase in production

* Introduced system of stage inspections in production to improve quality control resulting in fewer job rejections; increased profits by 15%

1966-72
Trainee

* Received general training in various units of the company - planning, machine shop, G.I. foundry, non-ferrous foundry and pattern shop

EDUCATION: Regional Engineering College, Rourkela, India
                 1970 - BS, Mechanical Engineering

                 Specialized Courses:
                   Industrial Organizations and Works Management
                   Refrigeration Engineering (Theory)
                   Automobile Engineering (Theory)

                 Sacred Heart College, Ernakulam, India
                 1963 - Pre-degree

PETER CHU MING
10 Ashley Avenue
Norwich, NY 10523
(914) 592-6320

OBJECTIVE: ENGINEER - MECHANICAL/THERMODYNAMIC

Seeking staff position with opportunity to advance to consulting engineer

SUMMARY: More than eight years experience in design, fabrication and installation of air conditioning duct and equipment. Expert at taking off specs and bidding from architects' drawings. Knowledge of manufacturer equipment. Shrewd negotiator with sub-contractors. Able supervisor of mechanics and junior engineers. Capable draftsman. Skilled in design and research and quality control of precision mechanical parts.

RELEVANT EXPERIENCE:

1970 to   BIG FOUR ENTERPRISE AND ENGINEERING COMPANY, Taipei, Taiwan
1978
General Manager/Mechanical Engineer

*   Operated as prime air conditioning contractor on four textile factories

    - Bid on and negotiated contracts from specifications
    - Designed, fabricated and installed sheet metal duct lines
    - Installed and started up air conditioning equipment ordered from manufacturer
    - Supplied maintenance and repair service after installation and during operation

*   Operated service of installation, maintenance and repair for commercial and residential construction, and maintenance and repair service for industrial installations

*   Managed plant with supervision of sales force, office personnel and engineering and mechanical specialists

1962 to   RESEARCH INSTITUTE OF TECHNOLOGY (1966-1970)
1970   PRODUCTS SERVICE, COMBINED SERVICE FORCES (1964-1966)
           CHINESE GOVERNMENT ARSENAL (1962-1964)
           Taipei, Taiwan

Mechanical Engineer

*   In high security position of military research and testing

*   Supervised control of inventory in factories, and of material purchased from US Government under aid program

*   Supervised quality control of manufactured precision mechanical parts for adherence to close tolerance for interchangeability, according to military specifications

EDUCATION: Ordnance Engineering College, Taipei, Taiwan
1960 - BS, Mechanical Engineering
Course work included: Industrial Engineering, Industrial Management, Plant Layout and Time/Motion Studies

Taiwan Provincial Taipei First Professional Technical School
Electrical Engineering

Willing to relocate

ROBERT STEVENS
1573 Palm Springs Blvd.
Miami, Florida 33182
(305) 890-5261

OBJECTIVE: SENIOR ENVIRONMENTAL SCIENTIST

SUMMARY: Experienced in trace element and inorganic compounds
                analysis in particulate and liquid samples.

                Comprehensive knowledge of Atomic Absorption
                Spectroscopy (AA), Ion Chromatography (IC), X-ray
                Photoelectron Spectroscopy (ESCA), and various wet
                chemical methods.

                Working knowledge of EPA methods and Level I and
                Level II procedures.

EXPERIENCE: ENVIRONMENTAL SCIENTIST
1976 to   APR Corporation Jensen Beach, Florida
Present   *   Evaluate sampling and analysis techniques used
                    in Environmental Assessment Programs

                *   Design experimental programs and conduct back-
                    ground research on collection techniques for
                    volatile trace metals, current uses and potential
                    applications of ion chromatography, and the
                    effect of ammonia on the sampling and analysis
                    of sulfur oxides and nitrogen oxides

                *   Participated in design and construction of sample
                    steam generator to simulate flue gases of varied
                    chemical composition, temperature and flow rate

                *   Principal investigator in program to characterize
                    total suspended particularities (TSP) for total
                    volatiles and selected anions and metals

                *   Assisted in development of an ashing-fusion
                    technique to prepare cellulose filter samples
                    for analysis of silicon by atomic absorption

EDUCATION: HARVARD UNIVERSITY, Cambridge, MA
                1976 - A.B., Engineering and Applied Physics
                       Concentration in Environmental Sciences

HERMAN SCHWARTZ . 628 Newbridge Avenue . Staten Island, New York 10310

(212) 727-5321

OBJECTIVE: ENGINEERING MANAGEMENT

SUMMARY: More than 15 years hands-on experience in electronic systems engineering. Innovative conceptual designer, acutely cost-conscious with proven ability to complete project within budget limitations. Capable coordinator of inter-departmental activities. Excellent supervisor of technical personnel. Have security clearance at secret level.

PROFESSIONAL HIGHLIGHTS:

1970 to Present

ISRAEL AIRCRAFT INDUSTRIES, LTD.
Yahud, Israel

Senior Project Engineer MBT Division (1971-Present)

* Manage projects involving the design, development, production and installation of microwave, radar, antenna and other systems for commercial, government and classified military use

* Designed and developed, from prototype through production, microwave system and antenna equipment for EW application in ECCM

  - Wrote proposal, sold it to government and followed through on execution

* Prepare PERT and long-lead programs

* Coordinate purchasing, design and production departments; effect expedited delivery of equipment; supervise staff of ten engineers and technicians

* Updated and maintain accurate testing programs and equipment

Senior Development Engineer - Elta Electronics Div.(1970-71)

* Charged with design and system control of two radar systems - one for ship and land base use and the other for airborne use, in X-band frequency

1967-70

NORDEN DIVISION, UNITED AIRCRAFT CORPORATION
Norwalk, CT

Development Engineer

* Designed Beacon receiver for A-6A radar system and AMTI equipment

* Analyzed F-111D video systems for computer-oriented go-no-go philosophy program; established final acceptance specifications for system

* Met deadlines required for delivery of equipment; executed and manufactured to specifications

* Effected saving of $100,000 in costs through judicious selection of components and vendors

* Supervised test engineers, technicians and production personnel

208

1962-67   LITCOM DIVISION OF LITTON SYSTEMS, INC.
New York and Maryland

Project Engineer   (1964-67)

* Designed and developed HF receivers

* Ran complete on-site final acceptance testing of
  high-performance SSB communications system and trained
  personnel for U.S. Government installation

* Credited with saving six months work and a year of
  development time through expedited procedures

Electrical Engineer   (1962-64)

1959-62   RCA COMMUNICATIONS, INC.
New York, NY

Electro-Mechanical Designer

* Designed circuits and worked on packaging and layouts
  (PC boards for amplifiers, transmitters, receivers,
  motor controls, talker hybrid units and ARQ equipment)

1956-59   WESTERN UNION TELEGRAPH COMPANY
New York, NY

Senior Electro-Mechanical Draftsman

* Worked on schematics and finished wiring and assembly
  drawings for cabinets, carrier equipment and switching
  systems

MILITARY: U.S. Army - 1954-55
Sergeant - Communications

EDUCATION: University of Maryland, College Park, MD
1962 - BSEE

Brooklyn Polytechnic Institute
City College of New York
Course work toward BSEE

MEMBER: Institute of Electrical and Electronics Engineers

Willing to relocate and/or travel

CAESAR HABIB . 77-02 67th Avenue . Jackson Heights, NY 11372 . (212) 424-7539

OBJECTIVE: INDUSTRIAL CHEMIST - PHARMACEUTICALS

A production, quality assurance or research/development position
in the pharmaceutical field

SUMMARY: More than ten years experience as a chemist involved in drugs, pharmaceuticals and cosmetics. Expert in qualitative and quantitative analysis with thorough knowledge of USP, NF and non-official compendia.

Instruments Used:

Viscometer	Gas/water separation index
UV, GC, IR, TLC	Reid vapor pressure
ORD; CD (Cary 14, 60)	Spectrofluorometer

PROFESSIONAL HIGHLIGHTS:

1974 to   NEW YORK POLICE DEPARTMENT, New York, NY
Present
Chemist - Crime Laboratory

* Charged with analysis of physical evidence for use in criminal
  proceedings

  - Quantitative and qualitative organic analysis of unknown
    street samples

  - Analysis of illicit pharmaceutical preparations

  - Analysis of intermediates, solvents, reagents and drug products
    from clandestine laboratories

  - Physical comparison of evidence such as unknown tablets, trace
    particles and ballistics

* Successfully defended analyses before lower and supreme courts at
  local and federal levels in establishing guilt or innocence of
  defendant

* Improved analytical procedures to produce more timely reports

* Direct work of assistant chemists, junior chemists and technicians
  during periods of heavy activity

Concurrent   ST. JOHN'S UNIVERSITY INSTITUTE OF PHARMACEUTICALS, New York, NY

Pharmaceutical Chemist (Part time)

* Performed analyses for New York State Board of Pharmacy as a
  consultant

  - Determined legality of dosages and conformation with USP and
    NF standards in both quality and quantity

  - Acted on customer complaints regarding compliance

* Developed improved analytical procedures and techniques for
  various non-official pharmaceutical preparations

1971-74   PURDUE FREDERICK PHARMACEUTICAL COMPANY, Yonkers, NY

Analytical Chemist - Quality Control Laboratory

* Worked with vitamins, aspirin, surgical scrub solutions, laxative tablets, capsules, lotions and ointments
    - Thoroughly familiar with all wet methods of analysis
* Ran quality assurance tests on raw materials, intermediates and finished products
* Checked dosages and conducted stability studies

1969-71   ELIZABETH ARDEN COSMETIC COMPANY, New York, NY

Production Chemist

* Developed formulae for lotions, creams, lipsticks, loose powder, pressed powder and foundations
* Supervised manufacture of thousands of pounds of product on production line
* Supervised and directed technicians on problem products; personally checked the operations of large batches
* Became expert in all aspects of color matching and contrasting shades of makeup
* Worked under Director of Quality Control for six month period solving particular problems in color matching
* Developed solution to problem of stability in one cream

EDUCATION: St. John's University, College of Pharmacy, New York, NY
1980 - PhD Candidate, Industrial Pharmacy
    Thesis: "Microencapsulation"

St. John's University, School of Chemistry, New York, NY
1975 - MS, Chemistry
    Thesis: "Effect of Divalent Salts (Magnesium, Calcium) on the
        Confirmation and Configuration of Bovine Serum Albumin"

Ain Shams University, School of Science, Cairo, Egypt
1966 - BS, Chemistry

LANGUAGES: Bilingual - English/Arabic

JANET PIERCE

400 Schenck Avenue	Great Neck, NY 11021	(516) 487-9530

OBJECTIVE: Seeking position offering advancement in the field of genetics

EXPERIENCE:

1977 to 1980

MONTREAL CHILDREN'S HOSPITAL, Montreal, Quebec, Canada

<u>Cytogenetic Technician</u> and <u>Tissue Culture Technician</u>

* Set up and cultured amniotic fluids; added colcemid and harvested when indicated
* Prepared, stained and screened slides under microscope
* Photographed metaphase cells; enlarged and printed pictures
* Cut the karyotype
* Used tissue culture techniques to make poor growth cultures successful thus eliminating need for repeat taps
* Set up skin biopsies and prepared cells for biochemical analysis
* Maintained cell bank of mutant fibroblast strains and diseases; shipped worldwide on request; thawed and froze fibroblasts
* Participated in diabetic research related to the development and morphology of the fetal pancreas
  - Assisted in removal of fetal pancreas; digested pancreas to obtain islets; cultured islets and prepared them for electron microscopy
* Developed technique for successful growth of bloody amniotic taps
* Initiated quality control of individual bags of flasks
  - Identified cell attachment problem

1976 to 1977

CIRCO CRAFT, INC., Granby, Quebec, Canada

<u>Chemical Analysis & Quality Control Technician</u>

* Organized lab for testing and adjusting concentrations of metal solutions for printed circuit board manufacturer
* Tested thickness and quality of electroplated metals

1975 to 1976

McGILL UNIVERSITY, Montreal, Quebec, Canada

<u>Microbial Genetics Technician</u>

* Prepared all chemicals and maintained equipment used in 400-student per week laboratory
* Tested mutant bacterial strains and verified necessary calculations by conducting eight separate experiments, among them:
  - UV irradiation and repair of DNA (mutagenesis)
  - Mapping of genes on the E. Coli chromosome by interrupted conjugation

Continued

McGILL UNIVERSITY (Continued)

* Proposed system and adapted equipment for automated method of successfully pouring agar media dishes under sterile conditions

Summer
1974

LONG ISLAND JEWISH MEDICAL CENTER, NY

Microbiology Technician Trainee

EDUCATION: State University of New York, Stony Brook, NY
1975 - BS, Medical Technology

Alton Jones Cell Science Center, Lake Placid, NY
1978 - Seminar in Prenatal Diagnosis

LANGUAGES: French

REFERENCES:

Available upon request

FRANCES DAVISON . 2500 York Avenue . New York, NY 10021 . (212) 288-7356

OBJECTIVE: Seeking a position employing my experience in investigative drug research and project systems design

SUMMARY: Registered professional nurse researcher with intensive experience in clinical administration. Adept at problem analysis with ability to develop systems for efficient records management. Knowledgeable about testing techniques and legal requirements. Demonstrated expertise in human resource management. Highly experienced in research into drug quality control and effectiveness of recommended dosage.

MEDICAL RESEARCH/ADMINISTRATION HIGHLIGHTS:

1973 to Present

MEMORIAL SLOAN-KETTERING HOSPITAL, New York, NY

Clinical Research Coordinator (1976 to Present)

* Responsible for development, coordination and human resource management of federally-funded cancer treatment research project

- Report directly to board of clinical investigators; determine and initiate appropriate action based on their requests

- Design systems for administration, record-keeping and control of experimental drug program

- Develop procedures for patient recruitment, evaluation, dosage administration; follow up testing of participants

- Organize and work in liaison with participating surgeons, clinics and laboratories

- Solve special scheduling, transportation and communication problems as well as counseling terminally ill patients and their families

- Designed toxicity sheet, label for experimental tablet and patient schedule cards to facilitate and simplify record-keeping and communications

- Train medical fellows as back-up administrators

* Assist with clinical administration of 30 additional protocols

- Coordinate appointments; document tests and dosages according to legal and protocol requirements

- Monitor patients and assess dosage requirements and referrals

- Developed systems for identification of incomplete records, indexing and chart procurement; evaluated information required for efficient usage of records desk

* Developed and administered two-year breast study

- Wrote problem analysis and offered solutions in paper submitted to Chiefs of Staff and discussed in interdepartmental meeting

- Initiated system for following day-to-day changes in patients' toxicity levels

Continued

MEMORIAL SLOAN-KETTERING HOSPITAL (Continued)

- Designed label for medication vials according to legal specifications; organized effective systems for patient follow-up

* In addition to official job responsibilities, accomplished extensive reorganization of general record-keeping

- Set up log book to document work flow and staff use of time for funding

- Designed and re-designed numerous charts, forms, cards and labels

- Reorganized responsibilities of entire staff to achieve full productivity during crisis caused by 40% personnel shortage

- Simplified reordering of supplies and drugs by preparing coded catalogs

Clinical Research Nurse/Chemotherapy Department (1973-1976)

* Prepared and administered experimental drug therapy; monitored and evaluated patient status both in and out of hospital

NURSING EXPERIENCE:

1969-1973   NEW YORK STATE REGISTRY, New York, NY
Private Duty Nurse

KINGS COUNTY HOSPITAL CENTER, Brooklyn, NY
Assistant Clinical Instructor (1970-1971)

* Taught respiratory medicine and respiratory intensive care to senior nursing students (both theory and practice); designed techniques for teaching decision-making skills

* Supervised student nurses in clinical care; assessed and graded performance; conducted individual evaluation conferences

Staff Nurse/Intensive Care Unit (1969-1971)

* In charge of intensive care unit; supervised entire night staff for 600-bed service

1967-1968   DOCTORS HOSPITAL, Freeport, NY
Nurses Aide/Medicine and Surgery (while in school)

EDUCATION: Current - Marymount Manhattan College, New York, NY
(Earned 99 credits toward BS in Nursing, attending school part time)

Kings County Hospital Center School of Nursing, Brooklyn, NY
1969 - Nursing Diploma

Nassau Community College, Garden City, NY
1966 - Liberal Arts/Nursing Program

CERTIFICATION:
Registered Professional Nurse

MICHAEL FRIER   120 West 86th Street, #4A   Home 212-724-6572
                      New York, NY 10025   Work 212-650-7530

<u>FACILITIES PLANNING</u> for consulting and development, real estate, construction firm or government planning agency.

SUMMARY
Facilities Planner with over 10 years in planning and development for major New York City medical center. Management authority over as many as ten ongoing projects with combined budgets of up to $750,000, involving sophisticated medical and research facilities. Experienced at obtaining government approvals, certificates of need and variances. Effective client consultant and director of architects, engineers and general contractors.

1971 to
Present

MONTEFIORE HOSPITAL, New York, NY
Office of Facilities Planning & Design
<u>Project Manager</u>
Responsible for all phases of the planning and implementation of major facility changes.

Facilities
Planning

* Create and direct construction, renovation and space utilization projects to facilitate institutional development
  - Design programs which reconcile desires of client departments with facility objectives
  - Determine available resources and administer budgets ranging from $50,000 to $100,000
  - Review architectural and engineering proposals to achieve maximum cost-effectiveness
  - Schedule, direct and monitor work of architects, engineers, consultants and interior designers

* Fully knowledgeable about New York Department of Health Building codes and other state regulatory agencies and local planning regulations

Major Building
Programs

* Assisted Director of Planning with development of major building programs
  - These included a $100,000,000 500-bed hospital facility, a 30 story, $10,000,000 residence and a 10 story, 100 suite professional practice building

* Wrote and presented proposal to New York City Environmental Agency for $3,000,000, 600-car garage
  - This was the only such proposal approved by Agency since its inception

Long Range
Planning

* Developed currently implemented long range plan in 1975 for future development of hospital and its building

(MONTEFIORE Cont'd)

Space Planning   * Designed comprehensive computerized 2 year, $100,000 space
inventory to achieve efficient space management

Construction   * Projects up to 15,000 square feet with budgets ranging to
Management $750,000
- Put projects out to bids
- Negotiate contracts and approve changes
- Monitor costs and schedules
- Inspect work to ensure adherence to plans and specifications
- Deal with general contractors and subcontractors

1970-1971   Stevens, Smith & Partners, New York, NY
Architects and Hospital Consultants
Health Planner

Long-Range   Developed long-range plans for Bronx Municipal Hospital Center, NY,
Planning   Norwich Hospital, Norwich, CT, Backus Hospital, Greenwich, CT.

* Prepared comprehensive studies serving as basis for long-range
building programs:
- Studied demography, patient origins, physician manpower, community
objectives, transportation, ambulatory care, delivery systems,
long term care and available health and community resources

1966-1970   Taught for New York City Board of Education, served in Peace Corps
in India, traveled through Mid East, Europe and Mexico

Education   NEW YORK UNIVERSITY, New York, NY
1965-1966   Completed course work for MA, Philosophy
        New York University Fellowship

KENYON COLLEGE, Gambiar, OH
1965:   BA, Philosophy (cum laude with high honors in Philosophy)
       Woodrow Wilson Scholar

Professional Courses:

New York University - Urban and Health Planning, Construction
   Technology and Management
New School for Social Research - Urban Planning and Real Estate

Willing to relocate, free to travel

BERNARD REESE   600 Rosedale Avenue   White Plains, New York   (914) 946-7357

OBJECTIVE: PHARMACEUTICALS: Market Research and Development

SUMMARY: Eight years diversified experience in clinical and immunological cancer research. Candidate for Master's degree
in marketing. Master's degree in immunology and Bachelor's
degree in biology/chemistry

EXPERIENCE: INMAN INSTITUTE, New York, NY
1969 to   Senior Research Assistant (1974 to Present)
Present
* Conduct experimental immunological research (in-viro
   and in-vitro)

* Write experimental papers

* Direct laboratory and staff of approximately 15 MDs,
   PhDs, technicians, students and volunteers

* Prepare annual budget of $250,000

* Administer $100,000 annual laboratory purchases from
   pharmaceutical companies

* Write grant papers

* Interview job applicants

Research Assistant (1969 to 1974)

* Developed formally adopted creative procedures for performing perfusion techniques in live animals

   - Performed immunological preparation associated with
      liver and pancreas transplantation surgery in dogs
      and cats

   - Performed microsurgery in rats

   - Ran Alpha Feto Protein Immune-Electropheresis of
      serum proteins from patients suspected of having liver
      malignancy

* Responsible for some laboratory administration laboratory administration

EDUCATION: NEW YORK UNIVERSITY, New York, NY
              Present - MBA candidate, Marketing
              1978 - MS, Immunology

              BOSTON UNIVERSITY, Boston, MA
              1969 - BS, Biology

              UNIVERSITY OF ROME, Rome, Italy
              1969 - Summer courses at School of Medicine

              FAIRLEIGH DICKINSON UNIVERSITY, Teaneck, NJ
              1968 - Summer course in Advertising

EXTRA-CURRICULAR ACTIVITIES:

              Worker in University Hospital Volunteer Plan
              Orientation advisor and guidance counselor

              President, Boston University International Folk Dance Club

LANGUAGES: Italian - read/speak

LEWIS LEE SHUN

200 Smithtown Road   Yorktown Heights   New York   NY   10598   (914) 245-5662

OBJECTIVE: To obtain a research or management position utilizing my education and expertise in international economics, monetary economics, and finance.

SUMMARY: MA in Economics with specialization in International and Monetary. Economist, Government of Republic of China. Research at University of Florida. Bilingual: English, Mandarin Chinese.

RELEVANT
EXPERIENCE:
1976 - 1978   Research Assistant, UNIVERSITY OF FLORIDA
                                   Gainesville, FL

--Assistant to economist Michael Connelly, performing the research function for papers and projects on foreign exchange, economics, and other international studies.

--Sole responsiblility for evaluation and selection of new source books for economics, international finance, and business administration for University of Florida library.

--Simultaneously worked toward MA in the fields of International and Monetary Economics.

1975 - 1976   Economist (GS-11 equivalent level)
               ECONOMIC PLANNING COUNCIL OF REPUBLIC OF
               CHINA. Taipei, Taiwan

--Organized, wrote, and edited reports for the director of the Council on international trade, new developments, and the effect of monetary devaluation--much of it having to do with the United States, Canada, Asia, and Europe.

--Published two reports for the Republic of China: (1) "The Effects of Devaluation" (2) "A Comparison of Taiwan-Korean Trade Patterns."

Instructor, THE NATIONAL CHUNG-HSING UNIVERSITY
           Taiwan

--In addition to my position as a staff economist, taught "Money and Banking" and "International Economics" courses at the University.

--Developed curriculum for both courses, based upon U.S.-published texts.

OTHER
EXPERIENCE:
1978 - 1979   Part-time retail sales work
               Washington, DC

EDUCATION: MA, University of Florida, 1978
Major: Economics, International & Monetary

Graduate Work, Cornell University, 1973-1974

BA, National Taiwan University, 1971
Major: Economics

PERSONAL: Married. No children. Willing to travel. Permanent U.S. resident

Developing a Successful Marketing Plan

You have followed all the rules. Your résumé is as good as it can be, for the specific audience you had in mind. Let's now determine how to make the best possible use of it. This will depend, as mentioned in Chapter 2, on why you wrote it.

First of all, are you accelerating or changing careers? The strategies are different. Accelerating is much easier, so let's deal with it first.

Strategies for Accelerating

If you are trying to get further faster in the same field, you probably are seeking an interview for a position you either *know* is available or you think *might* be, now or in the near future. For either option, the most effective approach is to keep in mind and utilize the three levels of information listed in Chapter 3: knowledge of industry, knowledge of company, and knowledge of position.

Knowing what's out there obviously maximizes your chances of getting the job you want. Moving from the obvious to the less obvious, consider the following sources:

- [ ] Employment agencies
- [ ] Executive recruiters
- [ ] Newspaper want ads and business section display ads
- [ ] Business and trade publication articles and want ads
- [ ] Industry or function journals and newsletters
- [ ] Industry association officers
- [ ] Former colleagues and "friends of friends" networks

Let's take them in turn.

Employment agencies. Reputable agencies specializing in your field are worth contacting, but should not be depended on too heavily. Send a résumé and letter to those you've identified as the best of them, call within a decent interval for an interview (so at least one placement counselor knows you personally), and then forget about it.

Employment agencies work for the corporations and private institutions that give them job orders, and therefore can't be expected to go out of their way for you. It's important to take enough time to interview with each agency to which you send a résumé, though, so that it has a "card" on you, filed with each résumé. Each applicant is rated by appearance (so dress as you would for a job interview), personality, and experience. A résumé by itself will get lost in any agency's voluminous files. When stapled to a card indicating that you have interviewed there, however, it permits you to remain "live" for any openings the agency gets in the next several months.

If you are in the following fields, there is likely one or more agencies in your metropolitan area specializing in positions appropriate for you:

Accounting/Finance	Personnel
Advertising	Public Relations
Banking	Publishing
Brokerage	Retailing
Data Processing	Sales
Health Care/Pharmaceutical	Technical/Scientific
Legal	Textile/Apparel

Executive Recruiters. Our advice regarding "headhunters" is similar to that for employment agencies. Their allegiance is to their clients, understandably, rather than to any individual applicant. If you are willing to come up with 30 percent of your current annual salary as a "finder's fee," on the other hand, you can probably be assured of the same level of attention the recruiters afford their corporate clients.

Some of you who have been contacted by a recruiter may remember being vaguely irritated that first time to be told about a great new job just as you were beginning to enjoy the best one you ever had. That happens. Don't expect them to be there when you need them. Most recruiters lure "fast trackers" from their clients' competitors and companies with similar product/service lines to that of their clients.

Recruiters like to *solicit* résumés, not receive them unasked. If they hear from you first, you are perceived to be vulnerable with your current employer, or even unemployed (even though you may not have alluded to your job status in a cover letter). The reason is not so much that you are tainted professionally by being—at worst—between jobs, but that you are a tougher "sell" to the client. Most recruiters would rather not spend the extra time it takes to neutralize the negatives of pitching an out-of-work applicant or one whose job is in jeopardy. An executive who has to be pried from his current position is a much lower risk and a more prized commodity.

Most recruiters do accept résumés, however, and indeed keep them. And because they have to stay on top of industry/company/position trends, they can be excellent source people.

Call the recruiter for an interview a week or so after you send in a résumé, and see if you can steal a half hour of time. Do enough brain picking to get a sound estimate of your intrinsic marketability and the current state of the market for someone with your background and aspirations.

Newspaper ads. Responding to a newspaper ad is much like buying a lottery ticket: the cost is low and the payoff high, but the odds of winning are even higher. The employers' screeners first scan résumés as much to exclude the unacceptable as to identify the qualified. Their instructions usually are to pick out the top ten or twenty-five résumés from the hundreds they read, so that interviews can be set up accordingly.

Their checklist usually is inviolable, because they are simply following orders. So if you like the sound of the job but fall short on more than one of the stated criteria, applying probably will be a waste of your time. Papering the gap between your qualifications and the minimum listed by writing a long cover letter won't help either. Either rewrite your résumé to fit the specifications of the opening (honestly, that is—anything less will catch up to you, eventually), or keep looking until you find a better match.

As to want ads in particular, be sure you look under all the appropriate categories, and do it consistently. Some companies advertise by function, others by industry, still others by job title. A public relations writer, for example, conceivably could find openings appropriate to ability under "Public Relations," "Corporate Communications," "Corporate Relations," "Copywriter—Public Relations," "Speechwriter," and "Writer," as well as under the various industry and individual agency listings. Get in the habit of regularly cross-checking all categories that could pertain to you.

Be familar with those weekdays your metropolitan papers gang their display ads in a discrete employment section. The *Wall Street Journal* lists employment opportunities and employment services every Tuesday, for example; The *New York Times* on Wednesdays and Sundays.

Business and trade publication articles and want ads. Spend a half-day every week at the best public library available to you, so you can assemble an intelligence system effective enough to anticipate trends that may in turn trigger job openings.

Go through business magazines such as *Fortune*, *Forbes*, and *Business Week* regularly, as well as your particular trade magazines. Take notes on companies that interest you and individuals in them who may make good contacts for you some day. Check the back-of-the-book classifieds for openings you may want to follow up.

Industry or function journals and newsletters. Those you can't find at the library, subscribe to. Use them as you would business and trade publications.

Industry and function association officers. Membership directories are great sources for identifying leaders in your field who could be valuable contacts for you. If you don't know of a directory listing your industry or function membership, talk to a reference librarian or consult the *Directory of Directories* (Gale Research Company), published semi-annually.

Networks. To draw a lead on companies where you have discovered openings or believe they are about to occur, contact former colleagues or friends in other companies to see who knows somebody in power at each target company.

Raised to its highest, most organized form, this systematic contacting is called "networking." (It's an effective strategy for career changers as well, so you'll be referred back to this section if you're thinking of plunging ahead to those paragraphs.)

Most female executives and professionals are great networkers. Many males don't even know the term. One reason for this is that women as a group have had it far rougher in the business world than have their male counterparts, owing to various forms of sexual discrimination. They've been the Outs; men the Ins. As a result women have learned to cope and scramble in an alien world, a bit like fish learning to walk on land. So they're less reluctant to ask the right questions of anyone who can help them break down the barriers.

Male executives generally talk to a handful or so of former colleagues to see where the jobs are, but rarely do they exploit the networking technique to its fullest. Many groups of female executives meet regularly just to exchange business cards and broaden their network base.

But the technique is beginning to spread. A noted former radical excoriated in the sixties by a large segment of society for his anti-establishment behavior, helped broaden the networking concept in the early eighties by taking over a large New York discotheque on off-nights. By promising both professional and social introductions to attending male and female executives, he generated the exchange of thousands of business cards leading to proposals of various kinds—many of them for jobs.

Male reluctance to networking has been partly attributed to the eggshell egos some say go with the gender. This is probably true, although the job hunt exposes anyone—male as well as female—to vulnerability in the extreme. And this is the case even for those changing positions of their own volition. Most executives feel best about themselves when they are secure, productive, well-compensated team members. They feel worst about themselves, understandably, when this security is taken away.

Strategies for Career Change

A complete analysis of career change requires a book of its own, but several basic steps will help point you in the right direction.

You're probably thinking of a change because you're bored beyond belief; are burned out; are miscast; or just would prefer a different professional way of life after ten or fifteen years doing what you're doing.

Jumping *from* is easy. You just quit, or—consciously or subconsciously—get or allow yourself to be fired. Jumping *to* is the tough part.

First you need to make two lists. List A should contain all of the things you like about your existing function, company, position, and industry. List B should contain all of the things you can't stand about what you are doing, in these same categories. The ideal change, it will come as no surprise to you, will include all of the List A items and none from List B. This won't happen, of course. To come as close to this ideal as you can, though, is your reasonable goal.

If you're lucky, the adjustment will be a minor one: moving to a company that gives you a freer hand in the same function and industry, for example; doing what you do for an organization larger—or smaller—than yours, or in a different geographical setting.

Slightly more difficult, but manageable, are position changes other than "straight ahead." One Career Clinics client who had risen through the commercial real estate and building management ranks to vice-presidency of a large New York commercial real estate concern said the fun had gone out of his work. His most challenging years, he said, were at the building management level where he had to juggle working relationships with various unions and state and local regulatory bodies, as well as solve dozens of variegated day-to-day problems. His more elevated executive position gave him considerable policy-making power and paid extremely well, but bored him to the point that he hated to come to work in the morning. He wanted to return to where the action was, even if it involved a pay cut.

His problem was to find such a job without appearing to have lost his drive and ambition. It might seem to some, for example, that he had peaked professionally and was willing to settle for fewer responsibilities and less challenge—when in fact the opposite was true. With the appropriate résumé, cover letter, and list of targeted prospects, he reached his goal. (His résumé appears on pages 198-199; his cover letter on page 246.) Within three months he was appointed building manager of the Empire State Building.

More difficult, and impossible to cover in a book of this scope, are changes that involve function or—in many cases—industry. If you realize after working with data or "things" for ten years that you would prefer to work more with people, you may have to complete additional necessary training or appropriate courses in your spare time. Plan to spend a year or more making this happen, including enough networking and information interviewing to be sure you remain on the right track.

Putting It Together

You've heard of the hidden job market? No need to pay thousands of dollars to the large career service companies that advertise access to the "90 percent of job vacancies...available that the average job searcher does not know about." Their claims of inside information from corporations that for some reason share this knowledge with them but don't get the word out to "the average job searcher" are false.

The hidden job market is simply the wealth of positions that don't get advertised because they are filled first by individuals who have done the homework outlined in this chapter, and are tapped into the networks we've mentioned. There is no need to advertise, after all, if one or more qualified candidates for a position are *known* to exist and be available.

Be that candidate. In any company you'd like to work for, find one or more people in a position to provide inside information. To help you determine whether an opening exists or might be coming up, get answers to the following questions, and any others you can think of:

☐ Is there an impending merger or acquisition?
☐ Is expansion a probability—or the addition of one or more product or service lines?
☐ Are sales up—and staying there?
☐ Is activity scheduled that leads to one of your strengths?
☐ Have you identified a problem area that your background would help solve?

Set up an interview with your contact person if you need additional information, then send your résumé and an appropriate cover letter to the line officer or department head who will be doing the hiring.

Cover Letters That Sell 6

A cover letter is a personal letter in the sense that it introduces you *personally*—whether it is addressed to a box number in answer to an ad or sent to an individual who has personally requested it. As such, each must appear to have been written solely for the eyes of the addressee, even if it is but one of five hundred you have sent out.

This is important because it gives you the opportunity to neutralize the impersonally written résumé by introducing you in more human terms. Each cover letter should highlight your strengths specifically in light of the opportunity you are addressing.

No better model exists for constructing your cover letter than the four-paragraph sales letter prescription offered in Business English classes decades ago: 1. command attention; 2. sustain interest; 3. assure conviction; 4. incite action. Whether you do this in more or fewer than four paragraphs will depend on the circumstances. Those four components, however, should all be there.

Command attention. The most effective way to get the reader's attention is to state your business in as forceful and succinct a way as you can. Are there exceptions? Of course. An advertising copywriter, for example, expected to write winning copy every time she puts typewriter to paper, might start off with her best headline, followed by a couple of sentences telling how well it sold the product. Other situations will vary with the purpose of the letter, as described later in the chapter.

Sustain interest; assure conviction. Consider these not as discrete paragraphs, but rather two inherent elements often combined in the body of the letter. Those of your credentials—accomplishments, responsibilities, skills, professional record, and education—that you know to be of particular importance to your reader should be laid out with the appropriate emphasis and in appropriate sequence, with specific examples as they apply. See the samples included later in the chapter for varying kinds of circumstances.

Incite action. Notice in all of the sample letters that follow (except for replies to blind newspaper ads) that the writer requests an interview—and further, indicates his or her intention to follow up with a phone call to personally petition for an interview.

This is important. First of all, with the number of résumés hitting the desk of hiring line executives or institutional supervisors, it is unlikely your letter will trigger an immediate return call unless the opening is current and you are right for it. Essential as it is for an organization to seek out the best people, the press of day-to-day responsibilities often pushes this need down the list of professional priorities.

Saying you will call to request the interview increases your chances of getting it. The absence of a reply to your letter is of itself a negative response, obviously. By calling, you force a *direct* negative response (if this be the case) and eliminate the possibility of *passive* rejection. No chance now that the addressee lets your letter work its way down to the Pleistocene level of his In box and dooms it to inaction.

Cover Letter Situations

Most of your mailings will fall under one of the five following categories, so the remaining pages of this chapter consist of specific tips for each situation, followed by sample letters written for Career Clinics clients under the same circumstances:

☐ Newspaper ad replies
☐ Executive recruiter/employment agency inquiries
☐ Corporate/institutional cold calls
☐ Slight-career-change cold calls
☐ "I'm back in the job market" re-introductions

Newspaper ad replies. All ads won't require your attention in equal measure. When you see one you think you are perfect for, though, give it an extra effort.

Go over the ad's requirements thoroughly. Assume that they have been rank ordered, and deal with each as sequenced in the ad. Write and rewrite a description of those accomplishments, skills, and responsibilities that relate specifically to each requirement, until you have eliminated all excess words. Communicate your strengths clearly and succinctly. Work on your transitions until each idea flows effortlessly to the next. Below is an ad from the Business section of the *Sunday New York Times* that was of particular appeal to a client. The letter he sent in reply can be found on page 231.

COMMUNITY RELATIONS/ PUBLIC PARTICIPATION

Large East Coast environmental firm is seeking an individual to set up and coordinate community relations/public participation program for hazardous waste management project. Candidate must have an extensive background in community relations work, public participation techniques, local and national media relations and in the technology of waste management. Salary is commensurate with background and experience.

Send resume, salary history and requirements, and supporting material in confidence to:

Y 7427 TIMES 10108
An Equal Opportunity Employer M/F

You might try experimenting with a mailgram for the occasional ad meriting special attention—and also likely to attract résumés in the hundreds. One done for an export executive can be found on page 232.

Finally, don't send your ad response off immediately. Letting it sit for a few days will give you a chance to read it with a fresh eye and make improvements at leisure. The first week or so after the ad's publication, it will attract bagfuls of replies. Wait until the first wave subsides, in about a week or so. Your letter and résumé will get more attention and be more carefully read.

Executive recruiter/Employment agency inquiries. Get in touch with the best of each (the quality and quantity of jobs they list is a good clue), keeping in mind that few employment agencies handle many jobs above the $50,000 salary level. To check out recruiters who are likely to have something at your level and in your field, write or call the American Management Associations (135 W. 50th Street, New York, NY 10020; (212) 586-8100) for a copy of their *Executive Employment Guide*. For $10.00 they'll send you a list of more than 125 executive recruiters nationwide (several with offices worldwide), including addresses, phone numbers, special fields covered if any, minimum salaries of positions handled, and an indication as to whether each accepts résumés or will accede to an interview regarding opportunities in general.

Make the principal purpose of your letter to set up a conversation with one recruiter in each firm—best, in person; second best, by phone. Reconcile yourself to the reality that your chances of matching the specifications of any current search assignment are probably one in one thousand. What you want is information, as well as the opportunity to favorably impress an individual with the power to call you about a client opening six months from now.

Start by calling each target search company within visiting distance, and talk with—or get the name of—the highest ranking individual available. Just get a name and title, and "permission" to send in a résumé. Make your cover letter brief, highlighting major strengths, and follow with a phone call in ten days to set up an interview if you can. On page 233 is a sample letter sent to a recruiter for this reason.

Corporate/Institutional cold calls. If your universe of prospects is a large one, it will be impossible to include a paragraph or more tailored to the express needs of every organization. Decide first how much research on individual companies you are willing to undertake.

Let's say there are ten companies you are extremely interested in, and another fifty you want to contact because a real possibility exists that there is a spot for you—or soon will be. Thoroughly research the top ten companies and write letters indicating your awareness of a particular—and recent or imminent—expansion, merger, acquisition, or market repositioning, and your ability to help the company implement or maximize it. On page 234 is an example of this type of letter.

For the remaining fifty or more organizations it may be enough to simply address each letter to the appropriate person, and then mention the company's name once or twice during the body of the letter. More effective, if you can take the time, is to rank order the companies, complete in-depth research on them, ten at a time, and write your letters as you would for the top ten. Most letter houses with word processing equipment can do this for you for about $1 per letter, including addressing the envelopes. Obviously it is important to have the letters typed individually rather than printed, even if you do go to a word processor. Form letters get thrown out before they're read. On pages 235-242 are some corporate cold call letters for the two situations described above.

Slight-career-change cold calls. If you are making a transition between two related fields, your résumé obviously should be written to minimize the differences between your current and future professions or positions—and indeed use the terminology of the field you are working to get into. The letter you write to accompany the résumé, similarly, should pick up on accomplishments valued equally by current and future employers and stay away from the differences.

The closer your new career is to the old one the easier your task is, obviously. There will be more to draw from your past, and less to hypothesize about your future. In any case the format of the letter accompanying your résumé is basically the same as for any other cover letter. On pages 243-248 are a few examples.

"I'm back in the job market" re-introduction letters. Most executives and professionals make at least one dreadful career mistake during their forty and more years of ladder climbing and tightrope walking. Now and then the greener grass wilts without warning. A pre-employment promise goes unfilled; an unanticipated personality or workplace conflict sours an otherwise promising venture. These things happen.

Many of them, sadly, don't have to happen. Sometimes asking the right question in the final interview will uncover a potential stumbling block large enough to change an acceptance to a rejection. But that's another story, touched on in a bit more detail in Chapter 7.

If you find yourself in an untenable position, get out as gracefully and as quickly as you can—in a way that doesn't arouse your current employer's suspicions in the process, obviously. Don't bite the bullet and do a miserable three to five when you could be advancing professionally and happily elsewhere. Re-establish your network and get the word out subtly that you'd rather be somewhere other than where you are. The letter on page 249 is one way to do this.

ROBERT M. SMICK
590 Mordeca Street   Silver Spring, MD 20850
Home: [301] 968-2402   Office: [202] 747-9201

July 6, 1983

Y7427 TIMES 10108
C/O The New York Times
229 West 43rd Street
New York, NY 10036

Ladies/Gentlemen:

This letter is in response to your ad in the June 21 Business Section of
The New York Times for someone to head up your Community Relations/Public
Participation program.

For the past six years I have served as Executive Director for the Board on
Minorities in Engineering & Sciences, National Academy of Sciences. In this
position I am responsible for coordinating the efforts of 65 corporations,
15 federal agencies, and 112 universities to implement a science manpower
policy utilizing $4,000,000 annually. I call upon the cooperation of promi-
nent leaders from government, industry, academic institutions, and civic
organizations to accomplish the Board's goals.

The public participation techniques I find most useful flow from an identification of the issues and the subsequent identification of competent, expert
witnesses to present informed views regarding these issues. These data
result in reports, symposia, and news conferences to inform the public. I
have worked closely with the print media, and have appeared on television
and radio talk shows in support of various issues espoused by the Board.

My background in chemistry and the Board's relationship with other divisions
of the Academy have provided me with the basic tenets of hazardous waste
management. A short time ago, in fact, I brokered a contract between DuPont
and a small environmental engineering firm for an environmental impact study
on waste disposal that resulted in a mutually satisfying relationship for
both parties.

My resume is enclosed. I look forward to hearing from you so that we may
take the discussions of this challenging position one step further.

Sincerely,

Robert M. Smick

Robert M. Smick
RMS/mg

THE WALL STREET JOURNAL
BOX EJ-991

MY QUALIFICATIONS MATCH YOUR NOVEMBER 17 AD FOR CORPORATE VICE PRESIDENT

AND DIRECTOR OF INTERNATIONAL SALES. HAVE 20 YEARS EXPERIENCE COVERING

EXPORT SALES, CORPORATE DEVELOPMENT, INVESTMENT ANALYSIS, VENTURE CAPITAL,

AND STOCK BROKERAGE. EARNED WHARTON MBA 1958 AND UNIVERSITY OF TEXAS BBA

1957, BOTH MAJORS IN FINANCE AND BANKING.

FOR PAST THREE YEARS HAVE BEEN OPERATING OWN CORPORATION, A MANUFACTURERS'

EXPORT DISTRIBUTION AND REPRESENTATIVE FIRM. HAVE ALSO SERVED AS PRESIDENT

OF GREATER CLEVELAND REGION INTERNATIONAL TRADE DEVELOPMENT ASSOCIATION.

EARLIER INITIATED EXPORT SALES FOR A NORTH CAROLINA MANUFACTURER OF

BUILDING MATERIALS AND AN OHIO MANUFACTURER OF LASER-ENGRAVED PRESTIGE

ADVERTISING SPECIALITIES AND CORPORATE GIFTS. WAS A CO-FOUNDER FOR BOTH

IN 1969 AND REMAIN AN ACTIVE DIRECTOR.

KINDLY TELEPHONE (414) 298-4133 TO DISCUSS THIS POSITION.

Rollin Payne

ROLLIN PAYNE

14 Panther Place
Stamford, Connecticut 06814
August 15, 1983

Dear Sir:

Among your clients may be one or more contemplating entry into the export market, or who has limited experience therein.

As founder and managing director of Tremont International, I currently represent or distribute for dozens of manufacturers who, until our relationship, had never before sold overseas. My intention is to take this expertise -- together with more than 20 years of financial and investment management background -- to a manufacturer ready to begin exporting.

My concept of exporting is designed to minimize cost and red tape, and at the same time maximize profit. You can see by the attached resume that my specific accomplishments in this area are considerable, and range over a variety of consumer and industrial product areas.

Within the next few days I will call to see when you might be available to discuss with me what prospects exist for meeting principals of firms you now represent.

Thank you for your consideration.

Sincerely,

Jarvis Henry

Jarvis Henry

JL/rm

10 Tyrolia Lane
Lawrence, New York 11559
September 3, 1983

Mr. Paul Bergeson
President
Acme Stores, Inc.
655 Fifth Avenue
New York, New York 10036

Dear Mr. Bergeson:

Your recent acquisition of the Bandow chain would indicate an intent to pursue southeastern market opportunities more vigorously than you have in the past several years. I believe that my retail management background would complement your long-range strategy for Acme very effectively.

For the past 10 years I have put together a record of which I am quite proud, including six years at Loud & Schwartz culminating in a senior vice presidency and membership on both the Executive Committee and Management Board.

As you will see on the enclosed resume, most of my accomplishments are quantifiable, including sizable volume and gross margin increases in every position of leadership I have held. In a single year at Loud & Schwartz, for example, the profit ranking of the division I led improved from tenth to first.

These are far from single-handed achievements, obviously. One of my strengths is the ability to recognize and utilize the best talent available, and to extend the decision-making process so as to offer middle managers-- and sometimes even those below them--a stake in determining or refining company policy.

I will call within the next week or so to see if you agree that our mutual interest would be served by a personal meeting, and if so, to see when your schedule permits it.

Sincerely,

Douglas Frisk

Douglas Frisk

Encl.

859 Hobart Street
San Francisco, CA 94110
(415) 875-0922

Mr. Kenneth Rivera
Senior Vice President
Florida State Bank at Orlando
801 N. Lemon Avenue
Orlando, FL 32800

Dear Mr. Rivera:

In approximately three months I am moving to Orlando with my family, and am bringing with me 15 solid years banking experience--the last eight in branch operations management. I would like particularly to utilize this experience with the Florida State Bank at Orlando.

As Branch Manager I currently supervise 20 employees, including nine tellers, at the largest branch of the Federal Mutual Savings Bank, in San Francisco. I serve as an officer of this bank, as well.

As you will see from the enclosed resume, I am well rounded in the workings of NOW and money market accounts, and am extremely strong in the use of systems to reduce overtime and increase both efficiency and customer relations.

I am in the process of planning an exploratory trip to Orlando sometime in late May, and would like very much to meet you and learn of any opportunities that may exist at the Florida State Bank at Orlando for someone with my background and potential. I look forward to hearing from you. Because the precise timing of my move is not certain, I have not yet informed my employer of my intention to move. I would, therefore, appreciate your confidentiality in this regard.

Sincerely,

Marcia J. Shin

Marcia J. Shin

Encl.

24 West 65th Street
Brooklyn, New York 11020
September 12, 1983

Mr. R. B. Ashton
Vice President for Merchandising
Loud & Schwartz
1821 Broad Street
Philadelphia, PA 20171

Dear Mr. Ashton:

For the past four years I have assumed positions of increasing responsibility for both domestic and import retail furniture buying, and am now ready for additional challenge.

At G. Dixon and Company I supervise all aspects of retailing from product purchase to merchandising for bedroom, dining room, occasional and lifestyle furniture. Revenues in this department run in excess of $2 million annually. In the Lifestyle Department alone I increased volume from $400,000 to more than $1 million in one year.

I have a particularly strong color and design sense and am able to identify a potentially successful product with a high degree of accuracy. As you will see from the enclosed resume, another of my strengths is in the area of effective and creative merchandising.

It is my hope to bring these qualifications to Loud & Schwartz. Toward this end I will call you within the next week or so to see when your calendar permits a personal interview.

Sincerely,

Phyllis Sublett

Phyllis Sublett

Enc.

FRANCIS C. HOLLAND   P.O. BOX 663   NORTHPORT, CT 06490

October 29, 1983

Mr. Frederick R. Gloeckner
Vice President & General Manager,
  Export Sales & Services
General Electronics
3135 Weston Turnpike
Northfield, Connecticut 06431

Dear Mr. Gloeckner:

I would like the opportunity to put my nine years of marketing and sales experience to work for General Electronics.

My years with the Learning Corporation of America have been marked by consistently increasing levels of responsibility and achievement. In each of the three positions I have held, departmental sales have increased dramatically. Moreover, I have been responsible for opening market areas previously unknown to the company. The problem is that my current product line -- educational films -- is not in a growth stage, nor is it likely to be so in the foreseeable future.

For this reason I am seeking new challenges, and have selected General Electronics as one company whose dynamic marketing position is unparalleled. Within the next few days I will be calling you to determine when your schedule will permit us to discuss a sales or marketing management position with your firm.

Sincerely,

Francis C Holland

Francis C. Holland

43 Racine Avenue
Skokie, Illinois 60076
January 3, 1984

Mr. Russell Hendrickson
Executive Vice President
Thatcher and Thatcher
48 Greenwich Avenue
Greenwich, Connecticut 06830

Dear Mr. Hendrickson:

The enclosed resume summarizes my background as follows:

> Extensive experience working directly with heads of Fortune 500
> corporations, federal agencies and the Congress. Skilled in
> assessing importance of specific issues and designing successful
> issues-oriented actions.

This is the strongest two-sentence case I can make toward convincing you of
my potential value as a key public affairs or government relations manager
for Thatcher and Thatcher.

What I do best is to analyze problems accurately, and then marshal the appropriate resources to solve them. The arena in which I am most effective
is in the protection and fostering of corporate interest--either as a
spokesman to the public, or in influencing the passage of legislation or
regulations best reflecting that corporate interest. One of my major responsibilities as Executive Director, Board on Minorities in Engineering and
Sciences is to work with Cabinet and federal agency heads, as well as with
members of Congress, to formulate and influence the passage of laws and
regulations regarding issues affecting the Board's objectives and policy.

On both a day-to-day and long-range basis I direct the planning, organization
and administration of the Board. I organized a national symposium that
included 800 prominent leaders from government, industry, academic institutions, and civic organizations. I plan and chair semi-annual meetings for
35 corporate leaders to address national manpower problems.

I am particularly interested in working for a company like Thatcher and
Thatcher because it will allow me to use all of my background--technical,
scientific, educational, and public and legislative affairs.

I look forward to discussing with you the possibility of a position with
Thatcher, and will call within the next week or so to see when your schedule
might permit a personal interview.

Sincerely,

Harry K. Ellis

Harry K. Ellis

Enc.

35 Lyndon Way
Cromwell, New Jersey 07841
November 10, 1983

Dear _____:

Within the next six weeks my wife and I will be moving to Ventura
County, where I intend to put to use my 20 years of financial
management experience in the health care field.

I am writing to see if there is an opening--either now or in the
immediate future--for a professional with the skills and achievements I have to offer.

My strengths include a heavy background in grants application and
analysis, budget forecast and maintenance, staff supervision, and
problem solving.

Upon my arrival in California I will call to see if you believe
our mutual interest might benefit from a personal meeting.
Enclosed is a copy of my resume for your information.

Sincerely,

Barton R. Nelson

Barton R. Nelson

Encl.

455 Ocean Parkway, Apt. 1C
Brooklyn, New York 11218
September 15, 1983

Mr. Harry Martinez
Executive Director
Foster Labs, Inc.
Anderson Blvd.
St. Charles, IL 60134

Dear Mr. Martinez,

With more than ten years clinical chemistry experience as a
graduate biochemist in hospital settings, I am seeking a position as a technical representative or specialist. I am
thoroughly familiar with the chemicals used for general and
special tests in hospitals and doctors' offices and all of
their applications. I am also expert in the use and promotion
of testing equipment.

My resume can only highlight my qualifications. A personal
interview will assure you of my potential value to your company. I will call you in a few days to set an appointment.

Sincerely yours,

Irene Seanor

Irene Seanor

Enc.

310 West 30th Street
New York, New York 10001
April 20, 1983

Mr. Phillip Mitchell
Director of Marketing
Worthington Electronics
Manheim Road
Secaucus, N.J. 02471

Dear Mr. Mitchell:

The state of the art in the electronics market changes at such
a rapid pace that aggressive marketing and astute product
management are essential if high profitability is to be achieved.
I offer a background of more than twenty years in the field of
electro-mechanical products.

My ability encompasses concept and design and includes complete
product management through the entire production process. In
addition, I have worked with engineers, designers and product
managers in U.S. and foreign manufacturing plants to bring in
production schedules for high volume sales of most profitable
items.

The enclosed resume hits the high points. Perhaps we can get
together and talk in detail of my potential value to your
organization. I will call you in a few days to arrange an
appointment for a personal interview.

Sincerely yours,

Clarence Weber
Clarence Weber

Encl.

19 Wingate Road
Cleveland, Ohio 12345
February, 1 1983

Mr. Charles Close
Executive Vice President
T. Clark and Company
Sugar Grove, IL 60134

Dear Mr. Close:

The enclosed resume highlights significant accomplishments of my 11 years of
sales and marketing management. I am looking now for a greater challenge,
and believe you will agree that my record justifies such an expectation.

In seven years with Foraldo Corporation I rose from western regional manager
of the Epcraft Division to vice president of a group overseeing all five of
the firm's tool divisions. This position involved the development and management of a nationwide organization of 92 manufacturers' rep firms and 10
direct sales managers, and supervision of a staff of 250.

The sales incentive program I established at Foraldo resulted in a 13% increase in annual sales and helped set new corporate records in gross profit
levels. I have a keen sense of cost control, and am particularly strong in
the structural reorganization of profit centers to increase efficiency and
productivity.

My goal is to join a firm that requires the immediate use of these skills
whether to increase a rate of established growth or to effect a turnaround
situation.

Within the next week or so I will call to see whether you agree that our
mutual interests would be served by exploring this matter further, and if
so, when your calendar might permit time for a personal interview.

                                        Sincerely,

                                        John A. Larson

Encl.   John A. Larson

411 Market Place
Boston, MA 09296
May 12, 1983

Mr. Samuel Insull
Vice-President for Corporate Affairs
Sunco Oil Company
60 West 42nd Street
New York, NY 10042

Dear Mr. Insull:

After four years of public affairs and press work with both the White House
and as an aide to the Governor of Massachusetts, I am eager to return to corporate life once again.

I offer a unique combination of public and private sector experience. Most
recently, my work as lead advance for Vice President Mondale, Rosalynn Carter,
and Mrs. Mondale has given me the opportunity to handle press and protocol
matters both domestically and abroad. My charge has been to manage the sen-
sitive--and potentially inflammatory--relationships when representatives from
different cultures, societies and religions meet and mix. This calls for a
high order of organizational skills, tact, and attention to detail.

As special assistant to the president of Arnoco Industries I single-handedly
organized a Government Relations conference at which were set industry standards that ultimately influenced crucial federal legislation. My corporate
experience also includes five years with Dean Witter as both a registered
representative and Executive Assistant to the President, and a customer service position with Merrill Lynch.

This combination of public and private sector experience has been excellent
preparation for a position in corporate communication/public affairs--possi-
bly involving legislative liaison at federal, state and local levels. I look
forward to discussing this prospect with you, and will call within the next
few days to see when your schedule permits such a conversation to occur.

Sincerely,

Martha Buchanan

Martha Buchanan

Encl.

43 Crescent Lane
Port Washington, New York 11050
June 5, 1983

Mr. Jake Smith
Editor-in-Chief
The Viking Press
16 E. 46th Street
New York, New York 10077

Dear Mr. Smith:

Is one of your new publications being delayed in startup for lack of
qualified editorship? Is one of your existing periodicals foundering,
or not running at peak efficiency or quality for a similar reason?

If the answer is "yes" in either case, I think it would be to our mutual
advantage to talk. I have a solid 20 years writing and editing experience
to draw on -- all in the areas of business, finance, and insurance. I
have conceived new magazine ideas, managed the gestation periods, and
brought inaugural issues to the black of print.

Moreover, as you'll see from page two of the enclosed resume, my current
freelance client base is both varied and prestigious.

I have considerable talent and commitment to offer some very special and
specialized audiences, and would appreciate the opportunity to discuss
this with you personally. I'll give you a call within the next week or
so to see when it might be convenient for us to meet.

                                        Sincerely,

                                        Albert Magnus

                                        Albert Magnus

Encl.

2803 Chesapeake Street
Washington, D.C. 20008
April 3, 1983

Mr. James Clark
Vice President for Programming
Extension Cablevision, Inc.
1007 Post Road East
Westport, CT 06880

Dear Mr. Clark:

For the past three years I have been involved in television programming and production at Hayden Lurch Associates, as part of my job as Manager of the Audio-Visual Department. My immediate goal is to apply this valuable background--as well as my current freelance videotape producing experience--to the needs of station WXYZ.

While at Hayden Lurch I have coordinated productions from start to finish for such clients as Sun Company, Inc. and Burroughs, including budgeting, scripting, editing, production work, and talent coordination. In addition I prepare departmental budgets, develop concept proposals for client selection, and supervise both creative and administrative personnel.

I have the respect of both colleagues and clients for overall effectiveness, on-schedule and under-budget performance, and quality of final product. My reason for wanting to leave Hayden Lurch--and public relations in general--is an intense desire to focus my skills and expertise full time in the field of television.

Within the next few days I will call to see if you agree that it would be advantageous for us to meet and discuss a position with WXYZ, and if so, to schedule a time that is convenient for you. My resume is enclosed.

Sincerely,

Rollin Ashton

Rollin Ashton

Enc.

465 West End Avenue
New York, New York 10023
January 23, 1984

Mr. Richard Fairbank
Vice President for Operations
Ackroyd and Fisher
369 Lexington Avenue
New York, New York 10010

Dear Mr. Fairbank:

Over the past five years I have grown at Dakota Realty from Building Superintendent of a single building to Vice-President and Director of Operations for six commercial buildings-- including the ICC Building on Fifth Avenue and the MCA- Universal Building at 445 Park Avenue. My accomplishments over this period are considerable, as you will see from the enclosed resume, and include responsibility for a 55% increase in revenue for the 445 Park building during my tenure there as building manager.

My purpose for writing is to acquaint you with my background and indicate my availability for a building management position-- for either a prestigious office building or a corporate head- quarters. My credentials are impeccable, and I am willing to discuss any current or imminent openings with you at your convenience.

I will call you over the next week or so to see when you might be available for a personal interview.

Sincerely,

Juan S. Geisler

Encl.   Juan S. Geisler

62 Marsh Street
Chicago, Illinois 60602
December 7, 1983

Mr. Verner Anderson
President and General Manager
WGBW TV
14 Rockville Plaza
Detroit, Michigan 51073

Dear Mr. Anderson:

For the past 15 years I have co-directed Datus Productions, a film, television and audio/visual production company I co-founded to serve clients in publishing, advertising, and other manufacturing and service industries. As you will see on the enclosed resume, my clients include McGraw-Hill, Young & Rubicam, Amerada Hess, and American Express.

My interest at this point of my career is to devote fewer energies to building a business and more to developing product. I have determined that the way to do this is to work with one "client" only--and do it full time.

This decision is reached from a position of strength: I have eight active clients and a number of additional projects under development. The point is, I have product development skills I am not utilizing as much as I want to.

Please look over my resume to see if any of my skills and accomplishments match your current or imminent needs. I'll call you in a week or so to see when your calendar permits a personal meeting.

Thanks for your time.

Sincerely,

Tilden Meyers

Tilden Meyers

Encl.

15 Cayaka Street
Los Angeles, CA 90057
December 29, 1983

Dear_____:

For more than twenty years I have built a record of solid accomplishments
in the business of education--as a financial officer, a human resources
manager, and as a senior operating executive. I would like to offer this
experience to the executive management or human resources operation of
(name of company)   .

At two colleges in the past twelve years, I devised a considerable number
of bold, innovative management programs. They improved efficiency, reduced
costs, eliminated problems, and unsnarled administrative tangles. At the
same time, the academic programs were maintained and improved. My com-
petencies range from administering complex federal programs to negotiating
labor contracts and disputes; from supervising the revision of a school's
complete legislative structure to instituting and administering a college-
wide energy conservation and deferred maintenance program.

I look forward to discussing with you the several ways in which my experience,
talents, and services could be of use to (name of company). I will call
next week to see when your calendar permits scheduling an appointment.

Sincerely,

Robert O. Levinson

Robert O. Levinson

45 Hunter Lane
Grand Rapids, MI 49505
April 18, 1983

Mr. Clarence Halter
President
Animated Industries, Inc.
4641 Boardwalk
Dallas, Texas 41414

Dear Mr. Halter:

Four months ago you and I discussed an opportunity at
Animated, and you were kind enough to set up meetings
with Jack Conde and Ernest Soderstrom. Shortly there-
after, as you know, I accepted a position with Spring-
born & Sons, where I am now.

For reasons I will go into when we meet, I would like to
re-open our discussions. If you think such a conversation
would be mutually beneficial, I'll call next week to see
when you have a half hour or so of free time.

Sincerely,

Jerry Lake

Jerry Lake

Winning Interview Techniques

You were asked to be interviewed because an executive, personnel director, or other representative of the employer felt that the company's interest would be served by knowing more about you. Your résumé indicates to them that you are qualified; now they are trying to determine if you are the *best* qualified.

With this in mind, you must now convince them that it is in their best interest to hire you. You must present yourself in such a manner that the interviewer will feel that your assets and abilities are superior to those of any other candidate.

Surprisingly, and sadly, the job does not always go to the most qualified. It is possible to predict with some reliability which candidates will receive not just one, but many job offers. We have analyzed the common denominator each of these "winners" possesses: It is a first impression that projects honesty, sincerity, and enthusiasm. Given two or more candidates with virtually indistinguishable credentials, the job will almost invariably go to the individual projecting the more positive and enthusiastic image.

Creating the Right Impression

Because the first impression you make will carry through the entire interview and greatly determine its outcome, it is of vital importance to create the most positive image possible. Your physical appearance, mannerisms, vocabulary, attitude, and nonverbal communication all contribute to the impression you make.

How does one convey sincerity? By being honest, open, and real. Be yourself. Take the attitude that the company needs you, and feel confident. This starts the self-fulfilling prophecy. *Feel* successful and chances are better that you *will* be successful.

Any form of role-playing that projects a personality other than your own will likely lead to a disastrous interview. There is no way to predict what kind of person the employer is looking for, and if in fact you knew, it is highly unlikely you could keep up the charade for the duration of the interview.

Do Your Homework

Because the interview is such a crucial part of the hiring process, take the time to prepare yourself completely. This preparation will add to your feeling of self-confidence and generate a positive, successful interview with the best chance of a job offer.

Learn as much as possible about your prospective employer—who the officers, directors, or partners are and what the firm's complete product or service line is. Be sure of the company's reputation, and get as much information as you can about past and upcoming mergers, acquisitions, and new market possibilities.

Any library can offer a wealth of information. Use such directories as *Standard and Poor's*, *Dun and Bradstreet*, and *Moody's*. (Names of additional business directories can be found on page 259.) The business periodical Index will help you find any recent press coverage.

Try to read both current and back issues of any trade journals that deal with your industry and the company or companies you are interested in.

Handling Tough Questions

Though every interview is different, all will include one or more questions you'd just as soon not have to answer. The interviewer will be listening not only for content, but sincerity, poise, and ability to think quickly, as well.

Spend some time before the interview developing answers to those of the following questions you think might give you trouble. Some of them are tough and fair. Some of them are tough and unfair.

Be mindful of the fact that everyone has an "obnoxious question threshold" past which he or she cannot, *should* not go. A question you consider opprobrious calls for an appropriate response. For example, if you find it offensive to take a lie detector test, say so. Never compromise strongly held values to make interview points. It may be that your resolve, not your honesty, is being tested. But if it *is* your honesty that is being tested, feel perfectly comfortable to politely end the interview forthwith, on the appropriate grounds that you prefer not to work for a company whose values obviously differ so markedly from your own.

With a friend, your husband or wife—or even a tape recorder—go through questions you think you might be asked. Prepare answers you can give extemporaneously. The wording and substance of these questions will vary to reflect your particular set of circumstances. Review them in light of potential trouble spots in your background, and prepare for those few that may cause you problems in an interview.

1. What did you enjoy most about your last position?
2. What did you like least about your last position?
3. What do you consider your most outstanding achievement?
4. How well do you work under pressure?
5. How well do you get along with your peers?
6. How ambitious are you?
7. How good are you at motivating other people?
8. What kinds of problems do you enjoy solving?
9. What do you think you could contribute to the company (or association, hospital, etc.)?
10. How often have you been ill in the past five years?

11. Are you willing to take a physical exam?
12. Are you willing to take a series of personality (intelligence, aptitude) tests?
13. Are you willing to take a lie detector test?
14. What do you consider your greatest strengths?
15. What do you consider your greatest weaknesses?
16. In what ways do you think your weaknesses would interfere with the position we're trying to fill?
17. Why do you want to change jobs?
18. Were you ever fired? If so, why?
19. Would you consider relocating?
20. How do you explain the gaps (if any) in your employment record?
21. How do you spend your free time?
22. Are you active in community affairs? If so, describe your participation.
23. What were the last three books you read?
24. What newspapers do you read?
25. To what magazines do you subscribe?
26. What is your definition of success?
27. Where do you expect to be with your career in five years?
28. What is your attitude about working for a woman (man, if female) or a younger person?
29. What did you learn from your last position?
30. How did you get along with your previous boss (or staff)?
31. Why do you want to work for this company?
32. What are your hiring techniques? Describe some of the people you've hired, their positions, and why you hired them.
33. What skills do you think you possess that would be beneficial to this company?
34. What motivates you?
35. Do you work better alone, or as part of a team?
36. What are your long-range career objectives?
37. What are your short-term objectives?
38. Would you describe yourself as creative? What are some examples of your creativity?

Other Interview Potholes

If you have sent out several different versions of your resume, each targeting your achievements and experience to a particular kind of employer, review the appropriate version—and cover letter—to help you anticipate any tough questions as effectively as possible.

If you are between jobs, your reasons for leaving the last one will undoubtedly come up at the interview. Organize your thoughts on this subject before the interview. Preparing for the toughest possible questions will provide you with the confidence you need to do your best.

If you were fired, tell the simple truth. In these times of retrenchment, bankruptcies, mergers, relocations, and layoffs, firing is replacing baseball as the national pastime. Chances are that your prospective boss is no stranger to the experience and will find it easy to empathize if you deal with your situation honestly.

If you were fired because your performance was in question, answer truthfully and try to transmit the extent to which you made this a learning experience. Never offer unsolicited negative comments about any staff member, or about your former or present employer.

If you are presently employed, you will be asked why you want to change jobs, and specifically why you would like to work for the company you're visiting. Again, be brief, exact and direct. Wanting to move up, earn a higher salary, join a larger (or smaller) organization, a desire to relocate, or make a career change—all are appropriate reasons to be looking for a new job. The research you have done about the particular employer will help you point out why you feel positive about the interviewing company and how you think you can make a positive professional impact on it soon after coming on board.

To sum up, be as honest during your interview as you were writing your résumé. It is tempting to exaggerate, distort a little, tell a little lie or a half truth, but making yourself seem better or other than you are is a dangerous game. First of all, it's going to be virtually impossible for you to be consistent once you've injected a shot of fiction into your autobiography. Second, and more importantly, once you're caught in a lie—no matter how slight—you've lost your credibility; maybe even your reputation.

We remember referring a publicist to a major corporation. Her résumé was first-rate, and the interview good enough for her to accept a splendid offer. After six months she received a 20 percent salary increase. Several months later, however, the personnel department checked out the information on her résumé and on the company's application form. She had said she had worked for a certain employer for three years when in reality she had been there for only one year. Even though she was doing a fantastic job and her boss respected her work highly, she was fired. The company—not unlike many other employers—had a policy of terminating any employee found to be untruthful on the application form. The vice-president who had hired her was as upset as she, the irony being, he revealed, that he would have taken her on even if he had known she had worked for company X for only one year. And though he was high on the company ladder, he couldn't change company policy.

Nervous is Natural

If you experience a slight case of the jitters before and during your interviews, you're in good company. Though you've gone through the experience a dozen times or more, putting yourself in this vulnerable position can be an unsettling experience. We've found, as have colleagues all over the country, that an overwhelming majority of job-seekers view the interview as the most stressful phase of the job search.

Unfortunately, most job candidates experience the interview as an acid test of their abilities and self-worth. Such an attitude is extremely anxiety-producing and tends to create a negative reaction from the interviewer. If you're nervous, don't get more nervous about being nervous. (Easy for us to say, right?) But just go with it. The interviewer expects some nervousness on your part and usually he or she will try to help you through it.

It may help for you to view the interview as a meeting between two equals, a buyer and a seller, to explore what each has to offer the other. If you can convey the feeling early that you have something the company wants, you will establish parity in a hurry. Always keep in mind a feeling of equality between you and the interviewer. Being too humble or subservient is as bad as being arrogant. Be a good listener, but ask any questions that will help you find out how close you and the company are to a possible match—and what you can tell them that might tip the scales in your favor, if this is a job you want.

Compensation

Never begin salary negotiations until you are relatively certain you have a job offer. When asked about your present or last compensation packages, answer concisely, including all bonuses and perquisites. If you feel you were or are underpaid, mention that as one reason for wanting to change jobs. Never, however, insinuate that you were exploited or victimized by an employer. Playing victim can backfire on you.

When discussing your present minimum salary requirements, stay flexible. If you know what salary range is being offered, put your salary expectations at the high end of that range. Remember, the interview is a screening process. If your minimum salary requested is considerably higher than the employer intends to pay, this alone could knock you out of the running.

Don't get boxed into a specific figure before you have to. Always talk in $5,000 to $10,000 ranges. If the interview has gone superbly, aim high and then negotiate. If you are in doubt about the range the employer is considering and are asked what your salary expectations are, answer the question with one of your own. "I'm glad you brought up the subject of compensation. What range do you see for this job?" Then negotiate from there.

Finally, never make a decision at the interview—whether it's the first, second, or third. Say: "I appreciate your offer, and will give it serious consideration. May I call you on Tuesday with my decision?" This gives you a chance to weigh any other serious offers, and also to reflect more thoroughly on this one. You may come up with a question that affects your decision—and even the composition of the job itself.

Which Job Do You Take?

8

The tricky thing about handling your first job offer is knowing whether to hold out for a better one, or squeeze that bird senseless while it's still in your hand. Odds are you won't have to decide in isolation, unless this is the first solid opportunity you've had since severance pay ran out three weeks ago. And even then, unless you're down to zero cash reserves, you'll be better off saying no if the position is dead wrong for you and you realize it before the employer does. No point in reaching for this book again before you need to.

How to decide, then, supposing subsistence is not your number one problem? Even if you feel you've been offered a dream position, delay your final decision for a few days to provide some perspective. Thank your prospective boss for the offer, as we said in the last chapter, and tell him or her you'll be back to him in a few days—but mention, and stick with, a specific day. Unless the organization is in a crisis condition (which if you're hearing for the first time is an even better reason to stall), your request will be honored and you'll have a chance to weigh the offer both intrinsically and against any others you may have.

What You Need to Know

Complete your research. Any open questions about the organization and the position that are either hanging fire or to which you haven't received satisfactory answers should be resolved now. For example: Under what circumstances did your predecessor leave—if this is not a new position. If the reason was one of chemistry or personality conflict between him and your new boss, get to the bottom of it. Ask the person who held the job previously, if he is accessible. Any workways or points of view the two of you share that may have been inimical to his corporate health could serve you up the same fate. Decide which is more important to you, those particular values or the job.

Dollar signs bedazzle. Look carefully at the flip side of your highest paying offer. Don't give up in potential and prestige what you might be gaining in a monthly paycheck. Analyze the entire compensation package, including benefits and perquisites, to be sure that a lower salary with excellent fringes may indeed not be more remunerative in the long run. Ask your accountant or lawyer to help steer you through the thornier issues.

If you view this position as a way station to greater professional advancement down the road, be sure the experience and accomplishments you stand to attain aren't clouded by accepting more money for a position that may weaken your next résumé.

Trust your instincts. When all the evidence is in, count on your gut reaction to deliver a decision in your best interests. Maintain the professional ties that bind, however, so if you realize in six months that you've made a terrible mistake you can swallow your pride and announce your renewed availability (as in the Chapter 6 "I'm back in the job market" re-introduction letters).

May the best possible position be yours.

Corporate Information Directories

These directories can be found in the reference section of any good library. Some may be available only in a business library.

Ayer Directory of Publications
Chamber of Commerce Publications
Directory of Corporate Communications Executives
Directory of Manufacturers (geographical listings)
Dun & Bradstreet's Million Dollar Directory
Encyclopedia of Associations
Encyclopedia of Business Information
F and S Index of Corporations and Industries
Fitch Corporation Manuals
Fortune Double 500 Directory
How to Find Information About Companies
Index and Listed Stock Reports
Literary Marketplace
MacRae's Blue Book
Magazine Marketplace
Martindale Hubbard
Moody's Industrial Manual
National Association of Independent Schools
National Trade and Professional Associations of U.S. and Canada
Newsletter Yearbook/Directory
O'Dwyer's Directory of Corporate Communications
Printing Trades Blue Book
Redbook of Regional Corporations
Standard & Poor's Corporation Records, Industrial
Standard & Poor's Security Dealers of North America
Standard Directory of Advertising Agencies
Statistical Abstract of the U.S. Department of Commerce
The Uncle Sam Connection, a Guide to Federal Employment
Thomas Register of Manufacturers
United States Government Manual
Walker's Manual of Far Western Corporations

More selected BARRON'S titles:

DICTIONARY OF FINANCE AND INVESTMENT TERMS
John Downes and Jordan Goodman
Defines and explains over 2500 Wall Street terms for professionals, business students, and average investors.
Paperback $8.95, Canada $11.95/ISBN 2522-9, 495 pages
"This is an invaluable fog-cutter for investors."
—*William S. Rukeyser, Managing Editor,* FORTUNE *Magazine*

DICTIONARY OF REAL ESTATE TERMS
Jack P. Friedman, Jack C. Harris, and Bruce Lindeman
Defines over 1200 terms, with examples and illustrations. A key reference for everyone in real estate. Comprehensive and current.
Paperback $8.95, Canada $11.95/ISBN 3898-3, 224 pages

REAL ESTATE HANDBOOK
Jack P. Friedman, Jack C. Harris, and Bruce Lindeman
A dictionary/reference for everyone in real estate. Defines over 1500 legal, financial, and architectural terms.
Cloth $19.95, Canada $27.50/ISBN 5758-9, 700 pages

HOW TO PREPARE FOR REAL ESTATE LICENSING EXAMINATIONS-SALESPERSON AND BROKER, 3rd EDITION
Jack P. Friedman and Bruce Lindeman
Reviews current exam topics and features updated model exams and supplemental exams, all with explained answers.
Paperback, $9.95, Canada $13.95/ISBN 2996-8, 340 pages

BARRON'S FINANCE AND INVESTMENT HANDBOOK
John Downes and Jordan Goodman
This hard-working handbook of essential information defines more than 2500 key terms, and explores 30 basic investment opportunities. The investment information reflects new Federal Tax Act provisions effective in 1987. Cloth $21.95, Canada $29.95/ISBN 5729-5, 864 pages
"...an excellent investment guide...almost any serious investor will want this book."—*Christian Science Monitor*

BARRON'S FINANCIAL TABLES FOR BETTER MONEY MANAGEMENT
Stephen S. Solomon, Dr. Clifford Marshall, and Martin Pepper
Pocket-sized handbooks of interest and investment rates tables used easily by average investors and mortgage holders. Paperback
Savings and Loans, $5.50, Canada $7.95/ISBN 2745-0, 272 pages
Real Estate Loans, $5.50, Canada $7.95/ISBN 2744-2, 336 pages
Mortgage Payments, $5.50, Canada $7.95/ISBN 2728-0, 304 pages
Stocks and Bonds, $5.50, Canada $7.95/ISBN 2727-2, 256 pages
Comprehensive Annuities, $5.50, Canada $7.95/ISBN 2726-4, 160 pages
Canadian Mortgage Payments, Canada $8.95/ISBN 3939-4, 336 pages
Adjustable Rate Mortgages, *Jack P. Friedman and Jack C . Harris*
$5.50, Canada $7.95/ISBN 3764-2, 288 pages

All prices are in U.S. and Canadian dollars and subject to change without notice. At your bookseller, or order direct adding 10% postage (minimum charge $1.50, Canada $2.00), N.Y. residents add sales tax.

Barron's Educational Series, Inc.
250 Wireless Boulevard, Hauppauge, NY 11788
Call toll-free: 1-800-645-3476, in NY 1-800-257-5729
In Canada: Georgetown Book Warehouse
34 Armstrong Ave., Georgetown, Ontario L7G 4R9